10-11-76

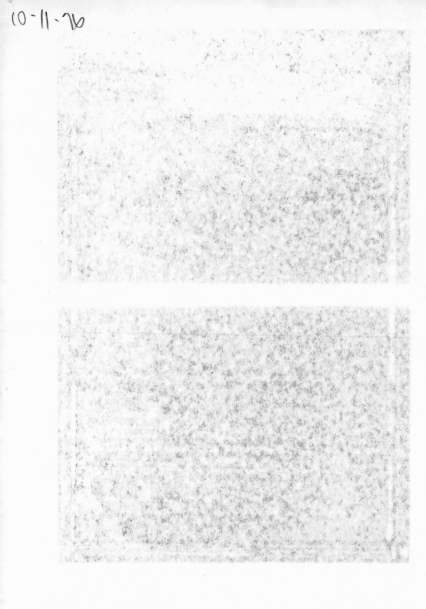

Encyclopedic Directory

of

Ethnic Newspapers and Periodicals

in the United States

Encyclopedic Directory

of

Ethnic Newspapers and Periodicals in the United States

Second Edition

Lubomyr R. Wynar

and

Anna T. Wynar

Libraries Unlimited, Inc. — Littleton, Colo. — 1976

LIBRARIES UNLIMITED, INC.
P.O. Box 263
Littleton Colorado 80120

Library of Congress Cataloging in Publication Data

Wynar, Lubomyr Roman, 1932-
    Encyclopedic directory of ethnic newspapers and
periodicals in the United States.

    Includes indexes.
    1. Ethnic press—United States—Directories.
I. Wynar, Anna T., 1944-   joint author. II. Title.
Z6953.5.A1W94   1976   [PN4882]   070.4'84'02573
ISBN 0-87287-154-1   76-23317

PREFACE

In 1972 the first edition of the *Encyclopedic Directory of Ethnic Newspapers and Periodicals in the United States* was published by Libraries Unlimited, Inc. The publication, which was well received by both librarians and students of ethnicity, was selected by the American Library Association as one of the best "Reference Books for 1972." This new updated and completely revised edition of the directory, appearing in the Bicentennial year, aims primarily to serve not only scholars engaged in the study of the American society and ethnic groups but also librarians involved in reference service and the building of ethnic collections. This edition has been revised and expanded: new ethnic groups and new titles have been added, and defunct publications have been omitted. Also, a new section on the multi-ethnic press is included.

Ethnic newspapers and periodicals constitute the major source of information on the cultural heritage and historical development of individual ethnic groups in the United States. Because of this, they may be regarded as unique primary and secondary sources for historical and sociological study of the American people and their culture.

In 1975, the *Encyclopedic Directory of Ethnic Organizations in the United States* was published, constituting the first comprehensive source of information on ethnic organizations in this country. The present volume on the ethnic press serves as a companion reference tool to that work.

The main objective of this directory is to identify the newspapers and periodicals published by various ethnic groups in the United States and to describe their content and bibliographical features.

The directory consists of the following parts:

1. Preface
2. Introduction
3. Nature of the Ethnic Press
4. Fifty-two sections covering the ethnic press
5. Appendix (statistical analysis of each individual press)
6. Title index

1934182

It is hoped that this updated second edition of the directory will serve as an indispensable tool for reference departments in libraries, for government agencies, and for students analyzing the various aspects of ethnicity in the United States.

ACKNOWLEDGMENTS

A number of persons contributed either directly or indirectly to the completion of this work. First of all, our gratitude is due to all editors and publishers of ethnic newspapers and periodicals who cooperated in our survey by submitting relevant data on the ethnic press and by completing the questionnaire. Special appreciation is expressed to Nikolay Altankov of the University of

California, Helvi Mesenberg of Boulder, Colorado, Lois Buttlar of Kent State University, Vytis Bieagus of Denver, John Cadzow of Kent State University, and Jungnam Kwon of Kent State University for supplying important information on the ethnic press. Special thanks are due to Anne Elizabeth Smith and Genevieve H. Scott, who assisted in checking the questionnaires, and also to Ann Harwell for copy editing of the manuscript. The staff of the Center for the Study of Ethnic Publications at Kent State University deserves special recognition for their assistance in this project.

TABLE OF CONTENTS

To Natalia

INTRODUCTION

METHODOLOGY

The data provided in this *Encyclopedic Directory* are based on a comprehensive survey of ethnic newspapers and periodicals in the United States, a survey conducted from March 1975 through January 1976. For that purpose a special questionnaire was prepared and distributed to all known editors and publishers of the ethnic press in this country. The addresses of these editors were obtained from the first edition of the directory (1972), from the files of the Center for the Study of Ethnic Publications in the United States at Kent State University, and from the editors of ethnic publications. In all, 1,455 questionnaires were mailed to known addresses of ethnic publications. Two follow-up letters were mailed to editors who did not respond. A total of 1,095 questionnaires were returned and analyzed; as a result of this analysis, 913 entries were included (182 publications were excluded because they did not meet the criteria of the directory). The listing of 64 titles was based on secondary sources, particularly on information received from ethnic organizations. The total number of publications listed in the directory is 977. It should be pointed out that some of the returned questionnaires contained only partial answers (in particular, circulation figures were omitted). Unfortunately, some ethnic editors failed to participate in the survey; despite follow-up attempts we were unable to obtain enough information to justify including these publications in the present directory.

SCOPE OF THE ENCYCLOPEDIC DIRECTORY

In scope, this bibliography is limited to 63 ethnic groups, arranged in 51 sections; a separate chapter is devoted to the multi-ethnic publications.

The present revised edition of the *Encyclopedic Directory* covers the presses of eight groups that were not included in the first edition: Argentinian, Basque, Egyptian, East Indian, Iranian, Irish, Pakistani, and Scottish. In addition, new sections cover the Asian press, the Scandinavian press, and multi-ethnic publications. The statistical analysis of the results of our 1975/76 survey of ethnic presses is presented in the section entitled "Nature of the Ethnic Press," which deals with the bibliographical control and present status of the ethnic press in the United States.

The following ethnic presses and types of publications were excluded from this directory:

1. American Indian press;
2. Black American press;
3. Non-English professional and trade publications that are published not by ethnic groups but by American institutions (e.g., industries, businesses, universities, etc.) for a professional and trade clientele rather than for the ethnic reader;
4. Ethnic newspapers and periodicals that did not return the questionnaire and for which additional information could not be found in secondary sources.

Our survey revealed that the American Indian press and Black American press are already covered in other directories, so the present work simply provides references to these directories (see pp. 34 and 48). Actually, these two presses, because of the quantity and diversity of their publications, deserve separate encyclopedic directories. It should be stressed that the emphasis in this directory is on ethnic groups that have continued to publish in non-English languages, although the Irish and Scottish presses have been included. In a few instances, newspapers and periodicals published by organizations that are not ethnic in nature have been included because they are designed specifically for an ethnic readership.

The content analysis of individual publications was based on the editor's statement and on *de visu* examination of individual titles. Most editors supplied examination copies of their publications.

ARRANGEMENT

Periodicals and newspapers are arranged alphabetically within separate ethnic sections. These sections usually consist of two parts: 1) publications that are either entirely in the native language or that are bilingual (i.e., published in both the native language and English), and 2) titles published entirely in English. Cross references ("see" and "see also") are included where necessary. The multi-ethnic publications are listed alphabetically in the first section of this directory.

A comparison of the number of titles published in English by an individual ethnic group with the number of titles that are published in the native language or that are bilingual sheds valuable light on the degree to which each group has retained its native language.

Exceptions to the arrangement by individual ethnic groups are made for three presses—Arab, Spanish, and Jewish. The first two are arranged on the basis of the linguistic principle only and are not subdivided into the individual ethnic groups existing within the Arab- and Spanish-speaking worlds. Thus, the Arab press includes publications by Egyptians, Lebanese, Palestinians, and Syrians as well as Pan-Arabic publications. The Spanish press includes the publications of Argentinians, Cubans, Mexicans (Chicanos), and Puerto Ricans. Necessary cross references are provided for these presses. The section on the Jewish press is divided into four parts: Hebrew and Hebrew-English publications; Yiddish and Yiddish-English publications; Jewish publications in German; and Jewish publications in English.

The Appendix contains statistical analyses of individual ethnic presses.

ENTRIES

A complete entry provides information in the following sequence: 1) title of the publication; 2) translation of the title (if the title is not in English); 3) year of origin; 4) editorial address; 5) telephone number; 6) editor's name; 7) language(s) used in publication; 8) sponsoring organization; 9) circulation; 10) frequency; 11) annual subscription rate; 12) annotation.

As we pointed out earlier, a few editors failed to complete all items on the questionnaire. In such cases the abbreviation "n.i." (no information) is provided. Our policy with respect to diacritical marks has been to follow the editor's usage as reflected on our questionnaire. A sample entry is provided below:

NAS GLAS. **Our Voice.**   1910–
    6401 St. Clair Avenue   (216) 361-0886
    Cleveland, Ohio 44103

Editor: Margot A. Klima   Circulation: 7,800
Sponsor: American Mutual Life Association   Frequency: semi-monthly
Language: English and Slovenian   Subscription: $2.00

Contains general news of interest to Association members—mainly social events sponsored by the organization. Some insurance news and features, ethnic news, senior citizen news.

All titles are transliterated into the roman alphabet. If the editor failed to provide the transliteration, Library of Congress transliteration tables were used. All titles include English translation unless the title is in English or is the same in English as in the original language.

Each brief descriptive annotation of an individual title is based on the editor's statements and a *de visu* examination of the relevant publication. If the title and bibliographical information were self-explanatory, or if no statement of content was available, then no annotation was provided.

STATISTICAL DATA

Statistical analyses of individual ethnic presses are included in an appendix. Additional statistical charts are presented in the introductory article "Nature of the Ethnic Press."

INDEX

The index lists title entries arranged in straight alphabetical order, with ethnic press designation. Figures cited after the entries refer to the item number assigned to the title.

The table of contents serves as a subject index.

NATURE OF THE ETHNIC PRESS

The survival of ethnic communities and ethnic life in the United States is largely a result of the continued existence of the ethnic press, which in most cases is sponsored by various ethnic organizations and institutions. Close examination of an ethnic community reveals that to a very large extent the degree of structural complexity of that particular group is determined by the types and characteristics of existing organizations and their publications, especially newspapers and periodicals. The ethnic press maintains the "ethos," or "spirit," behind an ethnic way of life. It provides an important glimpse of the extent of organization within the ethnic community, thus serving as one of the more *reliable* indices of not only the historical development or the structure and nature of a particular ethnic group, but also the degree of its assimilation and acculturation. Only through the study of the ethnic press and its immense influence on ethnic communities can the total picture of "ethnicity" emerge, for the contents of these ethnic publications reflect the realities of an "ethnic existence."

Before analyzing the historical background, role, nature, and present status of the ethnic press, it is necessary to comment briefly on terminological problems and to define what is meant by the concept of "ethnic press."

QUESTION OF TERMINOLOGY

The term "ethnic press" is often used interchangeably with "immigrant press," "foreign language press," "foreign press and publications," and "nationality press." The acceptance and usage of these terms has led to misconceptions and to negative connotations regarding the American ethnic press. For example, while it may be true that many existing ethnic publications have their origins in immigrant publications, they are not necessarily "immigrant" in nature, by virtue of the fact that they are now being published by second or third generation ethnic Americans and not by newly arrived immigrants. Thus, the term "immigrant" press is too limited and cannot be applied to many ethnic titles being published in present-day America. Although numerous ethnic titles were initially published by immigrants and basically served to fulfill immigrant needs, other ethnic publications do not have their roots in immigrant beginnings. Rather, such publications were initiated for a particular ethnic readership which, due to the process of time, could no longer be regarded as *immigrant* in nature. Specifically, publications in this category were introduced by second, third, and even fourth generation native-born Americans who strongly identified with their ethno-racial origins. The notable example here is the Black press, which witnessed its most rapid growth during the 1960s, but examples of such publications may also be found within other ethnic groups. The purposes of publications within this particular category are to serve native-born *ethnic* rather than foreign-born *immigrant* needs.

The terms "foreign press," "foreign language press," and "nationality press" also fail to describe correctly the American ethnic press; instead, they tend to promote varying degrees of hostile sentiments toward ethnic publications. Since the ethnic press is sponsored by American ethnics, either native-born or naturalized, the term "foreign" cannot be used in its definition. The ethnic press, which is clearly an

14

American product, should not be confused with titles published by foreign governments and their agencies, which are "foreign" in the true sense of the word.

The term "foreign *language* press" is also incorrect when applied to American ethnic publications. Although English is the official language of the United States, many Americans also claim other non-English languages as their native or mother tongue. To them the use of their native language is by no means interpreted as constituting a "foreign" act or as using a "foreign" language. Often in ethnic communities it is common for English to be the second language learned by the individual. If one keeps in mind that American society is composed of individuals from diverse national, religious, and racial backgrounds, then one should accept the notion that the American nation is in fact a multi-lingual society, within which the English language occupies the dominant status. Thus, in order to avoid furthering such misconceptions as "non-American," "anti-American," and "alien" regarding the ethnic press, it is necessary to eliminate the terms "foreign," "foreign language," and "nationality" when defining the publications sponsored and published by American ethnics.

The terms "American ethnic press" and "American ethnic publications" are the most logical ones to use when referring to the publications of the various ethnic groups in the United States. In regard to general language identification, terms such as "American ethnic English-language publications," "American ethnic non-English language publications," and "American ethnic bilingual publications" are far more appropriate as descriptions of the ethnic press in the United States. Concepts such as "American Polish language publications," "Ukrainian-American publications in English," "Italian-American publications in non-English," etc., tend to identify ethnic publications even more specifically in terms of a particular group, while at the same time emphasizing their *American* origin. In general, the *American* ethnic press may be defined as consisting of newspapers and periodicals published either in English, in non-English, or bilingually, published by ethnic organizations or individuals in the United States, and specifically aimed at an ethnic readership. The contents of such publications are primarily designed to satisfy the needs and interests common to persons of a particular ethnic group or community.

HISTORICAL DEVELOPMENT OF THE ETHNIC PRESS

Despite the importance of the ethnic press in the study and comprehension of the pluralistic character of American society, only marginal attention has been focused on this topic.[1]

The historical development of the American ethnic press covers at least 244 years, beginning with the German bimonthly *Die Philadelphische Zeitung*, published in Philadelphia by Benjamin Franklin in 1732. It is rather difficult to establish a firm periodization of the historical development of the ethnic press in the United States. Its growth is directly related to the immigration process of the eighteenth, nineteenth, and twentieth centuries. The second half of the nineteenth century witnessed a rapid growth of ethnic newspapers and periodicals, many of which were sponsored by religious bodies, by ethnic fraternal and other organizations, and by individual initiative. During this period ethnic publications reflected the common concerns, interests, and needs that arose as a result of the migration process, and it therefore constituted an *immigrant* press.

The following chronological chart outlines the early development of the ethnic press in terms of individual ethnic groups.

Year	Title	Ethnic Affiliation	Place of Publication
1739	Germantauner Zeitung	German	Germantown, Pa.
1776	The New York Packet and American Advertizer	Irish	New York
1789	Courier de Boston	French	Boston
1823	The Jewish Journal	Jewish	New York
1827	Freedom Journal	Black American	New York
1828	The Cherokee Phoenix	Indian	New Echota, Ga.
1832	Cymbro America	Welsh	New York
1835	El Crepusculo	Spanish	Taos, N.M. (then Mexico)
1847	Nordlyset	Norwegian	Muskegon, Wisc.
1847	Skandinavia	Scandinavian	New York
1849	L'Eco d'Italia	Italian	New York
1853	Szamüzottek Lapja	Hungarian	New York
1857	Scottish American Journal	Scottish	New York
1860	Slovan Amerykansky	Czech	Racine, Wisc.
1861	Pella's Wekoblad	Dutch	Pella, Iowa
1861	Amerikansko-Slovenske Noviny	Slovak	Pittsburgh, Pa.
1863	Echo z Polski	Polish	New York
1869	Alaska Herald	Russian	San Francisco
1870	Die Juedishe Zeitung	Jewish/Yiddish	New York
1872	Det Danske Pionner	Danish	Omaha, Nebr.
1876	American Suomainen Lehti	Finnish	Hancock, Mich.
1879	Lietuwiszka Gazieta	Lithuanian	New York
1884	Slavenska Sloga	Serbian	San Francisco
1886	Ameryka	Ukrainian	Shenandoah, Pa.
1887	A Uniao Portugueza	Portuguese	Oakland, Calif.
1887	Arekag	Armenian	Jersey City, N.J.
1891	Chinese World	Chinese	San Francisco
1891	Amerikansky Slovenec	Slovenian	Chicago
1891	Ensei	Japanese	San Francisco

Year	Title	Ethnic Affiliation	Place of Publication
1891	Napredak	Croatian	Hoboken, N.J.
1892	Kawkab America	Arabic (Syrian)	Boston
1892	Neas Kosmos	Greek	Boston
1896	Amerikas Vestnesis	Latvian	Boston
1897	Eesti America Postimmees	Estonian	New York
1903	Tribuna	Romanian	Cleveland
1905	Hanin Sisa	Korean	Honolulu

In the twentieth century the ethnic press expanded to include such groups as the Byelorussians, Bulgarians, Rumanians, Filipino, Turkish, and others. It was also during this century that a vast number of ethnic publications passed from the stage of being primarily *immigrant* oriented, and thus classified as the *immigrant* press, and evolved into the American *native* ethnic press, published by native-born ethnic Americans and serving their new and changing needs and concerns. The twentieth century also witnessed the emergence of new ethnic titles, initiated by native-born American ethnics, which had not evolved from earlier published immigrant newspapers or periodicals.

Unfortunately, there are no reliable historical statistics on the ethnic press in terms of circulation and number of publications. The following table attempts to present the approximate number of ethnic publications (excluding Indian and Black) issued between 1884 and 1975.[2]

Table 1. Number of Publications, 1884-1975

Year	Number of Titles
1884	794 (Park)
1900	1,163 (Park)
1917	1,323 (Park)
1930	1,037 (Fishman)
1940	1,092 (Chyz)
1960	698 (Fishman)
1970	903 (Wynar)
1975	960 (Wynar)

One of the single most important characteristics of the ethnic non-English press has been its high mortality. For example, Jerzy Zubrzycky found that in the United States between 1884 and 1920, 3,444 newspapers were started and 3,186 discontinued.[3] However, he later qualifies this statement by observing that the disappearance of an ethnic newspaper is often the result of a merger. His conclusion is correct, but it would be more meaningful if he had provided comparative statistics on the mortality of the non-English ethnic press as compared to the regular American press. Basically the growth and decline of the American ethnic press, especially in regard to non-English titles, has been directly related to the immigration policies of the U.S. government[4] and the immigration influx. In general, it may be stated that during the 244 years of its existence in the United States the ethnic press was characterized by fluctuation. Many publications were initiated only to be discontinued or to merge with other periodicals. Many, however, survived and continue to constitute important primary source material for the study of ethnic groups in the United States.

ROLE OF THE ETHNIC PRESS
AND TYPES OF PUBLICATIONS

The major function of the ethnic press lies in its role as the principal agent by which the identity, cohesiveness, and structure of an ethnic community are preserved and perpetuated. It is by providing this sense of shared identity and common consciousness that the ethnic press serves as the cementing element within the community. Although an ethnic community experiences changing needs and shifting priorities throughout its existence, the press's role as the major cementing factor remains always constant, in spite of the fact that it also mirrors the altering concerns.

The role of ethnic newspapers and periodicals as educational tools cannot be underestimated. As such, they are the vehicles through which the common concerns and purposes within ethnic communities are defined. The functions of the press, as one of the major educational agents within the ethnic community, change as the ethnic community evolves from a primarily immigrant society to that of an established native American ethnic community. While the community still remains in its immigrant stage, the press serves primarily as the major tool of adjustment. By printing American news, describing the American way of life, and interpreting the conditions, customs, laws, and mores of the new society, the immigrant press eases the process of adjustment and consequently hastens the assimilative process. While the immigrant press acts as an agent of assimilation, at the same time it also functions as a force that retards assimilation. This latter role, the slowing of the assimilative process, results from the press's tendency to preserve the ethnic culture and identity by encouraging language retention, stimulating a continued interest in the country of origin, and sustaining involvement in ethnic community affairs within the host country.

Once the community has evolved from an immigrant society to an established native ethnic society, the importance of the press in the adjustment process of new arrivals diminishes. The needs of the community, which were once primarily of an immigrant nature (i.e., revolving around questions of successful adjustment) become transformed into different interests and purposes. The new and evolving objectives, which in general tend to be common to members of an ethnic society, are continuously defined and redefined by the press. It is by identifying these common concerns that the ethnic press preserves the cohesiveness and identity of the community as it undergoes various changes within its internal structure. Since most members of the ethnic community are no longer viewed as immigrants, the new concerns are centered not on adjustment problems, but rather on the need to preserve the ethnic identity and community within the larger social order and to establish a socioeconomic and political power base that will assure the community's existence. A few examples of such new interests are the protesting of discriminatory practices within various social institutions; the election of political figures who are sensitive and responsive to the specific ethnic needs; the improvement of the socioeconomic status of the ethnic community; preservation of the ethnic heritage and language within a constantly changing society; etc.

By educating the ethnic readership in these common concerns, the press assures the continuation of the ethnic society. Thus, while on one hand it promotes the full and equal participation of the ethnic community within the larger order, at the same time it encourages retention of the distinctiveness that differentiates the community from the dominant society. In general, the existence of the ethnic press is assured as long as its readers' needs remain unfulfilled within the framework of the existing social institutions and as long as their concerns are not voiced in the pages of the dominant press media.

The types (defined on the basis of content) and the number of ethnic newspapers and periodicals vary from group to group. Consequently, no generalizations can be made, from one group to another, about the number or the subject matter of publications. For example, the survey data reveal that some groups (Assyrians, Cossacks, Georgians, etc.) report the publication of only one newspaper or journal, while other groups publish well over one hundred (e.g., there are more than 140 Jewish publications listed here). On the basis of content, the publications can be classified into the following broad categories, which are not necessarily mutually exclusive:

General Newspapers and Periodicals

Publications in this group focus on the various activities, events, positions, and issues occurring within the ethnic community on international, national, regional, and local levels. In addition to providing coverage of events in the home country, the publications also provide coverage, in capsule form, of major world and national events, especially in the non-English-language editions. Some also include poetry, short stories, and items that can be classified as cultural or educational, which usually appear in specially designated columns. The largest number of ethnic publications falls into this category, which also has the highest circulation figures.

Special Purpose or Specific Interest Publications

This broad category contains the greatest variety of publications on the basis of content. Into this group one may place the following types of materials:

Political and ideological publications are published by organizations, groups, or individuals that identify with a particular political ideology or party. All coverage of either general news or specific events tends to be from the perspective of the ideological position of the publisher. Such publications usually serve as the official organ of the political group in question. In addition to covering organizational activities, they also tend to present the group's official stand on all social, educational, economic, political, and other issues. These publications are intended for either the organizational membership or for a larger readership. Many focus on political conditions in the home country as well as on "ethnic" politics within the United States.

Fraternal publications provide coverage of the projects, activities, and state of affairs of the organizations and their many lodges, and may also report on members' activities.

Religious publications may appear in the form of short bulletins, newspapers, or journals. Their dominant theme is religious. In addition to covering the affairs and activities of the denomination and providing spiritual guidance and information on official church positions, they also cover a variety of topics from a specific religious perspective. These publications are sponsored by the churches or parishes, by religious orders, or by the laity.

Scholarly and academic publications are usually published by scholarly societies. They can be devoted to a particular branch of knowledge (e.g., history, literature, economics, medicine, engineering, etc.) or they can take a cross-disciplinary approach. Publications covering more than one discipline are usually published by scholarly "umbrella" organizations. The single-discipline journals are sponsored by specific professional societies. Scholarship is the aspect most emphasized.

Educational periodicals are usually sponsored by ethnic schools or parent-teacher associations. Their purposes are to inform the community of ethnic educational activities, to stimulate interest in ethnic educational systems, and to serve as the forum for analyzing the future development of ethnic schools in this country.

Professional and trade publications often appear in the form of bulletins. They are published by ethnic professional or trade organizations (e.g., librarians, journalists, physicians, etc.). The contents cover organizational activities, purposes, future projects, and reports on individual members.

Cultural publications are devoted to a broad and popular presentation and interpretation of the ethnic cultural heritage, tradition, history, literature, art, music, drama, entertainment, etc.

Youth-oriented publications are often cultural in nature, but they are aimed directly at the ethnic youth. In general, they promote pride in the ethnic heritage, solidarity, and the retention of the culture and language. Usually they are sponsored by various youth organizations and report on organizational activities and events. They are published for different age levels.

Women-oriented publications are also often cultural in nature, with the dominant theme centering on women-oriented issues. Contents vary from recipes and ethnic folk art to analysis of social problems affecting women.

Sports and recreational publications are primarily bulletins published by sporting organizations; they report on club activities.

Veterans' publications, sponsored by veterans' organizations, provide coverage of organizational and membership activity. Articles on past national wars are also included.

Bibliographic periodicals provide listings, discussions, and reviews of new books and other communication materials published by the various ethnic organizations and individuals.

All the above-mentioned materials are published by various ethnic organizations such as fraternities; professional and trade associations; synagogues, churches, religious orders, and lay groups; women's associations; scientific, scholarly, cultural, and educational societies; social and recreational groups; veterans' organizations; political clubs and ideological groups; welfare and charitable societies; and umbrella organizations. They also may be sponsored by individual initiative.

The scope also varies from one publication to another. Many provide coverage of international and national events and are intended for a national or even international ethnic readership. Others confine their content to local or regional community affairs and are usually published by local societies specifically for local readership. As mentioned previously, some publications deal only with a specific interest, and these fall into an exclusive category. Many others, however, reflect mixed contents and cannot be placed under one particular grouping. Also, it is not uncommon for fraternal orders, political organizations, religious denominations, women's groups, etc., to publish materials that can be classified as general, cultural, educational, youth-oriented, etc. Therefore, although there can be a relationship between the type of sponsor and the nature of the publication's contents, in many cases this kind of correlation does not exist.

PRESENT STATUS OF ETHNIC PRESS

As we pointed out earlier, bibliographical control of the ethnic press has tended to be an ignored area of research. This neglect may be measured in terms of the number of surveys of the ethnic press that have been conducted and published, and in the number of directories that list ethnic newspapers and periodicals.

An older reference tool, *Ayer Directory*, has been listing ethnic periodicals since 1884. It currently maintains a separate section, "Foreign Language Publications," which includes some ethnic periodicals and newspapers along with non-ethnic trade and professional titles published in various languages. The included titles are not arranged by individual ethnic groups but on the basis of foreign language. This "foreign language" criterion adopted by *Ayer* is not adequate either for the bibliographical control or for the sociological and historical study of ethnic publications, since the same language may be used by several different ethnic groups. Also, *Ayer Directory* cannot be considered as a dependable reference publication for the ethnic press because it omits many ethnic titles and its information in many instances is incomplete.

Another directory that lists ethnic publications is *Editor & Publisher International Year Book*. Like *Ayer Directory*, it contains a separate section, "Principal Foreign Language Newspapers Published in the United States"; but it omits many major ethnic publications and cannot be considered as dependable.

The American Council for Nationality Service sporadically publishes mimeographed lists of ethnic publications. The 1974 listing includes 646 titles, but many of these entries contain incomplete or outdated information and several ethnic groups are ignored. Its major failing is the omission of many ethnic titles.

The following table of ethnic groups, selected at random, compares the number of titles listed in various reference publications with the number listed in this *Encyclopedic Directory*:

Table 2. Comparison of Coverage

	Number of Titles				
Ethnic Press	1975 Editor & Publisher	American Council for Nationality Service 1974	Ayer 1974	Ayer 1975	Encyclopedic Directory 1976
Albanian	2	4	2	1	7
Arabic	11	15	3	3	28
Byelorussian	0	2	0	0	14
Latvian	2	2	2	2	13
Lithuanian	12	39	20	20	43
Polish	17	49	23	25	53
Ukrainian	7	31	12	11	76

It is obvious that there is a need for periodic surveys of ethnic publications in the United States, and this need provided the impetus for our second major survey of the ethnic press, which resulted in the publication of this edition of the *Encyclopedic Directory*. Although it lists about 90 percent of the existing ethnic newspapers and periodicals, even this directory is not fully complete. When compared to other reference publications, however, the *Encyclopedic Directory of Ethnic Newspapers and Periodicals in the United States* can be considered as the most complete listing of ethnic publications.

The statistical data presented here, based on the information gathered during our survey, reflect the present status of the ethnic press in the United States. Special statistical tables for each ethnic group are included in the appendix, arranged under three major categories: native language, bilingual, and English language publications. Within each category the material is subdivided according to frequency of publication.

Out of the 960 publications listed in Table 3, 386 are published in non-English languages (circulation 2,781,694); 246 are bilingual (circulation 2,076,611); and 328 are published in the English language (circulation 4,205,057). The total circulation figure for these three groups is 9,063,362 copies (see Table 3).

Table 3. Ethnic Publications by Language and Frequency

	Native Language	Bilingual	English	Total
Daily	35	12	3	50
Semi-weekly	8	4	2	14
Weekly	98	59	80	237
Semi-monthly	32	27	22	81
Monthly	96	76	95	267
Bi-monthly	28	14	26	68
Quarterly	41	30	55	126
Semi-annually	8	7	10	25
Other	40	17	35	92
Total	386	246	328	960
Circulation	2,781,694	2,076,611	4,205,057	9,063,362

It should be noted that the circulation totals are only for those publications whose editors included the circulation figures in the questionnaire; they do not reflect the circulation of those publications for which this information was omitted. The determination of the circulation for individual ethnic publications presents quite a difficult task, since many ethnic editors and publishers do not submit their circulation figures to the Audit Bureau of Circulation, Verified Audit Circulation Company, or other agencies dealing with circulation. In this *Encyclopedic Directory* circulation figures are based primarily on editors' statements in the questionnaires and on annual publishers' statements in the publications themselves. At the same time, it should be stated that circulation of the ethnic press fluctuates from year to year, thus making it difficult to obtain reliable data.

The numerical strength of each individual ethnic press is presented in Table 4.

Table 4. Total Periodicals by Ethnic Group

	Daily	Semi-Weekly	Weekly	Semi-Monthly	Monthly	Bi-Monthly	Quarterly	Semi-Annually	Other	Total
Albanian	0	0	2	0	1	0	3	0	1	7
Arabic	0	1	9	2	10	3	2	0	1	28
Armenian	2	3	7	0	12	1	6	2	1	34
Asian	0	0	1	0	1	1	1	0	2	6
Assyrian	0	0	0	0	1	0	0	0	0	1
Basque	0	0	0	0	1	0	0	1	0	2
Belgian	0	0	1	0	1	0	0	0	0	2
Bulgarian	0	0	1	1	0	1	0	0	1	4
Byelorussian	0	0	1	0	1	2	2	3	5	14

Table 4. (cont'd)

	Daily	Semi-Weekly	Weekly	Semi-Monthly	Monthly	Bi-Monthly	Quarterly	Semi-Annually	Other	Total
Carpatho-Ruthenian	0	0	3	2	5	3	0	0	0	13
Chinese	13	1	7	2	3	1	1	2	1	31
Cossack	0	0	0	0	0	0	0	0	1	1
Croatian	0	0	3	1	1	2	2	0	3	12
Czech	1	0	11	1	14	1	4	0	1	33
Danish	0	0	1	2	3	1	2	0	0	9
Dutch	0	0	2	1	2	0	3	0	0	8
Estonian	0	0	1	0	1	1	0	0	0	3
Filipino	0	0	0	1	6	0	0	1	0	8
Finnish	0	3	3	0	1	0	1	0	1	9
French	0	0	3	1	1	2	2	0	1	10
Georgian	0	0	0	0	0	1	0	0	0	1
German	3	0	26	2	21	2	3	1	2	60
Greek	1	0	7	4	5	3	2	1	1	24
Hungarian	1	0	13	3	7	0	6	0	2	32
Indian	0	0	1	0	0	0	0	0	2	3
Iranian	0	0	0	0	0	0	0	0	1	1
Irish	0	0	3	0	0	0	1	1	1	6
Italian	1	0	17	6	12	4	5	1	2	48
Japanese	6	1	3	0	3	0	0	0	2	15
Jewish	2	0	47	9	38	7	25	1	12	141
Korean	2	0	2	3	0	1	0	0	0	8
Latvian	0	1	0	1	4	1	1	2	3	13
Lithuanian	2	2	4	6	10	5	5	2	7	43
Luxembourg	0	0	0	0	1	0	0	0	0	1
Norwegian	0	0	3	2	6	2	1	1	1	16
Pakistani	0	0	0	1	0	0	0	0	0	1
Polish	3	0	14	9	8	4	12	2	1	53
Portuguese	0	0	3	1	2	0	3	0	1	10
Romanian	0	0	0	1	5	1	0	0	0	7
Russian	2	1	1	1	7	3	4	1	6	26
Scandinavian	0	0	0	0	2	0	2	0	0	4
Scottish	0	0	0	0	2	0	1	1	0	4
Serbian	0	0	1	1	1	1	0	0	3	7
Slovak	0	0	5	2	12	1	2	0	2	25
Slovenian	2	0	1	2	5	0	1	0	0	12
Spanish	7	1	16	6	19	4	3	0	2	58
Swedish	0	0	6	3	9	0	1	0	1	20
Swiss	0	0	2	0	1	0	0	0	1	4
Turkish	0	0	0	0	4	0	1	1	0	6
Ukrainian	2	0	6	4	17	9	18	1	20	77
Welsh	0	0	0	0	1	0	0	0	0	1
Total	50	14	237	81	267	68	126	25	92	960

On the basis of this tabulation it is possible to determine certain trends in regard to various types of ethnic publications. Monthlies and weeklies are the most numerous types, followed by quarterlies, semi-monthlies, and dailies.

The total circulation for each individual ethnic press is presented in Table 5, which is arranged on the basis of circulation figures.

Table 5. Total Circulation by Ethnic Group

Ethnic Group	Circulation	Number of Publications
Jewish	3,016,235	141
Spanish	1,533,153	58
Polish	583,650	53
Italian	482,176	48
German	437,484	60
Greek	272,236	24
Hungarian	210,912	32
Norwegian	195,122	16
Ukrainian	179,638	77
Czech	164,302	33
Swedish	162,957	20
Slovak	158,096	24
Chinese	157,116	31
Lithuanian	153,628	43
Arabic	133,175	28
French	123,800	10
Armenian	112,866	34
Carpatho-Ruthenian	97,588	13
Japanese	92,948	15
Slovene	81,587	11
Dutch	79,850	8
Croatian	77,160	12
Russian	69,088	26
Irish	67,950	6
Portuguese	61,095	10
Filipino	50,450	8
Danish	49,250	9
Asian (general)	42,230	6
Serbian	39,460	7
Latvian	25,540	13
Finnish	23,069	9
Indian	16,000	3
Scandinavian	13,315	4
Romanian	12,549	7
Belgian-Flemish	11,855	2
Byelorussian	10,500	14

Table 5. (cont'd)

Ethnic Group	Circulation	Number of Publications
Turkish	9,397	6
Swiss	9,305	4
Bulgarian	8,319	4
Albanian	7,150	7
Korean	7,114	8
Basque	6,296	2
Scottish	6,000	4
Estonian	5,835	3
Welsh	2,000	1
Assyrian	1,700	1
Georgian	1,000	1
Luxemburg	650	1
Cossack	250	1
Iranian	not indicated	1
Pakistani	not indicated	1
Total	9,063,362	960
Multi-ethnic	49,922	17
Grand Total (ethnic and multi-ethnic)	9,113,284	977

It is interesting to note that the numerical strength of the circulation of individual ethnic presses is not directly correlated to the number of publications. For instance, the Italian press consists of 48 publications with a circulation of 482,176, while the Ukrainian press contains 77 titles with a total circulation of 179,638. Scholars of ethnicity should devote greater attention to the question of why some groups have high circulation figures but relatively few titles, while other groups publish a greater number and diversity of publications, yet reveal a smaller circulation figure. In studying this phenomenon social scientists should investigate each individual ethnic group and its historical and sociological development, and they should also determine the type and content of its press. The diversity of content may be directly related to factors such as the complexity of the internal social structure of the relevant ethnic community; the degree to which members of the group have a desire to preserve the group's ethnic identity and distinctiveness; the extent of differentiation between the social institutions, mores, and culture of the ethnic community and that of the host society; the degree to which existing dominant social institutions and communications media can fulfill perceived needs, concerns, and interests; the degree of alienation from the ethnic community and assimilation into the dominant social order, and vice versa; the importance of the press as a necessary part of ethnic community life; the socioeconomic and educational background of the community members; principal causes of the original emigration from the home country (i.e., whether politically or economically motivated); educational, social, and economic level of the original immigrants, and the ability of the ethnic community members to sustain economically a specified number of publications.

Important questions that have arisen and that should provoke further study relate to the geographical location of subscribers to the individual ethnic papers and journals. Is the subscription limited to the American ethnic subscribers, or does it also include ethnic subscribers from Canada and other countries of the world? It should be noted that many editors commented on the fact that their publications are popular in Canada and in other countries as well as in the United States. Is a particular title limited only to an ethnic readership, or is it also ordered by American public and academic libraries and by other non-ethnic institutions?

Other important points to consider involve the proper interpretation of the circulation numbers. Circulation figures should not be erroneously interpreted as constituting an equal number of individuals, especially when such numbers apply to total circulation figures within an ethnic group. For example, one cannot conclude that 153,628 individual Lithuanians read 43 titles, since one has no way of knowing how many of the individual readers subscribe to two, three, four, or more Lithuanian publications. The important point here is that caution should be exercised when interpreting the readership number. All of these important questions must be taken into account in any study of the ethnic readership of individual ethnic groups in the United States and abroad.

For the present, it seems that the ethnic press is here to stay and that it will continue to mirror the cultural pluralism of the American society. Its form, content, and functions are bound to alter as it continues to reflect the internal social changes that are constantly occurring within the ethnic communities. As a major force in ethnic life, the press should be subjected to further serious interdisciplinary research.

NOTES

[1] The most comprehensive study on the ethnic press was published by Robert Park in 1922: *The Immigrant Press and Its Control* (New York, Harper and Brothers, 1922; reprinted in 1971). Among other studies one should mention Edward Hunter's popular account, *In Many Voices; Our Fabulous Foreign-Language Press* (Norman Park, Georgia, Norman College, 1961); and Yaroslav J. Chyz's *225 Years of the U.S. Foreign Language Press* (New York, American Council of Nationalities Services, 1959).

There are several studies dealing with an individual ethnic press, such as Carl Wittke's *The German Language Press in America* (Lexington, University of Kentucky Press, 1957), and others.

[2] Statistical data are based on Park, *Immigrant Press*, p. 318; Joshua Fishman and others, "The Non-English and the Ethnic Group Press, 1910-1960," in *Language Loyalty in the United States* (The Hague, Mouton Co., 1966), pp. 66-69; Yaroslav J. Chyz, "Number, Distribution and Circulation of the Foreign Language Press in the United States," *Interpreter Releases*, No. 37, Ser. C., Oct. 13, 1943. Recent figures are taken from our own survey of the ethnic press.

[3] Jerzy Zubrzycki, "The Role of Foreign-Language Press in Migrant Integration," *Population Studies*, Vol. XII, 1958-59, p. 76.

[4] On immigration policies and law, see Frank Auerbach, *Immigration Laws of the U.S.*, 2nd ed. (Indianapolis, Bobbs-Merrill, 1961); and J. Wasserman, *Immigration Law and Practice*, 2nd ed. (Philadelphia, Joint Committee on Continuing Legal Education of the American Institute and the American Bar Association, 1973).

MULTI-ETHNIC PRESS
Multi-Ethnic and General Immigration Newspapers and Periodicals

1. **ETHNIC AMERICAN NEWS.** 1973–
   203 Plaza Building   (412) 391-8470
   Pittsburgh, Pennsylvania 15219

   Editor: Ivan Dornic   Circulation: 10,000
   Sponsor: Ethnos Publishers   Frequency: monthly
   Language: English   Subscription: $5.00

This newspaper publishes reports on "inside ethnic" affairs. The articles and reports touch on ethnic politics, the socioeconomic situation, folk culture, opinions, and heritage. It analyzes various trends and promotes civil rights and ethnic awareness among Americans of Slavic and southern and central European heritage.

2. **ETHNICITY.** 1974–
   111 Fifth Avenue
   New York, New York 10003

   Editor: Andrew M. Greeley   Circulation: n.i.
   Sponsor: Academic Press, Inc.   Frequency: quarterly
   Language: English   Subscription: $28.50

This interdisciplinary journal of the study of ethnic relations is "concerned with the persistence of diversity among human groups in an industrialized world and with promoting understanding of how various groups within society interact with each other" (editor's statement). Features scholarly articles on various ethnic groups in the United States and other countries.

3. **ETHNIC NEWSLETTER.**
   562 Davis Building   (301) 365-1713
   Washington, D. C. 20006

   Editor: Paul M. Deac   Circulation: n.i.
   Sponsor: National Confederation of   Frequency: irregular
       American Ethnic Groups   Subscription: n.i.
   Language: English

Prints reports and opinions on various topics, especially those relating to white ethnics.

4. **HERITAGE EXCHANGE.** 1974–
   71 East Ferry   (313) 872-2225
   Detroit, Michigan 48202

   Editor: Foster G. Braun   Circulation: 1,728
   Sponsor: Michigan Ethnic Heritage Studies   Frequency: bi-monthly
       Center   Subscription: $3.00
   Language: English

Contains national and local news about ethnic studies programs, curriculum development information resource materials, ethnic events and organizations, and ethnic Bicentennial activities. Brief articles on ethnicity.

5. **I & N REPORTER.** 1952–
   U. S. Immigration and Naturalization Service
   Washington, D. C. 20536

   Editor: Janet R. Graham   Circulation: n.i.
   Sponsor: U. S. Immigration and   Frequency: quarterly
       Naturalization Center   Subscription: $1.00
   Language: English

Contains articles on immigration and naturalization topics, recent court and administrative decisions, statistical data, and other relevant material on immigration.

6. IMMIGRATION BAR BULLETIN.　　　　　　　　　　1947–

50 Court Street, Room 1206
Brooklyn, New York 11201　　　　　(212) 624-5524

Editor: Edward Dubroff　　　　　　Circulation: 800
Sponsor: Association of Immigration and　　Frequency:
　　　Nationality Lawyers　　　　Subscription: free to association
Language: English　　　　　　　　　　　members

Features materials on laws of the United States concerning immigration, ethics, grievances, and other items concerning immigration legislation.

7. IMMIGRATION HISTORY NEWSLETTER.　　　　　1968–

690 Cedar Street
St. Paul, Minnesota 55101　　　　　(612) 296-5662

Editor: Carlton C. Qualey　　　　Circulation: 565
Sponsor: Immigration History Society　Frequency: semi-annual
Language: English　　　　　　　　Subscription: $3.00

Contains news items concerning immigration research in the United States and other countries. Also includes information on the activities of the Immigration History Society and bibliographical notes.

8. INTERNATIONAL MIGRATION REVIEW.　　　　　1964–

209 Flagg Place
Staten Island, New York 10304　　　(212) 351-8800

Editor: S. M. Tomasi　　　　　　Circulation: 2,300
Sponsor: Center for Migration Studies of　Frequency: quarterly
　　　New York, Inc.　　　　　Subscription: $14.50
Language: English

Covers scholarly "sociological, demographic, historical, and legislative aspects of human migration movements and ethnic group relations" (editor's statement). Contains articles on individual ethnic groups in the United States. Strong review and bibliographical sections included.

9. INTERPRETER RELEASES.　　　　　　　　　1924–

20 West 40th Street　　　　　　(212) 279-2715
New York, New York 10018

Editor: n.i.　　　　　　　　　Circulation: 1,000
Sponsor: American Council for Nationalities　Frequency: weekly
　　　Service　　　　　　　　Subscription: $25.00
Language: English

Contains articles and information on immigration and selected topics. Assists immigrants in naturalization procedure, providing information on legal regulations, court decisions and Congressional bills related to immigration policies. Statistical data and other relevant materials concerning immigration are also included.

10. JOURNAL OF ETHNIC STUDIES.　　　　　　1973–

High Street　　　　　　　　　(206) 676-3210
Bellingham, Washington 98225

Editors: Jeffrey Wilner and Jesse Hiraoka　Circulation: 715
Sponsor: College of Ethnic Studies　　Frequency: quarterly
Language: English　　　　　　　Subscription: $8.00

Contains articles and reviews on ethnicity and individual ethnic groups in the United States. "Preference given to articles applicable to present and future problems and situations" (editor's statement). Review section included.

11. MIGRATION TODAY.   1973–
   209 Flagg Place   (212) 351-8800
   Staten Island, New York 10304

   Editor: Lydio F. Tomasi   Circulation: 2,999
   Sponsor: Center for Migration Studies of   Frequency: monthly
      New York, Inc.   Subscription: $5.00
   Language: English

Contains news and articles on migration and ethnic communities in urban areas. Each issue contains editorials, a regular legal column, names and features in the news, and book reviews. Illustrated.

12. THE NATIONAL ETHNIC STUDIES ASSEMBLY NEWSLETTER.   1973–
   P. O. Box 1335, Cardinal Center
   Washington, D. C. 20036

   Editor: Richard Kolm   Circulation: n.i.
   Sponsor: National Ethnic Studies Assembly   Frequency: every 6 weeks
   Language: English   Subscription: n.i.

Provides information on various ethnic programs and the activities of the National Ethnic Studies Assembly, as well as available research projects in ethnic studies.

13. A NEW AMERICA.   1974–
   Box 48   (516) 628-8825
   Bayville, New York 11709

   Editor: Michael Novak   Circulation: 4,230
   Sponsor: Ethnic Millions Political Action   Frequency: 6 issues/year
      Committee (EMPAC)   Subscription: $5.00
   Language: English

Features brief articles on ethnicity and ethnic problems in the United States. It "supports a pluralism which enables each cultural group to appreciate its own legitimate history" (editor's statement). Special feature: section "People in the News."

14. NEWORLD MAGAZINE.   1974–
   1308 South New Hampshire Avenue   (213) 387-1161
   Los Angeles, California 90006

   Editor: Fred Beauford   Circulation: 3,000
   Sponsor: Inner City Cultural Center   Frequency: quarterly
   Language: English   Subscription: $15.00

Multi-cultural magazine of the arts. Contains articles on films, fiction, art, theatre, poetry, and music. Illustrated.

15. NEWSLETTER, NATIONAL CENTER FOR URBAN ETHNIC AFFAIRS.   1973–
   4408 Eighth Street, N. E.   (202) 529-5400
   Washington, D. C. 20017

   Editor: Andy Leon Harney   Circulation: 5,500
   Sponsor: The National Center for Urban   Frequency: quarterly
      Ethnic Affairs   Subscription: free
   Language: English

Covers the activities of the National Center for Urban Ethnic Affairs and the community groups associated with the Center, with news on community development, ethnic studies, education, and cultural affairs.

16. PENNSYLVANIA ETHNIC STUDIES NEWSLETTER.   1975–
   G-6 Mervis Hall
   University of Pittsburgh
   Pittsburgh, Pennsylvania 15260

Editor: Sandy Smeltz   Circulation: 15,000
Sponsor: University of Pittsburgh, Pennsylvania   Frequency: bi-monthly
         Ethnic Heritage Studies Center   Subscription: $9.00
Language: English

Includes brief articles and news items on various ethnic research projects and programs in Pennsylvania. This is the official publication of the Pennsylvania Ethnic Heritage Studies Center at the University of Pittsburgh.

17. SPECTRUM.   1975–
   826 Berry Street   (612) 373-5581
   St. Paul, Minnesota 55114

Editor: Michael G. Karni   Circulation: 2,000
Sponsor: Immigration History Research Center Frequency: 3 issues/year
         of the University of Minnesota   Subscription: free
Language: English

Spectrum is published "as a bibliographic guide to the holdings of the Immigration History Research Center and as an information source to the activities of the Center" (editor's statement).

AFRO-AMERICAN PRESS
See **Black American Press**

ALBANIAN PRESS
Albanian and Albanian-English Publications

18. DIELLI.   The Sun.   1909–
   25 Huntington Avenue, Room 412A
   Boston, Massachusetts 03116

Editor: R. Xh. Gurrazezi   Circulation: 1,650
Sponsor: Pan Albanian Federation of   Frequency: weekly
         America, "Vatra"   Subscription: $15.00
Language: Albanian and English

Articles on ethnic, social, cultural, and political issues of special interest to Albanians.

19. DRITA E VERTETE.   The True Light.   1958–
   54 Burroughs Street
   Jamaica Plain, Massachusetts 02130

Editor: Rt. Rev. Bishop Mark (Lipa)   Circulation: 1,200
Sponsor: Albanian Orthodox Diocese of   Frequency: monthly
         America   Subscription: $10.00
Language: Albanian

The official organ of the Canonical Orthodox Church for the Albanian Faithful, this monthly focuses primarily on the Orthodox faith, with coverage of the activities of the Bishop of the Albanian Orthodox Church and informative notes on the developments within various church communities. At times, articles dealing with Albanian culture, history, ethnic traditions, and religious practices are included. Current problems within Albanian communities in the United States are also explored.

20. JETA KATHOLIKE SHQIPTARE.   Catholic Albanian Life.   1966–
    4221 Park Avenue   (212) 878-5725
    Bronx, New York 10457

Editor: Rev. Msgr. Joseph J. Oroshi   Circulation: 600
Sponsor: Albanian American Catholic League   Frequency: quarterly
Language: Albanian and English   Subscription: $12.00

Features articles dealing with religious, social, cultural, and political issues relevant to Albanians in the United States. Includes Bible translations. Special section devoted to the activities of the Albanian Catholic Church. Illustrated.

21. LIRIA.   Liberty.   1941–
    397 B. W. Broadway   (617) 269-5192
    South Boston, Massachusetts 02127

Editor: Dhimitri R. Nikolla   Circulation: 1,200
Sponsor: Free Albania Organization   Frequency: weekly
Language: Albanian and English   Subscription: $10.00

Includes news on Albanian communities in the United States and Albania, international news, information on cultural and social events and on Albanian churches.

22. SHQIPTARI I LIRE.   The Free Albanian.   1957–
    150 Fifth Avenue, Room 1103
    New York, New York 10011

Editor: Vasil Germenji   Circulation: 2,000
Sponsor: Free Albania Committee   Frequency: quarterly
Language: Albanian   Subscription: voluntary contribution

Principally concerned with various developments in Communist Albania for the purpose of "explosing before the United Nations, the Assembly of Captive European Nations and other similar organizations in the Western world, the denial of human, political, and other rights of the Albanian people by the Communist regime" (editor's statement). Attention is also given to the resettlement problems of Albanian political refugees in the United States. Sections are devoted to political, cultural, religious, and social activities both in the United States and abroad.

23. ZËRI I BALLIT.   The Voice.   1950–
    158-23 84 Drive
    Jamaica, New York 11432

Editor: Begeja Halim   Circulation: n.i.
Sponsor: Balli Kombetar Organization   Frequency: quarterly
Language: Albanian   Subscription: n.i.

Contains political, cultural, and other articles of interest to Albanian community. Its major objective is to oppose Communism in Albania.

24. ZËRI I BEKTASHIZMËS.   The Voice of Bektashism.   1954–
    21749 Northline   (313) 287-3646
    Taylor, Michigan 48180

Editor: Tege Committee   Circulation: 500
Sponsor: First Albanian Bektashi Tekke in   Frequency: irregular
         America   Subscription: $2.00/copy
Language: Albanian and English

Contains materials concerning the philosophy and customs of a religious order whose aim is to explain the philosophy and customs of Bektashism in the United States.

AMERICAN INDIAN PRESS

The Indian press is not included in this Directory since the number of publications is too great to be listed in this publication. For information on the American Indian press the following sources should be consulted: Arnold Marquise, *A Guide to American Indians* (Norman: University of Oklahoma Press, 1974), Barry Klein, ed. *Reference Encyclopedia of the American Indian*, 2nd ed. Vol. 1 (New York, Todd Publications, 1973); *1975 Editor and Publisher International Yearbook, Ayer Directory of Newspapers and Periodicals* for 1975.

The American Indian Press Association (AIPA–1346 Connecticut Avenue, N.W., Room 306, Washington, D. C. 20036) coordinates the activities of the editors of the Indian press. It also publishes an annual *American Indian Media Directory*.

ARABIC PRESS

Editor's note: This section on the Arabic press in the United States includes newspapers and journals representing various Arabic nations (e.g., Egyptian, Lebanese, Iraqi, Syrian and Palestinian) published in Arabic and English.

25. AL-ALAM AL-JADID.   **The New World.**   1962–
4003 Edgeland
Royal Oak, Michigan 48073   (313) 549-8242

Editor: Yusuf E. Antone   Circulation: 5,300
Sponsor: Yusuf E. Antone   Frequency: weekly
Language: Arabic   Subscription: $15.00

Features news and articles on political, social, and religious life of Arabs in the United States and Arab countries. According to the editor the newspaper "is greatly respected in official as well as the popular circles." The editor has close connections with Iraq. Illustrated.

26. AL-BAYAN.   **The Statement.**   1910–
126 La Belle
Detroit, Michigan 48214

Editor: Raji Daher   Circulation: 1,000
Sponsor: n.i.   Frequency: weekly
Language: Arabic   Subscription: $20.00

27. HATHIHE RAMALLAH.   **This is Ramallah.**   1952–
P. O. Box 116
Dearborn Heights, Michigan 48127

Editor: Nadim S. Ajlouny   Circulation: 2,300
Sponsor: American Ramallah Federation   Frequency: monthly
Language: Arabic and English   Subscription: $10.00

Features articles on Palestinian problems and Arab refugees as well as Arabic poetry and short stories. News items on people of Ramallah.

28. AL-HODA.   **The Guidance.**   1898–
34 West 28th Street
New York, New York 10001

Editor: Fred G. Koury   Circulation: 2,750
Sponsor: n.i.   Frequency: semi-weekly
Language: Arabic   Subscription: $30.00

This paper, the oldest Lebanese newspaper in the United States, covers general and local news. It emphasizes politics, culture, and economy, but also includes news on Lebanese activities in the United States, Canada, and other countries.

29. AL-ISLAAH.   The Reform.   **1931—**
    260 West Broadway
    New York, New York 10013

    Editor: Alphonse Chaurize   Circulation: 1,000
    Sponsor: n.i.   Frequency: weekly
    Language: Arabic and English   Subscription: $10.00

Contains general news of special interest to Arabs. Most of the content of this weekly is devoted to editorials, rather than to news articles.

30. AL MAROONYYAH.   The Maronite Way.   **1962—**
    2759 North Lipkey Road   (216) 538-3506
    North Jackson, Ohio 44451

    Editors: James Elasmar and Elias Saadi   Circulation: 7,000
    Sponsor: National Apostolate of Maronites   Frequency: monthly
    Language: English and Arabic   Subscription: $5.00

Official Catholic organ of Maronites. Includes articles on Maronite Americans and Lebanon as well as poetry and fiction. One column is published in Arabic.

31. AL-MASHRIQ.   The Orient.   **1949—**
    56 Chandler,
    Highland Park, Michigan 48203

    Editor: Hanna Yatooma   Circulation: 1,010
    Sponsor: n.i.   Frequency: weekly
    Language: Arabic   Subscription: $12.00

Reports and reviews on current events of the Arab people throughout the world, plus editorial comments and opinions pertaining to major issues in the countries of the Middle East. It has an Iraqi-oriented philosophy. Includes coverage of cultural and social activities of Iraqis and other Arabic communities in the United States.

32. THE PALESTINIAN VOICE.   **1971—**
    6513 Hollywood Boulevard, No. 207
    Los Angeles, California 90028

    Editor: Mustafa Siam   Circulation: n.i.
    Sponsor: The Muslim Students' Association Frequency: monthly
    Language: Arabic and English   Subscription: $5.00

Features political, social, and other articles concerning Arab affairs as well as the Arab community in the United States. Emphasis is on Palestinian problems. Illustrated.

33. EL RA-ED NEWS.   The Pioneer.   **1975—**
    60 Hamilton Avenue, No. 8G   (212) 442-3128
    Staten Island, New York 10301

    Editor: Mamdouh Botros   Circulation: 2,000
    Sponsor: El Ra-ed Publications Corp.   Frequency: monthly
    Language: Arabic and English   Subscription: $7.50

Topics covered include economy, political and cultural life, and Arab communities in the United States, especially in New York, New Jersey, and Washington, D. C. Special attention is given to American investment in Arab countries.

34. AL-RISALA.   The Message.
    9 John F. Kennedy Highland Park
    Detroit, Michigan 48203

    Editor: Rev. "Imam" Hussein Karoub   Circulation: 600
    Sponsor: n.i.   Frequency: weekly
    Language: Arabic and English   Subscription: $12.00

Contains general and local news of interest to the Arab-Moslem community.

35. **SAOT MASR.   Voice of MASR (Egypt).**   1972–
    48 Prospect Street   (201) 963-3290
    Jersey City, New Jersey 07307

    Editor: William Elmiry   Circulation: 7,000
    Sponsor: Egyptian Community Center   Frequency: monthly
    Language: Arabic and English   Subscription: $10.00

Monthly newspaper for Arab communities in the United States and Canada. Most of the content is devoted to Mid-East problems. Features political, social, and cultural articles. The main objective of the paper is to "help the new Egyptian immigrants to a better social and cultural adjustment to the American society" (editor's statement).

Arabic Publications in English

36. **ARAB-AMERICAN ASSOCIATION NEWSLETTER.**   1972–
    P. O. Box 20041   (513) 751-3603
    Cincinnati, Ohio 45220

    Editor: Joyce W. Asfour   Circulation: 400
    Sponsor: Arab-American Association   Frequency: 10 issues/year
    Language: English   Subscription: free

Contains information and news about social, cultural, and educational activities of interest to members and friends of the Arab community of Greater Cincinnati. Reprints articles on the Middle East from other sources.

37. **ARAB JOURNAL.**   1953–
    2929 Broadway
    New York, New York 10025

    Editor: Maan Ziyadah   Circulation: 7,000
    Sponsor: Organization of Arab Students in the Frequency: quarterly
            United States and Canada   Subscription: $3.00
    Language: English

This publication features articles on political, cultural, and economic life of the various Arab countries.

38. **ARAB NEWS.**   1954–
    172 Atlantic Avenue
    Brooklyn, New York 11201

    Editor: Mrs. Hanan Watson   Circulation: 14,500
    Sponsor: Arab Information Center   Frequency: semi-monthly
    Language: English   Subscription: $2.00

Contains articles on political, cultural, economic, and religious life in the Arab countries, as well as information on international organizations–especially the United Nations and its stand on Palestine. Includes illustrations.

39. **CARAVAN WEST.**   1974–
    62 Webster Manor
    Webster, New York 14580

    Editor: Joan Abu Assaly   Circulation: 1,000
    Sponsor: Arab American Society of Rochester Frequency: bi-monthly
    Language: English   Subscription: free

Aims at promoting "understanding between the peoples of the United States and the Arabic nation" (editor's statement). Features educational, cultural, and other materials of interest to the Arab community.

40. **FREE PALESTINE.**   1969–
    P. O. Box 21096, Kalorama Station
    Washington, D. C. 20009

FREE PALESTINE (cont'd)
Editor: Aldeen Jabara
Sponsor: Friends of Free Palestine
Language: English

Circulation: n.i.
Frequency: monthly
Subscription: $5.00

Dedicated to the liberation of Palestine, it features political articles on the Palestinian struggle against Israel. Special coverage of Al-Fatah, the Palestinian national liberation movement.

41.   THE HERITAGE.
30 East 40th Street
New York, New York 10016

Editor: N. K. Basile
Sponsor: Heritage Press
Language: English

Circulation: 4,200
Frequency: weekly
Subscription: $15.00

Oriented toward the Lebanese community, this weekly includes international, national, and local news. The emphasis is on the Middle East; editorials and opinions are included.

42.   ISLAMIC ITEMS.   1972–
P. O. Box 7412   (202) 296-0749
Washington, D. C. 20044

Editor: Muhammad Tahir
Sponsor: Islamic Items, Inc. (independent)
Language: English

Circulation: n.i.
Frequency: weekly
Subscription: $25.00

Features brief articles on political, cultural, and social situation in Arab countries. Illustrated.

43.   AL-ITTIHAD.   The Unity.   1963–
200 Beacon Hill Drive, No. 3G   (914) 693-2031
Dobbs Ferry, New York 10522

Editor: Mohammad Zahirul Hassan
Sponsor: The Muslim Students Association of
                the United States and Canada
Language: English

Circulation: 5,000
Frequency: quarterly
Subscription: $6.00

Covers articles of interest to Muslims, discussing various socio-cultural and religious aspects. Publishes original research, poetry reviews, and excerpted articles. Includes columns for comments, book reviews, and letters to the editor.

44.   THE LINK.   1968–
475 Riverside Drive
New York, New York 10027

Editor: Rev. L. Humphrey Walz
Sponsor: Americans for Middle East
                Understanding, Inc.
Language: English

Circulation: 35,000
Frequency: bi-monthly
Subscription: free

Contains articles on various Arab countries as well as American-Arab relationships. "Aims at maintaining contacts among Americans who believe that friendship with the people of the Middle East is essential to world peace" (editor's statement). Illustrated.

45.   NEW LEBANESE AMERICAN JOURNAL.   1972–
16 West 30th Street
New York, New York 10001

Editor: Mary Mokarzel
Sponsor: New Al Hoda, Inc.
Language: English

Circulation: 10,000
Frequency: weekly
Subscription: $20.00

A Lebanese-oriented publication, it covers various events occurring in Lebanon and in Lebanese communities in the United States. Supersedes: *Lebanese American Journal.*

46. THE NEWS CIRCLE.　　　　　　　　　　　　　　　　1972–
　　　P. O. Box 74637　　　　　　　　　(212) 469-7004
　　　Los Angeles, California 90004

　　　Editor: Joseph Haiek　　　　　　　Circulation: 5,000
　　　Sponsor: Arabesque Publications　　Frequency: monthly
　　　Language: English　　　　　　　　Subscription: $8.00

Independent newspaper serving the Arab-American community. Contains articles on political issues, religious life, culture, economy, and other subjects. Also includes international, national, and local news.

47. THE OFFICIAL BULLETIN.　　　　　　　　　　　　　1932–
　　　1206 C & I Building　　　　　　　(713) 227-9181
　　　Houston, Texas 77002

　　　Editor: Kamal E. Atnone　　　　　　Circulation: 3,500
　　　Sponsor: Southern Federation of Syrian　Frequency: bi-monthly
　　　　　　　Lebanese American Clubs　　Subscription: free
　　　Language: English

News items concerning Southern Federation of Syrian Lebanese Clubs, including historical and other materials. Illustrated.

48. PALESTINE DIGEST.　　　　　　　　　　　　　　　1971–
　　　234 World Trade Center
　　　San Francisco, California 20009

　　　Editor: n.i.　　　　　　　　　　Circulation: n.i.
　　　Sponsor: League of Arab States, Arab　Frequency: weekly
　　　　　　　Information Center　　　Subscription: n.i.
　　　Language: English

A digest of the American and European press dealing with Palestine and Palestinians under Israeli occupation. Cites direct quotations.

49. SYRIAN-AMERICAN NEWS.　　　　　　　　　　　　1932–
　　　811 South Sierra Bonita Avenue
　　　Los Angeles, California 90036

　　　Editor: S. S. Mamey　　　　　　　Circulation: 7,400
　　　Sponsor: n.i.　　　　　　　　　Frequency: semi-monthly
　　　Language: English　　　　　　　Subscription: $5.00

News coverage of international affairs as well as events in Syria and the United States. Community oriented.

50. THE UNITY NEWSLETTER.　　　　　　　　　　　　1965–
　　　P. O. Box 26225
　　　Los Angeles, California 90026

　　　Editor: Gail Dibie (changes from year to year)　Circulation: 215
　　　Sponsor: American Arab Society　　Frequency: monthly
　　　Language: English　　　　　　　Subscription: single copy free
　　　　　　　　　　　　　　　　　　　　　with membership

Information about the American Arab Society–its "news and activities, past and future" (editor's statement).

51. THE VOICE.　　　　　　　　　　　　　　　　　　1972–
　　　600 New Hampshire Avenue, N. W., Suite 1175　(202) 333-6575
　　　Washington, D. C. 20037

　　　Editor: Helen Haje　　　　　　　Circulation: n.i.
　　　Sponsor: National Association of Arab Americans　Frequency: monthly
　　　Language: English　　　　　　　Subscription: $10.00

52. THE WORD.   1905–

358 Mountain Road
Englewood, New Jersey 07631

Editor: Rev. Stephen Upson   Circulation: 10,000
Sponsor: Syrian Antiochian Orthodox   Frequency: monthly
      Archdiocese   Subscription: $5.00
Language: English .

Features religious articles as well as information concerning the Syrian Orthodox Church and
its membership.

ARGENTINIAN PRESS
See Spanish Press

ARMENIAN PRESS
Armenian and Armenian-English Publications

53. AMSATERTIG.   Monthly Bulletin.   1912–

152 East 34th   (212) 685-3177
New York, New York 10016

Editor: Armine Mardiguian   Circulation: 1,000
Sponsor: Armenian Evangelical Church   Frequency: monthly
Language: Armenian and English   Subscription: $2.00

Contains news of the Armenian Evangelical community, including Armenian Evangelical churches
in the United States and especially in New York. From 1912 to 1934 this bulletin was published
only in the Armenian language.

54. ASBAREZ.   Arena Stage.   1908–

1501 Venice Boulevard   (213) 380-7646
Los Angeles, California 90006

Editors: Kristapol Pakradouni and   Circulation: 1,700
      Serge Samoniantz   Frequency: semi-weekly
Sponsor: ASBAREZ Publishing Co. of the   Subscription: $20.00
      Armenian Revolutionary
      Federation of California
Language: Armenian and English

Primarily a political newspaper, promoting and keeping alive the Armenian cause and culture.
It covers international, national, cultural, and scientific affairs; political commentaries; and
topics relating to Armenian communities, such as educational, cultural, and religious affairs.
The goals of this publication are "to propagate the Armenian culture, inform the Armenian
community of the state of Armenians worldwide, help achieve the goal of creating an independent, free and united Republic of Armenia, and to relate the Armenian community to the
affairs of the world" (editor's statement). English section of the newspaper was added in 1973.

55. BAIKAR.   Struggle.   1922–

755 Mount Auburn Street
Watertown, Massachusetts 02172

Editor: Nuba Berberian   Circulation: 2,140
Sponsor: Baikar Association, Inc.   Frequency: daily
Language: Armenian   Subscription: $20.00

Official publication of the Armenian Democratic Liberal Party. Contents include news of
international, national, and local events which are of special interest to Armenians. Features
political, social, and cultural articles.

56. ERITASSARD HAYASTAN.   Young Armenia.   1903–
    353 Forest Avenue   (201) 262-5363
    Paramus, New Jersey 07652

    Editor: Arsen V. Jerejian   Circulation: 2,000
    Sponsor: Social Democratic Hunchakian   Frequency: monthly
           Party of America   Subscription: $5.00
    Language: Armenian

Contains general news and political articles concerning Armenians throughout the world and especially in the United States.

57. GERMANIK.   1930–
    36-33 169th Street
    Flushing, New York 11358

    Editor: Andraniu L. P'olatyan   Circulation: 1,000
    Sponsor: Union of Marash Armenians   Frequency: quarterly
    Language: Armenian and English   Subscription: $3.00

58. HAI SIRD.   Armenian Heart.   1939–
    212 Stuart Street   (617) 542-0528
    Boston, Massachusetts 02116

    Editor: Astrid Sarafian   Circulation: 2,150
    Sponsor: Armenian Relief Society, Inc.   Frequency: quarterly
    Language: Armenian and English   Subscription: $2.00

This periodical, intended largely as an informative publication, is addressed primarily to members of the Armenian Relief Society and to its sympathizers and contributors. Articles cover the history and purposes of the organization and reports on meetings and functions of the Armenian Relief Society. Occasionally fiction or poetry in either language is published. Prior to 1973 it was published in Armenian only.

59. HAIRENIK.   Fatherland.   1899–
    212 Stuart Street
    Boston, Massachusetts 02116

    Editor: James H. Tashjian   Circulation: 3,400
    Sponsor: Armenian Revolutionary Federation Frequency: daily
           of America   Subscription: $16.00
    Language: Armenian

Oldest Armenian daily in the United States. National, international, local, and group news of interest to the Armenian population. Organ of the Armenian Revolutionary Federation of America. An Armenian weekly in English is published under the same title (1933–) and edited by the same editor.

60. HAYASTANYAITZ YEGEGHETZY.   Armenian Church.   1938–
    630 Second Avenue   (212) 686-0710
    New York, New York 10016

    Editor: Krikor Vosganian   Circulation: 4,500
    Sponsor: Diocese of the Armenian Church   Frequency: monthly
           of America   Subscription: $3.00
    Language: Armenian

Focuses on news concerning Armenian churches in the United States, but includes articles on Armenian literature, culture, and history. In 1959 an English edition was also introduced. Illustrated.

61. HOOSHARAR.   The Prompter.   1915–
    628 Second Avenue   (212) 684-7530
    New York, New York 10016

HOOSHARAR (cont'd)

Editors: Antranig Poladian (Armenian)
    and Bedros Norehad (English)
Sponsor: Armenian General Benevolent Union
    of America
Language: Armenian and English

Circulation: 10,000
Frequency: monthly
Subscription: $3.00

First published in Armenian in 1915; English edition introduced in 1929. Primarily a fraternal, welfare magazine. Features articles on Armenian culture, education, and other relevant topics concerning the Armenian community in the United States.

62. KIR-OU-KIRK. Letter and Literature. 1956–

114 First Street
Yonkers, New York 10704

(914) 237-5751

Editor: K. N. Magarian
Sponsor: Armenian Literary Society, New
    York, Inc.
Language: Armenian and English

Circulation: 2,500
Frequency: semi-annual
Subscription: free

Covers "the world of Armenian literature, past and contemporary. . . .As the publication of the A. L. S., it reports on the meetings, programs, and activities of the organization" (editor's statement).

63. LOUSAVORICH. Illuminator. 1938–

630 Second Avenue
New York, New York 10016

Editor: Rev. Garen Gdanian
Sponsor: St. Gregory Illuminator Church
    of Armenia
Language: Armenian and English

Circulation: 1,150
Frequency: weekly
Subscription: donation

In addition to news related to church and parish affairs, this weekly also includes religious and spiritual messages.

64. LRABER. The Armenian Herald. 1937–

39 West 32nd Street
New York, New York 10001

(212) 929-8335

Editor: V. Ghazarian
Sponsor: Armenian Progressive League
    of America
Language: Armenian and English

Circulation: 2,426
Frequency: semi-weekly
Subscription: $12.00

International, national, local, and group news, with emphasis on issues of special interest to Armenians.

65. MAIR YEGEGHETZI. Mother Church. 1940–

221 East 27th Street
New York, New York 10016

Editor: Rev. Moushegh Der Kaloustian
Sponsor: St. Illuminator's Armenian Apostolic
Language: Armenian and English

Circulation: 1,200
Frequency: monthly
Subscription: free

Objectives of the publication are to inform Armenians of church affairs, special services, and the activities of various church-affiliated groups. Information on donations, weddings, baptisms, and funerals is published. News is primarily of a local nature.

66. NOR ASHKAR. The New World. 1955–

151 West 25th Street
New York, New York 10001

NOR ASHKAR (cont'd)
Editor: Samuel H. Toumayan
Sponsor: Samuel H. Toumayan–individually
    owned
Language: Armenian and English

Circulation: 900
Frequency: weekly
Subscription: $5.00

Features news items concerning Armenians in the United States and in the world.

67. **NOR OR.** New Day.   1921–
    7466 West Beverly Boulevard, Suite 101
    Los Angeles, California 90039

Editor: Antnanig Antreassian
Sponsor: Nor Or Publishing Association
Language: Armenian

Circulation: 1,500
Frequency: semi-weekly
Subscription: $15.00

Includes political, social, and cultural articles related to Armenians in the world and the United States. Reflects the views of the Armenian Democratic Liberal Organization.

68. **PAP OUKHTI.**   1935–
    12813 Gay Avenue
    Cleveland, Ohio 44105

Editor: Gevorg Melitinetsi
Sponsor: Educational Association of Malatia,
           Central Executive Board
Language: Armenian

Circulation: 500
Frequency: quarterly
Subscription: $5.00

Literary magazine. Includes news items concerning Armenian writers and cultural life.

69. **PARI LOOR.** Good News.   1957–
    17231 Sherman Way   (203) 344-4860
    Van Nuys, California 91406

Editor: Father Shahe Semerdjian
Sponsor: St. Peter Armenian Apostolic Church
Language: Armenian and English

Circulation: 12,500
Frequency: monthly
Subscription: free

This church bulletin features information on various activities of the Armenian Church organizations. Also contains articles on education and other topics of interest to the Armenian community.

70. **PAROS.** Lighthouse.   1954–
    666 Richmond Road   (216) 381-6590
    Richmond Heights, Ohio 44143

Editor: Rev. Fr. Diran Papazian
Sponsor: St. Gregory of Narek Armenian Church
Language: Armenian and English

Circulation: 400
Frequency: monthly
Subscription: free

Provides information about parish life in particular and about Armenian community life of Greater Cleveland in general.

71. **PAROS.** Beacon.   1958–
    70 Jefferson   (401) 272-7712
    Providence, Rhode Island 02908

Editor: Reverend Father Haik Donikian
Sponsor: St. Sahag and St. Mesrob Armenian
           Apostolic Church
Language: Armenian and English

Circulation: 950
Frequency: monthly
Subscription: free

Includes diocesan news and religious articles. The major objective is "to reach and advise parishioners of the religious culture and social aspects of the Armenian Church in Rhode Island" (editor's statement).

72. SHOGHAGAT.   Drop of Sunlight.   1950–
    2215 East Colorado Boulevard   (213) 449-1523
    Pasadena, California 91107

Editor: Michael S. Matosian   Circulation: 500
Sponsor: St. Gregory Armenian Apostolic   Frequency: monthly
          Church of Pasadena   Subscription: free
Language: Armenian and English

Features articles on Armenian history and religion, church and community news, and activities of church organizations.

73. SOORHANTAG.   The Messenger.
    87 Salisbury Street   (617) 756-2931
    Worcester, Massachusetts 01609

Editor: Deacon Daniel Kochakian   Circulation: 800
Sponsor: The Armenian Church of our Saviour   Frequency: bi-monthly
Language: Armenian and English   Subscription: n.i.

Contains information on church activities as well as cultural life of Armenian community.

74. YETTEM.   Garden of Eden.   1971–
    P. O. Box 367   (209) 528-6892
    Yettem, California 93670

Editor: Rev. Fr. Vartan Kasparian   Circulation: 260
Sponsor: St. Mary Armenian Apostolic Church   Frequency: monthly
Language: English and Armenian   Subscription: free with church
          membership

This church-oriented publication has news items on Armenian community life and on materials related to Armenian education.

Armenian Publications in English

75. A.G.A.U. BULLETIN.   1921–
    116 38th Street   (201) 865-0057
    Union City, New Jersey 07087

Editor: Mike Megerdichian   Circulation: 1,000
Sponsor: Armenian General Athletic Union,   Frequency: semi-monthly
         USA, Inc.   Subscription: donation only
Language: English

Promotes athletics among Armenian-Americans. Illustrated.

76. ARARAT.   1960–
    628 Second Avenue   (212) 684-7530
    New York, New York 10016

Editor: Leo Hamalian   Circulation: 850
Sponsor: Armenian General Benevolent Union   Frequency: quarterly
         of America, Inc.   Subscription: $6.00
Language: English

Editorial objectives are to provide a vehicle for writers of Armenian ancestry, although authorship is not limited to only Armenian writers. Contents include articles, short stores, poetry, plays, book reviews, and illustrations. Topics include various facets of Armenian history and culture as well as problems of assimilation and acculturation of the Armenian ethnic community in the United States, with special issues on such topics as religion, contemporary fiction, education, and social sciences.

77. ARMENIAN AMERICAN OUTLOOK. 1962–
140 Forest Avenue
Paramus, New Jersey 07652

Editor: Rev. Dicran Y. Kassouny   Circulation: 5,200
Sponsor: Armenian Evangelical Association of   Frequency: quarterly
   North America   Subscription: $3.00
Language: English

Features religious and cultural articles.

78. THE ARMENIAN CHURCH. 1958–
630 Second Avenue   (212) 686-0710
New York, New York 10016

Editor: Jack Antreassian   Circulation: 8,500
Sponsor: Diocese of the Armenian Church   Frequency: monthly
   of America   Subscription: $3.00
Language: English

Articles on religion, history, and culture of Armenians. Contains news of the Armenian Church throughout the world. Illustrated.

79. ARMENIAN DIGEST. 1970–
P. O. Box 638
New York, New York 10001

Editor: Hagop Tankian   Circulation: 25,000
Sponsor: T & T Publishing Co.   Frequency: monthly
Language: English   Subscription: n.i.

Literary monthly.

80. THE ARMENIAN MIRROR-SPECTATOR. 1932–
755 Mount Auburn Street   (617) 924-4420
Watertown, Massachusetts 02172

Editor: Varoujan Samuelian   Circulation: 2,540
Sponsor: Baikar Association, Inc.   Frequency: weekly
Language: English   Subscription: $10.00

Covers Armenian cultural and religious activities, but general news is also included. The prime objective is "to make our readers aware of their national heritage, to be proud of the accomplishments of fellow-Armenians, and conscious of the fact that they, too, can achieve worthwhile things" (editor's statement).

81. THE ARMENIAN OBSERVER. 1971–
6646 Hollywood Boulevard
Hollywood, California 90028

Editor: Osheen Keshishian   Circulation: 4,500
Sponsor: Published by the Editor   Frequency: weekly
Language: English   Subscription: $8.00

Features articles on the social, cultural, and political life of Armenians. Illustrated.

82. THE ARMENIAN REPORTER. 1967–
42-60 Main Street
Flushing, New York 11355

Editor: Edward K. Boghosian   Circulation: 3,300
Sponsor: The Armenian Reporter, Inc.   Frequency: weekly
Language: English   Subscription: $9.00

This newspaper primarily reports various social, cultural, religious, and other activities of Armenian communities, in the United States and abroad. Special features include such

THE ARMENIAN REPORTER (cont'd)
sections as Views and Opinions, Letters to the Editor, Calendar of Coming Events, and Obituaries. Profiles of successful Armenian personalities are also printed.

83. **THE ARMENIAN REVIEW.** 1947–
212 Stuart Street
Boston, Massachusetts 02116

Editor: James H. Tashjian
Sponsor: Hairenik Association
Language: English

Circulation: 900
Frequency: quarterly
Subscription: $6.00

Literary-historical journal of Armenians. Its contents include historical articles, memoirs, political studies, commentaries, short stories, poetry, book reviews, editorials, and translations from Armenian language materials. The editorial objective is "support of the Armenian quest for an independent, free, united democratic Armenian State" (editor's statement).

84. **THE ARMENIAN WEEKLY.** 1933–
212 Stuart Street
Boston, Massachusetts 02116

Editor: James H. Tashjian
Sponsor: Hairenik Association
Language: English

Circulation: 2,600
Frequency: weekly
Subscription: $7.00

This newspaper presents materials of a social, cultural, political, and historical nature that are of interest to people of Armenian background. Its objectives are "to encourage the concept of an independent Armenian State, to urge the retention of the Armenian identity abroad, and to encourage the practice of citizenship in the United States and Canada" (editor's statement). Features include sections on national and international news, items of special interest to Armenians, editorials, columns, sports page, youth page, obituaries, letter forum, and translations from the Armenian language press.

85. **BULLETIN FOR THE ADVANCEMENT OF ARMENIAN STUDIES AND RESEARCH.** 1955–
175 Mount Auburn Street (617) 876-7630
Cambridge, Massachusetts 02138

Editor: n.i.
Sponsor: National Association for Armenian
           Studies and Research
Language: English

Circulation: 2,500
Frequency: semi-annually
Subscription: n.i.

Contains information on Armenian studies in the United States, special programs, grants, and other relevant information.

86. **THE CALIFORNIA COURIER.**
P. O. Box 966 (209) 264-9330
Fresno, California 93714

Editor: George Mason
Sponsor: n.i.
Language: English

Circulation: 2,500
Frequency: weekly
Subscription: $8.00

Features articles on Armenians in the United States, with special emphasis on California. International, national, and local news is included. Illustrated.

ASIAN PRESS
See also **Chinese Press, Filipino Press, Indian Press, Japanese Press, Korean Press, and Pakistani Press.**

Editor's note: Many scholarly and popular periodicals exist that deal with Asian affairs, and they are important in elucidating the historical and cultural background of individual Asian American groups in the United States. The following titles should be mentioned: *Journal of*

American Oriental Society (New Haven, 1943– .Q.); *Asia; A Journal Published by the Asian Society* (New York, 1964– .Q.); *Journal of Asian Studies* (Ann Arbor, 1941– .5/yr); *Literature East & West* (Austin, 1953– .Q.).

Asian Publications in English

87. AMERASIA JOURNAL.
3235 Campbell
University of California
Los Angeles, California 90024

Editor: n.i.
Sponsor: Asian American Studies Center
Language: English

Circulation: n.i.
Frequency: n.i.
Subscription: n.i.

88. THE ASIAN STUDENT. 1954–
P. O. Box 3223
San Francisco, California 94119

Editor: C. Y. Hsu
Sponsor: The Asia Foundation
Language: English

Circulation: n.i.
Frequency: weekly
Subscription: $3.00

Summarizes significant editorials from newspapers published in Asian countries, and covers international news about student and research activities. It is published "as a public service to Asian students in the U.S.A." (editor's statement).

89. BRIDGE: AN ASIAN AMERICAN PERSPECTIVE. 1971–
22 Catherine Street   (212) 964-6832
New York, New York 10038

Editors: N. T. Yung and Bill Wong
Sponsor: Basement Workshop Inc.
Language: English

Circulation: 5,000
Frequency: bi-monthly
Subscription: $5.00

Features articles on Asian-American communities, creative writings, Asian-American stories, news in brief, and other relevant topics covering the Asian-American experience in the United States. Also contains a review section and a guest column.

90. GIDRA. 1969–
P. O. Box 18046
Los Angeles, California 90018

Editor: n.i.
Sponsor: Gidra, Inc.
Language: English

Circulation: 2,230
Frequency: monthly
Subscription: $2.50

The purpose of this monthly is to inform the Asian-American community about cultural and political matters that concern them. It also contains historical articles related to the Asian-American experience in the United States.

91. JADE. 1974–
8240 Beverly Boulevard   (213) 653-5506
Los Angeles, California 90048

Editor: Gerald Jann
Sponsor: Jade Publications
Language: English

Circulation: 35,000
Frequency: quarterly
Subscription: $4.50

Contains popular articles on various phases of the Asian-American experience in the United States. *Jade* shows Asian Americans as "part of the society in which they work, live and raise their children" (editor's statement). Illustrated.

92. THIRD WORLD NEWS.
367 Memorial Union
University of California
Davis, California 95616

Editor: n.i.   Circulation: n.i.
Sponsor: Asian American Concern   Frequency: n.i.
Language: English   Subscription: n.i.

ASSYRIAN PRESS
Assyrian and Assyrian-English Publications

93. KOKHWA ATOURAIA.   **The Assyrian Star.**   1956–
P. O. Box 59309   (312) 728-6515
Chicago, Illinois 60659

Editor: Mike Rasho   Circulation: 1,700
Sponsor: The Assyrian American National Frequency: monthly
     Federation   Subscription: $10.00
Language: English, Assyrian and Arabic

"The purpose of this publication is to promote the Assyrian identity and culture within the
United States and throughout the world" (editor's statement). Features cultural, political,
and educational materials concerning Assyrian community, with the aim of retaining Assyrian
identity and at preserving the Assyrian language.

BALTIC PRESS
See Estonian, Latvian, and Lithuanian Presses

BASQUE PRESS
Basque and Basque-English Publications

94. THE BASQUE STUDIES PROGRAM NEWSLETTER.   1968–
University of Nevada Library   (702) 784-6086
Reno, Nevada 89507

Editor: William A. Douglass   Circulation: 5,000
Sponsor: The Basque Studies Program,   Frequency: semi-annual
     University of Nevada system   Subscription: free
Language: English

Provides information regarding the Basque heritage and news of the activities of the Basque
Studies Program at University of Nevada. It is directed primarily toward the Basque-American
community in the West and scholars involved in Basque studies.

95. VOICE OF THE BASQUES.   1975–
1900 Bella Street   (208) 342-8862
Boise, Idaho 83702

Editor: Brian K. Wardle   Circulation: 1,296
Sponsor: Voice of the Basques   Frequency: monthly
Language: English and Basque   Subscription: $8.00

Features articles on Basque history, culture, language, news of the clubs and organizations in
the United States, and other relevant information concerning Basque community. "The paper
is strictly social and cultural and avoids taking a political position" (editor's statement).
Illustrated.

BELGIAN AND BELGIAN-FLEMISH PRESS
Belgian and Belgian-Flemish Publications

96. **BELGIAN TRADE REVIEW.**   1946–
    50 Rockefeller Plaza   (212) 247-7613
    New York, New York 10020

    Editor: Albert A. Van Oppens   Circulation: 9,000
    Sponsor: Belgian American Chamber of   Frequency: monthly
             Commerce in the United States   Subscription: $7.00
    Language: Belgian

97. **GAZETTE VAN DETROIT.**   **Detroit Gazette.**   1914–
    11243 Mack Avenue
    Detroit, Michigan 48214

    Editor: Mrs. Godelieve B. Van Reybrouck   Circulation: 2,855
    Sponsor: Belgian Press Company   Frequency: weekly
    Language: Flemish   Subscription: $4.00

General news. Reports on the activities of Flemish organizations and individuals.

BLACK AMERICAN PRESS

The Black American Press is too comprehensive to be listed in the confines of this directory.
A number of other reference publications contain separate sections on the Black press: *1975
Editor and Publisher International Yearbook, Ayer Directory of Newspapers and Periodicals*
for 1975; *The Ebony Handbook*, by the editors of Ebony (Chicago: Johnson Publishing Co.,
1974). Also see *Black List: The Concise and Comprehensive Reference Guide to Black
Journalism, Radio, and Television, Educational and Cultural Organizations in the U.S.A.,
Africa, and the Caribbean*, 2nd ed. (New York: Panther House, 1974), Vol. 1.

In addition to these the National Newspaper Publishers Association, a Black American organization (3636 16th Street, Washington, D. C. 20010), also publishes, on a bi-annual basis,
Black Press Information Handbook.

BULGARIAN PRESS
Bulgarian and Bulgarian-English Publications

98. **AMERICAN BULGARIAN REVIEW.**   1952–
    35 Sutton Place   (212) 755-8480
    New York, New York 10022

    Editor: Nicholas Babanov   Circulation: n.i.
    Sponsor: American Bulgarian League   Frequency: irregular
    Language: Bulgarian and English   Subscription: free

99. **MAKEDONSKA TRIBUNA.**   **Macedonian Tribune.**   1927–
    542 South Meridian Street   (317) 635-2157
    Indianapolis, Indiana 46225

    Editor: Anton Popov   Circulation: 2,501
    Sponsor: Central Committee of the Macedonian   Frequency: weekly
             Patriotic Organization of the   Subscription: $10.00
             U. S. & Canada
    Language: Bulgarian and English

This newspaper deals primarily with news of various affairs in the Balkans. It also includes
editorial comments on both national and international issues. A section of the publication
is devoted to social and cultural activities of Bulgarians on the American continent. The main
objective of the newspaper is to "preserve the cultural and religious heritage of the Macedono-
Bulgarians on this continent and to work for the creation of a united and independent state
of Macedonia" (editor's statement).

100. NARODNA VOLYA. People's Will.   1937–
    5854 Chene Street
    Detroit, Michigan 48211

Editor: Bocho Mircheff   Circulation: 818
Sponsor: People's Will Co-operative   Frequency: semi-monthly
         Publishing Company   Subscription: $5.00
Language: Bulgarian and English

General news of special interest to Bulgarians. Also includes news items on various Bulgarian group and individual activities in the United States.

**101. SVOBODNA I NEZAVISIMA BOLGARIA. Free and Independent
Bulgaria.**   1949–
    109 Amherst Street
    Highland Park, New Jersey 08904

Editor: G. M. Dimitrov   Circulation: 5,000
Sponsor: Bulgarian National Committee   Frequency: bi-monthly
Language: Bulgarian   Subscription: $5.00

Features political and educational articles dealing with the independence of Bulgaria.

BYELORUSSIAN PRESS
Byelorussian and Byelorussian-English Publications

102. ABIEZNIK. News Letter.   1955–
    3441 Tibbett Avenue   (212) 549-5395
    Bronx, New York 10463

Editor: J. Zaprudnik   Circulation: 200
Sponsor: Byelorussian Institute of Arts and   Frequency: semi-annual, irregular
         Sciences   Subscription: free
Language: Byelorussian

This newsletter, the house organ of the Byelorussian Institute of Arts and Sciences, summarizes the activities of its membership and provides references and short annotations of publications pertaining to Byelorussian studies. Listings of the most important forthcoming events are published regularly. Occasionally exchange lists of materials available in the Institute's library are included, plus necrologies and short biographical data of deceased Institute members.

103. BELARUSKAYA DUMKA. Byelorussian Thought.   1960–
    34 Richter Avenue   (201) 246-3216
    Milltown, New Jersey 08850

Editor: Danilovich Anton   Circulation: 1,000
Sponsor: Byelorussian Publishing Society   Frequency: semi-annual
Language: Byelorussian and English   Subscription: $2.00

This journal surveys Byelorussian political life in the United States and in the free world; critically analyzes political events in the Byelorussian SSR; publishes political documents pertaining to the activities of Byelorussian organizations in the United States; and gives critical literary reviews and works of Byelorussian writers in the United States. It provides bibliographical listings of Byelorussian publications outside the Soviet bloc countries and gives obituaries of Byelorussian political leaders.

104. BIELARUS. Byelorussian.   1950–
    166-34 Gothic Drive   (212) 746-1971
    Jamaica, New York 11432

Editor: Stanislau Stankevich   Circulation: 2,100
Sponsor: Byelorussian-American Association,   Frequency: monthly
         Inc.   Subscription: $6.00
Language: Byelorussian

BIELARUS (cont'd)

Discusses Byelorussian national problems in the USSR; Byelorussian problems abroad, especially in the United States; American policy toward the USSR; and Byelorussian social, cultural, and economic life in the United States.

105. CARKOUNY SVIETAC. Church's Light. 1951—
192 Turnpike Road (201) 257-6478
South River, New Jersey 08882

Editor: Rev. Nikolai Lapitzki Circulation: 500
Sponsor: Church Committee of Byelorussian Frequency: irregular
Greek-Orthodox Church Subscription: $12.00
Language: Byelorussian

This paper surveys developments in the religious and cultural life of the Byelorussian community in the United States and outside the BSSR. It publishes research materials on the history of the Byelorussian church, occasional papers of literary and theological content, and obituary and biographical notes on prominent Byelorussian church and civic leaders.

106. HOLAS CARKVY. Voice of the Church. 1954—
401 Atlantic Avenue (212) 858-4560
Brooklyn, New York 11217

Editor: Michael Mickievich Circulation: 1,000
Sponsor: Byelorussian Autocephalic Orthodox Frequency: semi-annual
Church in America Subscription: $4.00
Language: Byelorussian

This publication of the Byelorussian Autocephalic Church prints research materials on the history of the Byelorussian church, philosophical works, and literary reviews of religious interest. Also included are reading materials for Byelorussian Sunday schools and surveys of activities of Byelorussian Autocephalic Orthodox Churches and affiliated organizations.

107. KAMUNIKATY. News of the Council of BNR. 1970—
166-34 Gothic Drive (212) 746-1971
Jamaica, New York 11432

Editor: J. Zaprudnik Circulation: n.i.
Sponsor: Council of Byelorussian Democratic Frequency: irregular
Republic Subscription: free to institutions
Language: Byelorussian

This newsletter of Byelorussian political parties centers around the Council of the Byelorussian Democratic Republic; it provides biographical information on Byelorussian political leaders.

108. KONADNI. Vigils. 1955—
3441 Tibbett Avenue (212) 549-5395
Bronx, New York 10463

Editor: V. Tumash Circulation: 300
Sponsor: Byelorussian Institute of Arts and Frequency: irregular
Sciences Subscription: $3.00
Language: Byelorussian

This is a paper devoted to Byelorussian literature, arts, and social sciences. It publishes new materials in literature, provides reproductions of art works, and includes extensive annotated critical bibliographies.

109. LITARATURNA-MASTACKI ZBORNIK. Literary-Art Review. 1969—
P. O. Box 1944
Trenton, New Jersey

Editor: Michael Sienko Circulation: 500
Sponsor: Publishing Company, "Rodny Krai" Frequency: quarterly
Language: Byelorussian Subscription: $2.00

LITARATURNA-MASTACKI ZBORNIK (cont'd)
This review, which analyzes developments in the Byelorussian community in the United States, also publishes new literary works and reprints of literary works.

110. **SIAUBIT.** The Sower. 1957–
  164 Broadway
  Fort Edward, New York 12828

  Editor: Rev. Francis Cherniawski   Circulation: 400
  Sponsor: n.i.   Frequency: bi-monthly
  Language: Byelorussian   Subscription: $5.00

This magazine publishes literary works, religious articles, and documents pertaining to the history of the Byelorussian Catholic Church. There are also book reviews and church events.

111. **VIALITVA.** Abbreviation of Great Lithuania (Vialika Litva). 1970–
  204 South Highway 18   (201) 249-2255
  East Brunswick, New Jersey 08816

  Editor: Peter Markouski   Circulation: 2,000
  Sponsor: Peter Markouski   Frequency: irregular
  Language: Byelorussian and English Subscription: $1.00

Prior to 1974 published under the title Vieča (*The Council*). Features political, historical, and economical, articles concerning the Baltic and Slavic populations in Eastern Europe, with special emphasis on Byelorussia. Promotes revolutionary movements in the Soviet Union.

112. **ZAPISY.** Annals (of the Byelorussian Institute of Arts and Sciences). 1965–
  166-34 Gothic Drive   (212) 549-5395
  Jamaica, New York 11432

  Editor: Stanislau Stankevich   Circulation: 500
  Sponsor: Byelorussian Institute of Arts and Frequency: annually
      Sciences   Subscription: $5.00
  Language: Byelorussian

A scholarly publication dealing with new research materials on Byelorussian culture, history, social studies, arts, economics, and sciences. The emphasis is on recent research investigations being performed outside the Soviet bloc countries. It provides critical reviews and analyses of recent events in Byelorussian cultural life as well as critical bibliographical surveys of publications pertaining to Byelorussian studies. It occasionally publishes special volumes in conjunction with affiliated institutions in Germany and Canada.

113. **ZMAHAR.** Soldier. 1970–
  9 River Road
  Highland Park, New Jersey 08904

  Editor: V. Wasilewski   Circulation: 500
  Sponsor: Byelorussian Veterans Association Frequency: weekly
      in U.S.A.   Subscription: $5.00
  Language: Byelorussian

Bulletin of the Byelorussian-American Veterans. It analyzes military achievements throughout the world and publishes documents and materials pertaining to the history of the Byelorussian army and various military units in Byelorussia.

Byelorussian Publications in English

114. **BIELARUSKAYA MOLADŹ.** Byelorussian Youth. 1958–
  P. O. Box 309
  Jamaica, New York 11431

  Editor: Raisa Stankievic   Circulation: 500
  Sponsor: Byelorussian-American Youth Frequency: quarterly
      Organization   Subscription: $4.00
  Language: English

BIELARUSKAYA MOLADŹ (cont'd)

The main objective of the paper is "to acquaint Byelorussian youth with their rich heritage" (editor's statement). Features articles on Byelorussian history, folklore, and culture. Also includes short stories and poetry written by the youth. Illustrated. Until 1972 was published in Byelorussian.

115. FACTS ON BYELORUSSIA. 1974–
Queens College, Room A 111 A, SGS
Flushing, New York 11367

Editor: Jan Zaprudnik Circulation: n.i.
Sponsor: Jan Zaprudnik Frequency: bi-monthly
Language: English Subscription: $7.00

Features historical and political articles on Byelorussia, with factual materials on Byelorussian culture, economy, and other subjects.

CARPATHO-RUTHENIAN PRESS

Editor's note: The Carpatho-Ruthenian community in the United States asserts itself as constituting a separate ethnic group, which embraces immigrants from Carpatho-Ukraine and the Lemkian region. Presently "Carpatho-Ruthenia" or "Carpatian Rus'" constitutes an integral part of the Soviet Ukraine. The Carpatho-Ruthenian press usually is published in a special jargon (lyazychiie) based on a mixture of Ukrainian, Russian, and Slovak dialects, and is printed in Cyrillic or Latin characters. The editors of these publications, in designating their language, use such terms as "Carpatho-Ruthenian," "Carpatho-Russian," "Ruthenian," and "Russian."

For a detailed discussion, see Wasyl Halich's *Ukrainians in the United States* (Chicago, University of Chicago Press, 1937), pp. 115-117, reprinted by Arno Press in 1970 and Walter C. Warzeski's *Byzantine Rite Rusins in Carpatho-Ruthenia and America* (Pittsburgh; Byzantine Seminary Press, 1971).

Carpatho-Ruthenian and Carpatho-Ruthenian-English Publications

116. CERKOVNYJ VISTNIK. **Church Messenger.** 1944–
145 Broad Street
Perth Amboy, New Jersey 08861

Editor: Very Rev. Stephen Sedor Circulation: n.i.
Sponsor: American Carpatho-Russian Frequency: semi-monthly
  Orthodox Greek-Catholic Diocese Subscription: $4.00
Language: Carpatho-Ruthenian and English

Religious topics, church news, and articles on religious education. The "Carpatho" section is published in Carpatho-Ruthenian dialect and in the roman alphabet.

117. KARPATSKA RUS'. **Carpathian Rus'.** 1927–
556 Yonkers Avenue
Yonkers, New York 10704

Editor: Nicholas Cislak Circulation: 2,488
Sponsor: Lemko Association of U.S. and Canada Frequency: semi-monthly
Language: Carpatho-Ruthenian Subscription: $7.00

This official organ of the Lemko-Soiuz, a fraternal organization features articles on Lemkos history, culture, and religion. Publishes materials on Lemko-Souiz. Illustrated.

118. LEMKOVINA. **Lemko Land.** 1971–
P. O. Box 131, North Station
Yonkers, New York 10703

Editors: Teodor Dokla and Stephen M. Kitchura Circulation: 1,000
Sponsor: Lemkovina Press Frequency: monthly
Language: Lemko dialect Subscription: $4.00

LEMKOVINA (cont'd)
Unofficial organ of the World Federation of Lemkos, which aims at cooperation between the Ukrainian organization "Organization for Defense of Lemkivshchyna" and the pro-Russian Lemkos. Features political, social, and other articles dealing with Lemkos in Ukraine, Poland, and the United States.

119. **PROSVITA. The Enlightenment.**   1917–
     613 Sinclair Street   (717) 342-3294
     McKeesport, Pennsylvania 15132

     Editor: Rev. Basil Shereghy   Circulation: 4,500
     Sponsor: United Societies of U.S.A. (Sobranie)   Frequency: monthly
     Language: English and Ruthenian   Subscription: n.i.

Promotes the interests of the Fraternal Benefit Society, with emphasis on church news and religious articles. Supersedes *Rusin* (*The Ruthenian*, 1910-1917).

120. **RUSSKIJ VISTNIK. Russian Messenger.**   1916–
     333 Boulevard of Allies
     Pittsburgh, Pennsylvania 15222

     Editor: V. Rev. John J. Miller   Circulation: 2,000
     Sponsor: United Russian Orthodox Brotherhood   Frequency: bi-monthly
              of America   Subscription: $1.50 (for 2 years)
     Language: Carpatho-Russian and English

Deals with news of important religious and social events and activities sponsored by Carpatho-Ruthenian parishes in the United States. Religious messages are also included.

121. **SVOBODNOYE SLOVO KARPATSKOI RUSY.   Free Word of**
     Carpathian Rus'.   1959–
     ˙ P. O. Box 509
     Mount Vernon, New York 10550

     Editor: Michael Turjanica   Circulation: 1,000
     Sponsor: n.i.   Frequency: bi-monthly
     Language: Russian   Subscription: $3.00

Material is primarily of a political and spiritual nature.

122. **VIESTNIK GREKO KAFT. SOJEDINENIJA.   Greek Catholic**
     Union Messenger.   1892–
     502 8th Avenue   (412) 682-3465
     Munhall, Pennsylvania 15121

     Editor: Michael Roman   Circulation: 18,000
     Sponsor: Greek Catholic Union of the U.S.A.   Frequency: weekly
     Language: Carpatho-Russian   Subscription: $2.00

This publication covers the religious, social, cultural, national, educational, political, and sports activities of members of the Greek Catholic Union of the United States. The first title of the weekly was *Amerikansky Ruskyi Viestnik* (The American Ruthenian Messenger).

Carpatho-Ruthenian Publications in English

123. **BYZANTINE CATHOLIC WORLD.**   1956–
     P. O. Box 7668   (412) 948-7156
     Pittsburgh, Pennsylvania 15136

     Editor: Rev. Msgr. Gregory Rommack   Circulation: 12,900
     Sponsor: Carpatho-Ruthenian Catholic   Frequency: weekly
              Archdiocese of Munhall,   Subscription: $5.00
              Pennsylvania
     Language: English

BYZANTINE CATHOLIC WORLD (cont'd)

This official publication of the Byzantine Catholic Archdiocese of Munhall features religious articles and news. Prior to 1965 it was published partially in Ruthenian, and also in Hungarian. Illustrated.

124. **EASTERN CATHOLIC LIFE.**   1956–
     101 Market Street
     Passaic, New Jersey 07055

     Editor: Very Rev. Msg. Thomas Dolinay   Circulation: 14,000
     Sponsor: Byzantine Rite Eparchy of Passaic   Frequency: weekly
     Language: English   Subscription: $4.00

Features religious articles and news of interest to the Catholic parishioners of the Eparchy of Passaic. Also publishes general national and international news.

125. **THE ORTHODOX CHURCH.**   1965–
     Route 25-A, P. O. Box 675   (516) 922-0550
     Syosset, New York 11791

     Editor: Very Rev. John Meyendorff   Circulation: 30,000
     Sponsor: Metropolitan Council of the Orthodox   Frequency: monthly
             Church in America   Subscription: $5.00
     Language: English

The main objective of the paper is "to keep members of the Orthodox Church in America informed of news in the Orthodox world" (editor's statement). Includes religious articles and news on Orthodox Church in America and in the world. Illustrated.

126. **PRAVDA.   The Truth.**   1902–
     1733 Spring Garden Street   (215) 103-2537
     Philadelphia, Pennsylvania 19130

     Editor: Stephen P. Kopestonsky   Circulation: 5,000
     Sponsor: Russian Brotherhood Organization   Frequency: monthly
             of the U.S.A.   Subscription: $3.50
     Language: English

This newspaper serves as the official organ of the Russian Brotherhood Organization. Its contents include reports and orders of the Board of Supreme Officers, the Executive Committee and subordinate lodges; articles dealing with the development of the Organization; general news items; and correspondence of particular interest to the members of the Organization. Prior to 1971 it was published in Carpatho-Ruthenian dialect.

127. **THE RUSSIAN ORTHODOX JOURNAL.**   1927–
     84 East Market Street   (717) 825-3158
     Wilkes-Barre, Pennsylvania 18701

     Editor: Peter Melnik   Circulation: 5,200
     Sponsor: Federated Russian Orthodox Clubs   Frequency: monthly
     Language: English   Subscription: $5.50

Covers theology of the Eastern Orthodox Church and the history and contemporary conditions of the church. Also relates activities of church clubs and members.

128. **SVIT.   The Light.**   1895–
     84 East Market Street   (717) 822-8591
     Wilkes-Barre, Pennsylvania 18701

     Editor: Basil Homick (manager)   Circulation: 1,500
     Sponsor: Russian Orthodox Catholic Mutual   Frequency: bi-monthly
             Aid Society   Subscription: $3.00
     Language: English

Prior to July 1972 most articles were published in Carpatho-Ruthenian dialect. Contains historical, cultural, and other materials concerning Ruthenian community and also features articles on organizational activities. Illustrated.

CHICANO PRESS
See Spanish Press

CHINESE PRESS
See also Asian Press
Chinese and Chinese-English Publications

129. CHENG YEN PAO.   Truth Semi-Weekly.   1967–
809 Sacramento Street
San Francisco, California 94108

Editor: Frank Y. S. Wong   Circulation: 9,000
Sponsor: Frank Y. S. Wong   Frequency: bi-weekly
Language: Chinese   Subscription: $14.00

Covers all topics of special interest to Chinese in the United States, including general news on world, national, and group events, and activities within Chinatown.

130. CHINESE AMERICAN PROGRESS (CAP).   1951–
2249 South Wentworth Avenue   (312) 225-0234
Chicago, Illinois 60616

Editor: Eugene Liu   Circulation: 1,500
Sponsor: Chinese American Civic Council   Frequency: semi-annual
Language: Chinese and English   Subscription: n.i.

Published for members of the Chinese American Civic Council. The publication aims at "citizenship, betterment, and intergroup understanding" (editor's statement). Illustrated.

131. CHUNG KUO SHI PAO.   The China Times.   1963–
103-105 Mott Street
New York, New York 10013

Editor: Kwei-sang Wang   Circulation: 11,687
Sponsor: The Meo Kuo Publishing Co.   Frequency: daily
Language: Chinese   Subscription: $33.00

Includes world news and news from the Chinatown, Taiwan, and Hong Kong. Anti-communist newspaper. Most important news from Taiwan are condensed here, and some typical Chinese stories are introduced. Almost all advertisements are from New York City Chinatown.

132. HONOLULU CHINESE PRESS.   1975–
1197 River Street   (808) 533-7817
Honolulu, Hawaii 96817

Editor: Mario Ma   Circulation: 1,000
Sponsor: Man-Key Publishing & Printing Co. Frequency: daily
Language: Chinese   Subscription: $10.00

Features articles on the Chinese community in Hawaii, but national and local news are also included. Illustrated.

133. HWA MEI JIH PAO.   The China Tribune.   1950–
210 Canal Street   (212) 964-6182
New York, New York 10013

Editor: T. Y. Hang   Circulation: 8,500
Sponsor: Chinese-American Cultural   Frequency: daily
            Corporation   Subscription: $21.00
Language: Chinese

Reports, reviews, important world events and U. S. news. Emphasizes news from Mainland China, Taiwan, Hong Kong, and Southeast Asia, as well as Northeast Asia. Anti-communist orientation.

134. HWA PAO.   Mott Street Journal.
241 Canal Street, Room 203
New York, New York 10013

Editor: n.i.   Circulation: n.i.
Sponsor: n.i.   Frequency: semi-monthly
Language: Chinese   Subscription: $8.00

Pro-communist newspaper that also includes some important news from Mainland China.

135. JIN SHAN SHYR PAO.   Chinese Times.   1924–
117-119 Waverly Place
San Francisco, California 94108

Editor: Kwai Fong Chan   Circulation: 10,000
Sponsor: The Chinese Times Publishing   Frequency: daily
          Company, Inc.   Subscription: $30.00
Language: Chinese

Contents include news items on domestic, foreign, and Chinese group affairs and events. Information on medical problems, editorials on various topics, stories, and poetry are also printed.

136. LIN HO JIH PAO.   The United Journal.   1952–
199 Canal Street   (212) 431-5999
New York, New York 10013

Editor: Chin-fu Woo   Circulation: 15,000
Sponsor: The United Journal, Inc.   Frequency: daily
Language: Chinese   Subscription: $30.00

Covers news from Asia and China, with material on Chinese ethnic organizations in the United States. Orientation is pro-Taiwan. Illustrated.

137. MAGAZINE OF THE CHINESE CULTURE ASSOCIATION.   1966–
P. O. Box 1271   (415) 948-2251
Palo Alto, California 94302

Editor: P. F. Tao   Circulation: 2,000
Sponsor: Chinese Culture Association   Frequency: semi-annual
Language: Chinese   Subscription: free/membership

Includes news and reports of Chinese Culture Association activities. Features short stories, poetry, essays, and other types of Chinese creative writing. Illustrated.

138. MEI JO JIH PAO.   The Chinese Journal.   1926–
7 East Broadway
New York, New York 10038

Editor: n.i.   Circulation: n.i.
Sponsor: Chinese-American World Publishing Frequency: daily
          Corp.   Subscription: $21.00
Language: Chinese

Includes world and national news, and news from the Chinese ethnic communities in the United States. Pro-Taiwanese government. Special coverage of news from Washington, D. C., and Taipei.

139. PA-MI-ER.   Pamir Magazine.   1963–
8122 Mayfield   (216) 729-9937
Chesterland, Ohio 44026

Editor: Peter Wang   Circulation: 7,040
Sponsor: Chinese American Cultural   Frequency: 8 issues/year
          Association   Subscription: $2.00
Language: Chinese

General information on Chinese communities in the United States.

140. SAN MIN YAT PO.   San Min Morning Paper.   1932–
    Chicago, Illinois 60616

Editor: Henry Pan   Circulation: 2,300
Sponsor: Kuo Min Publishing Company   Frequency: daily
Language: Chinese   Subscription: n.i.

141. SHAO NIEN CHUNG KUO CH'EN PAO.   The Young China Daily.   1910–
    49 Hang Ah Street
    San Francisco, California 94108

Editor: T. C. Ma   Circulation: 7,700
Sponsor: T. C. Ma   Frequency: daily
Language: Chinese   Subscription: $42.00

Covers national, international, and group news. Its prime objective is to keep the Chinese reader both here and abroad up-to-date on activities and events occurring in the nation.

142. SING TAO JIH PAO.   Star Island Daily.   1910–
    766 Sacramento Street
    San Francisco, California 94108

Editor: Aw Sian, c/o Robert Chang   Circulation: 9,500
Sponsor: n.i.   Frequency: daily
Language: Chinese   Subscription: $29.00

World and national news, news from Asia in general. Special material concerning Chinese community in Hong Kong. "The objective of our U. S. edition is to serve the general public of Chinese in U. S. and Canada" (editor's statement).

143. SING TAO WEEKLY.   Star Island Weekly.   1910–
    766 Sacramento Street
    San Francisco, California 94108

Editor: Aw Sian, c/o Robert Chang   Circulation: 9,500
Sponsor: Aw Sian   Frequency: weekly
Language: Chinese   Subscription: $29.00

144. SUN CHUNG KWOCK BO.   New China Daily Press.   1900–
    P. O. Box 1656
    Honolulu, Hawaii 96806

Editor: Yick Kam Leong   Circulation: 1,200
Sponsor: Chinese Democratic Constitutional   Frequency: daily
             Party   Subscription: $42.00
Language: Chinese

News items on international, national, local, and group affairs. Feature items on Chinese personalities are often included.

145. TAI PING YOUNG JOW BAO.   Chinese Pacific Weekly.   1946–
    809 Stockton Street, Suite 101   (415) 982-6748
    San Francisco, California 94108

Editor: Gilbert Woo   Circulation: 4,263
Sponsor: Chinese Pacific Publishing Co., Inc.   Frequency: weekly
Language: Chinese   Subscription: $7.00

This newspaper is "devoted to the improvement and progress of the Chinese community" (editor's statement). It contains commentaries and special news reports as well as feature articles dealing with the ethnic situation, events in China, and national and local affairs.

146. TSU KUO I CHOU.   Fatherland Weekly.
    100 West 32nd Street, 3rd floor
    New York, New York 10001

TSU KUO I CHOU (cont'd)
Editor: James Wei
Sponsor: China Publishing Company, c/o Chinese
         Information Service
Language: Chinese

Circulation: 1,200
Frequency: weekly
Subscription: gift

Condenses the most important news that has appeared in local Chinese newspapers in Taiwan.

147. TUNG HSI PAO.   **East/West.**   1967–
758 Commercial Street
San Francisco, California 94108

Editor: Kenneth Wong
Sponsor: East/West Publishing Company
Language: Chinese and English

Circulation: 4,985
Frequency: weekly
Subscription: $7.50

Topics covered include civil rights, youth movements, welfare, housing problems, working conditions, etc. The objective of the publication is to "serve the Chinese community in this country and to serve as a link between Chinese and English speaking worlds" (editor's statement).

148. WOR KUEN.   **Getting Together.**   1970–
P. O. Box 26229
San Francisco, California 94126

Editor: Staff
Sponsor: n.i.
Language: Chinese and English

Circulation: 2,000
Frequency: monthly
Subscription: $5.00

"The objective of the paper is to educate through past and current news, people, especially Asian people, as to the nature of fascism in the United States and the revolutionary alternatives" (editor's statement). Political in nature, the publication contains articles on Chinese-American and Chinese history, community news, the war, and liberation struggles. Illustrated.

Chinese Publications in English

149. AMERICAN CHINESE NEWS.
763 North Hill Street
Los Angeles, California 90012

Editor: Yin Po Lin
Sponsor: American Chinese News Company
Language: English

Circulation: 2,450
Frequency: weekly
Subscription: n.i.

150. BULLETIN OF THE CHINESE HISTORICAL SOCIETY OF AMERICA.   1966–
17 Adler Place
San Francisco, California 94133

Editor: Thomas W. Chinn
Sponsor: Chinese Historical Society of America
Language: English

Circulation: n.i.
Frequency: monthly
Subscription: members only

This publication is restricted to members of the Chinese Historical Society of America, and to other historical organizations on an exchange basis. Its contents deal primarily with the history of the Chinese in America and related subjects.

151. CHINA DAILY NEWS.
20 Elizabeth Street
New York, New York 10013

Editor: James Lee
Sponsor: China Daily News, Inc.
Language: English

Circulation: 3,100
Frequency: semi-weekly
Subscription: n.i.

152. CHINESE-AMERICAN WEEKLY.　　　　　　　　　　　　1942–
　　　199 Canal Street
　　　New York, New York 10013

　　Editor: Chin Fu Woo　　　　　　　　　Circulation: 9,000
　　Sponsor: Chinese-American Press　　　Frequency: weekly
　　Language: English　　　　　　　　　　Subscription: n.i.

153. THE CHINESE WORLD.　　　　　　　　　　　　　　1891–
　　　736 Grant Avenue
　　　San Francisco, California 94108

　　Editor: John S. C. Ong　　　　　　　Circulation: 7,500
　　Sponsor: Chinese World, Ltd.　　　　Frequency: daily
　　Language: English　　　　　　　　　　Subscription: n.i.

154. FREE CHINA REVIEW.
　　　100 West 32nd Street, 3rd floor
　　　New York, New York 10001

　　Editor: James Wei　　　　　　　　　　Circulation: 221
　　Sponsor: China Publishing Company, c/o Chinese　Frequency: monthly
　　　　　　Information Service　　　　　Subscription: $3.00
　　Language: English

155. FREE CHINA WEEKLY.　　　　　　　　　　　　　1963–
　　　159 Lexington Avenue　　　　　　　(212) 725-4950
　　　New York, New York 10016

　　Editor: Ying Lai　　　　　　　　　　Circulation: 7,000
　　Sponsor: Chinese Information Service　Frequency: weekly
　　Language: English　　　　　　　　　　Subscription: $2.50

The major objective of the magazine is "to present to the English-speaking public throughout the world significant events that take place in the Republic of China on Taiwan" (editor's statement). Covers politics, culture, economics, education, and other subjects. Illustrated.

156. HAWAII CHINESE HISTORY CENTER NEWSLETTER.　　　1970–
　　　111 North King Street, Room 410　　(808) 521-5948
　　　Honolulu, Hawaii 96817

　　Editor: Irma Tam Soong　　　　　　　Circulation: 800
　　Sponsor: Hawaii Chinese History Center　Frequency: quarterly
　　Language: English　　　　　　　　　　Subscription: $5.00

Contains information on Hawaii Chinese History Center activities.

157. MEI JO JIH PAO.　　The Chinese Journal.　　　　　1928–
　　　7 East Broadway
　　　New York, New York 10038

　　Editor: Hsuang Wu Kung　　　　　　　Circulation: 15,520
　　Sponsor: Chinese American World Publishing　Frequency: daily
　　　　　　Corporation　　　　　　　　　Subscription: $21.00
　　Language: English

Includes world and national news, and news from the Chinese ethnic communities in the United States. Orientation is pro-Taiwan.

158. UNITED CHINESE PRESS.　　　　　　　　　　　　1951–
　　　P. O. Box 1519
　　　Honolulu, Hawaii 96817

　　Editor: Kam Fui　　　　　　　　　　　Circulation: 3,225
　　Sponsor: United Chinese Press, Ltd.　Frequency: daily

UNITED CHINESE PRESS (cont'd)
Language: English   Subscription: n.i.

General, international, and national news of Chinese interest.

159. **VISTA.**
    100 West 32nd Street, 3rd floor
    New York, New York 10001

Editor: James Wei   Circulation: 195
Sponsor: China Publishing Company, c/o Chinese   Frequency: bi-monthly
        Information Service   Subscription: $1.80
Language: English

COSSACK PRESS
Cossack Publications

160. **KOZACHE ZYTTIA.**   The Cossacks' Life.   1953–
    602 Public Street   (401) 461-2948
    Providence, Rhode Island 02907

Editor: T. G. Bihday   Circulation: 250
Sponsor: n.i.   Frequency: quarterly
Language: Russian, Ukrainian and English   Subscription: $15.00

Until 1970 this periodical was published monthly. In January 1971 it became a quarterly. The journal is of a literary-political nature, dealing with the cultural and educational life of Cossacks in connection with their historical role.

CROATIAN PRESS
Croatian and Croatian-English Publications

161. **BULLETIN OF THE AMERICAN CROATIAN ACADEMIC CLUB.**   1960–
    P. O. Box 18081   (212) 361-3037
    Cleveland Heights, Ohio 44118

Editor: Tefko Saracevic   Circulation: 500
Sponsor: American Croatian Academic Club   Frequency: irregular
Language: English and Croatian   Subscription: free

The purpose of this publication is to report on the events and activities of the American Croatian Academic Club and on the various cultural activities of Croatians in the United States.

162. **CROATIA PRESS. A REVIEW AND NEWS BULLETIN.**   1947–
    P. O. Box 1767
    New York, New York 10017

Editor: Karlo Mirth   Circulation: 500
Sponsor: n.i.   Frequency: quarterly
Language: Croatian and English   Subscription: $6.00

This quarterly deals with current affairs in Yugoslavia, with emphasis on Croatia. The news covers political, economic, and cultural activities, and items on various activities of Croatian-Americans are also published. Sections of the periodical are devoted to bibliographies of Croatian publications worldwide. Between 1947 and 1952 the journal was published only in Croatian. in 1952 English language articles were introduced.

163. **DANICA.**   The Morning Star.   1912–
    4851 Drexel Boulevard   (312) 373-4670
    Chicago, Illinois 60615

Editor: Editorial Board   Circulation: 4,500
Sponsor: Croatian Center Association   Frequency: weekly
Language: Croatian   Subscription: $10.00

DANICA (cont'd)

This is one of the oldest Croatian newspapers in the United States. It provides news of interest to the Croatian community and promotes the cause of Croatian independence. Utnil 1945 this weekly was called *Hrvatski List i Danica Hrvatska.* It "sustains the cultural and religious values of Croatian emigrants, ties them to their homeland, and assists them to adapt to their new country" (editor's statement). Illustrated.

164. HRVATSKI KATOLICKI GLASNIK.   Croatian Catholic Messenger.   1941—
    4851 Drexel Boulevard
    Chicago, Illinois 60615

Editor: Fr. Gracijan Raspudic   Circulation: 2,000
Sponsor: Croatian Franciscan Fathers   Frequency: monthly
Language: Croatian   Subscription: n.i.

This monthly magazine published by the Croatian Franciscans features religious articles. Illustrated.

165. JUNIOR MAGAZINE.   **1940—**
    100 Delaney Drive   (412) 351-3909
    Pittsburgh, Pennsylvania 15235

Editor: Michael Grasha   Circulation: 15,500
Sponsor: Croatian Fraternal Union of America   Frequency: bi-monthly
Language: English and Croatian   Subscription: free to members

Provides coverage of social, cultural, athletic, and fraternal activities of the Croatian Fraternal Union throughout the United States and Canada. The objectives are to deal with issues pertinent to junior members of the Union. The publication also strives to "inculcate in those members an appreciation of the fraternal benefit system and an awareness of their ethnic background" (editor's statement).

166. NARODNI GLASNIK.   People's Herald.   **1907—**
    Chicago, Illinois 60608

Editor: Leo Fisher   Circulation: 910
Sponsor: Narodni Glasnik Publishing Company,   Frequency: weekly
    Inc.   Subscription: $6.00
Language: Croatian

Contents include news of social and political events, achievements in science, and interpretation of events and international relationships in order to promote "the understanding of American (and other) Croats and Yugoslavs in general of the conditions, customs, institutions, history, etc., of the United States" (editor's statement). This publication also includes items on the achievements of American Croats and other Yugoslavs in the fields of politics, science, sports, and labor.

167. NAŠA NADA.   Our Hope.   **1921—**
    125 West Fifth Avenue   (219) 885-7325
    Gary, Indiana 46402

Editor: Stanley Boric   Circulation: 6,250
Sponsor: Croatian Catholic Union Fraternal   Frequency: semi-monthly
    Benevolent Society   Subscription: $3.00
Language: Croatian and English

The purpose of this paper is "to perpetuate Croatian Catholic heritage in America and at the same time help educate and assimilate people to American life as good citizens" (editor's statement). It covers the cultural and social life of Croatian organizations in the United States and encourages fraternal activities.

168. TRUBLJAC.   The Trumpeter.   1972–
  1512 Lancelot   (806) 273-7225
  Borger, Texas 79007

  Editor: Charles Glavanic   Circulation: 600
  Sponsor: Croatian Philatelic Society   Frequency: quarterly
  Language: English and Croatian   Subscription: $5.00

Features articles on philately, numismatics, and history of Croatia, Bosnia, Yugoslavia, and the Balkan areas.

169. VJESNIK UJEDINJENIH AMERICKIH HRVATA.   Bulletin of United American Croats.   1960–
  550 West 50th Street   (212) 565-4300
  New York, New York 10019

  Editor: Krunoslav Masina   Circulation: 2,000
  Sponsor: United American Croats   Frequency: bi-monthly
  Language: Croatian   Subscription: $4.00

Focuses on political events that affect Croatians and Croatia. Sections cover news dealing with Croatia, editorials, comments, opinions, sports, education, cultural news, organizational news, and survey of the world press. The editorial policies and goals are "against Communism and for a free and independent Croatia" (editor's statement).

170. ZAJEDNIČAR.   The Fraternalist.   1904–
  100 Delaney Drive   (412) 531-3909
  Pittsburgh, Pennsylvania 15235

  Editor: John Herak, Jr.   Circulation: 40,200
  Sponsor: Croatian Fraternal Union of America Frequency: weekly
  Language: English and Croatian   Subscription: members only

The primary purpose of this publication is to cover events and activities of approximately 600 senior lodges and 400 junior groups ("Nests") affiliated with the Croatian Fraternal Union of America throughout the United States and Canada. News coverage deals with athletic, cultural, and educational activities. The publication also promotes the organization's insurance portfolio and disability, surgical, and hospitalization coverage.

Croatian Publications in English

171. AMERICAN–CROAT.   1964–
  P. O. Box 3025   (213) 795-3495
  Arcadia, California 91006

  Editor: Petar Radielovic   Circulation: 3,200
  Sponsor: Croation Information Service   Frequency: irregular
  Language: English   Subscription: $3.00

"The purpose . . . is to foster the cultural identity of Croats, to promote the legitimate freedom and independence cause of the Croatian nation . . . " (editor's statement). Contains commentary and documentation in the form of articles, reprints, reviews, letters, editorials, resolutions and recommendations.

172. JOURNAL OF CROATIAN STUDIES.   1960–
  P. O. Box 1767 Grand Central Station
  New York, New York 10017

  Editors: Jerome Jareb and Karlo Mirth   Circulation: 1,000
  Sponsor: The Croatian Academy of America, Inc. Frequency: annually
  Language: English   Subscription: $5.00

This is primarily a scholarly review which publishes articles pertinent to Croatian history and culture (literature, fine arts, music, sociology, economics, government and law, sciences, philology, and religion). Creative translations of Croatian short stories and poems, reviews of

JOURNAL OF CROATIAN STUDIES (cont'd)

recent books relevant to Croatian matters, and unpublished documents of Croatian historical and cultural significance (letters, diaries, and records) are also published.

CUBAN PRESS

See **Spanish Press**

CZECH PRESS

See also **Slovak Press**

Czech and Czech-English Publications

173. AMERICKE LISTY.   **American Letters.**   1962–
283 Oak Street
Perth Amboy, New Jersey 08861

Editor: Josef Martinek	Circulation: 1,600
Sponsor: Universum Press Company	Frequency: weekly
Language: Czech	Subscription: n.i.

Covers political, cultural, and social topics of interest to the Czech community.

174. BESIDKA SOKOLSKA.   **Sokol News.**   1892–
29-19 24th Avenue
Astoria, New York 11105

Editor: Bohuslav Zavorka	Circulation: 420
Sponsor: Czechoslovak Workingmen's Gymnastic	Frequency: monthly
Association	Subscription: $1.20
Language: Czech and English	

Focuses on current events within the Czechoslovak Workingmen's Gymnastic Association (SOKOL). Most of the news items deal with sports and physical fitness.

175. BRATRSKE-LISTY.   **The Brethren Journal.**   1902–
5905 Carleen Drive   (512) 452-3695
Austin, Texas 78731

Editor: Rev. Jesse E. Skrivanek	Circulation: 1,550
Sponsor: Unity of the Brethren in Texas	Frequency: monthly
Language: English and Czech	Subscription: $3.00

This journal publishes information concerning the activities of the Unity of the Brethren organization. Most of the articles deal with general religious interests and activities. Spiritual messages are numerous. A section of the publication also deals with vital statistics of members (births, deaths, baptisms, and weddings).

176. BRATRSKY VESTNIK.   **Fraternal Herald.**   1898–
1900 1st Avenue, N.E.   (319) 363-2653
Cedar Rapids, Iowa 52402

Editors: Henrietta Piskac Shutt (English) and	Circulation: 25,500
Anton Piskac, Sr. (Czech)	Frequency: monthly
Sponsor: Western Fraternal Life Association	Subscription: $2.00
Language: Czech and English	

This journal publishes reports on various activities of affiliated lodges and meetings of the Board of Directors and officers. Much of the material centers on the accomplishments of members of the Association, and biographies of deceased members are also printed. At times instructive and entertaining articles are included, especially when pertaining to Czech or Slovak history. Although the magazine is non-partisan in political matters, it does admit discussions of relevant issues. Illustrated.

177. ÚŘEDNÍ ORGAN JEDNOTY C.S.A. The CSA Journal.   1892–
2701 South Harlem Avenue, CSA Plaza   (312) 795-5800
Berwyn, Illinois 60402

Editor: Bill R. Cicovsky   Circulation: 18,500
Sponsor: Czechoslovak Society of America   Frequency: monthly
Language: Czech and English   Subscription: free/membership

The magazine contains editorials, a sports section, a family page, a juvenile page, and other materials concerning CSA. In 1967 it changed from the newspaper to magazine format. Illustrated.

178. DENNI HLASATEL. Daily Bohemian Herald.   1891–
1545 West 18th Street   (312) 226-3315
Chicago, Illinois 60608

Editor: Milo R. Tuma   Circulation: 6,281
Sponsor: None   Frequency: daily
Language: Czech   Subscription: $28.00

National, international, local, and general news, and editorials of interest to the Czechoslovak community in the United States. Also includes short stories and articles on Czech history. Illustrated.

179. HLASATEL. Bohemian Herald.   1891–
1545 West 18th Street   (312) 226-3315
Chicago, Illinois 60608

Editor: Milo R. Tuma   Circulation: 3,724
Sponsor: n.i.   Frequency: weekly
Language: Czech   Subscription: $14.00

Covers national and international events of interest to Czech people. Also includes Czech fiction. Special section includes "Letters from Readers." Illustrated.

180. HLAS JEDNOTY. Voice of the Unity.   1894–
6907 Cermak Road
Berwyn, Illinois 60402

Editor: R. J. Heukal   Circulation: 6,000
Sponsor: Unity of Czech Ladies and Men   Frequency: quarterly
Language: Czech and English   Subscription: $1.50

This publication focuses on matters pertaining to fraternal life insurance. Most of the space is devoted to letters from lodge officers reporting on fraternal activities. Short articles on various subjects and editorials are also occasionally included.

181. HOSPODAR. Farmer.   1889–
214 West Oak   (817) 826-5282
West, Texas 76691

Editor: Jerome Kopecky   Circulation: 7,344
Sponsor: Czechoslovak Publishing Company   Frequency: semi-monthly
Language: Czech   Subscription: $7.00

This farmers' magazine features articles on agricultural topics, general news, and other subjects of interest to the Czech community, including historial articles and Czech fiction.

182. KATOLIK. The Catholic.   1893–
1637 South Allport Street
Chicago, Illinois 60608

Editor: Very Rev. Alex Machacek   Circulation: 2,250
Sponsor: Bohemian Benedictine Order   Frequency: weekly
Language: Czech   Subscription: $7.50

KATOLIK (cont'd)

Contains articles on international, national, regional, and local news with emphasis on the Catholic Church and related topics. Historical and cultural themes pertaining to the origin of the Czechs, their American setting, and their contributions to the United States are also covered.

183. **KATOLICKY DELNIK.**   **Catholic Workman.**   1907–
    Box 277
    Dodge, Nebraska 68633

    Editor: Rev. Francis J. Oborny   Circulation: 15,584
    Sponsor: Catholic Workmen's Fraternal   Frequency: monthly
             Association   Subscription: $.50
    Language: English and Czech

Regular monthly features include decisions of the Supreme Executive Council; a list of new members; a list of mortuary claims; the Supreme Treasurer's Report of Receipts; disbursements and up-to-date assets; reports of State Executive Councils; news from branches; religious instructions for the Supreme Spiritual Directory; editor's comments and articles reprinted from other fraternal magazines.

184. **KJZT NEWS.**   1955–
    P. O. Box 1884
    Austin, Texas 78767

    Editor: Benita Pavlu   Circulation: 10,600
    Sponsor: Catholic Women's Fraternal of Texas   Frequency: monthly
    Language: English and Czech   Subscription: free to members

This journal functions as a means of communication between members of the Fraternal Benefit Society, the KJZT. Its contents consist primarily of items on the society's events and activities.

185. **LEADER-NEWS.**   1885–
    P. O. Box 907
    El Campo, Texas 77437

    Editor: Herschiel L. Hunt   Circulation: 5,000
    Sponsor: n.i.   Frequency: weekly
    Language: Czech and English   Subscription: $4.50

186. **NÁROD.**   **The Nation.**   1893–
    1637 South Allport Street
    Chicago, Illinois 60608

    Editor: Very Rev. Alex Machacek   Circulation: 2,060
    Sponsor: Bohemian Benedictine Order   Frequency: weekly
    Language: Czech   Subscription: $8.00

This publication, like *Katolik*, is published by the Bohemian Benedictine Order, and its contents are similar. However, it consists of two parts: Part one is published in the Czech language, as a Saturday edition, while Part two is published in English as a Sunday edition. *Narod* was a daily until 1956.

187. **NASINEC.**   **Fellow Countryman.**   1914–
    East Davila Street, P. O. Box 158
    Granger, Texas 76530

    Editor: Joe Maresh, Sr.   Circulation: 2,010
    Sponsor: Czech Catholic Union of Texas   Frequency: weekly
    Language: Czech   Subscription: free to members

188. **NEDĚLNÍ HLASATEL.**   **Sunday Herald.**   1891–
    1545 West 18th Street
    Chicago, Illinois 60608   (312) 226-3315

NEDĚLNÍ HLASATEL (cont'd)

Editor: Milo R. Tuma
Sponsor: Denni Hlsatel Publishing & Printing Co.
Language: Czech

Circulation: 3,400
Frequency: weekly
Subscription: $14.00

Similar in content to *Hlasatel*.

189. **NOVA DOBA.   New Era.**   1937–
     Chicago, Illinois 60608

Editor: Charles Musil
Sponsor: Nova Doba Publishing Company, Inc.
Language: Czech

Circulation: 1,198
Frequency: weekly
Subscription: $6.00

190. **NOVÝ DOMOV.   New Home.**   1894–
     Davilla Street
     Granger, Texas 76530

Editor: Walter Malec
Sponsor: Union of Czech Catholic Women of
         Texas
Language: Czech

Circulation: 3,067
Frequency: weekly
Subscription: $4.00

191. **NOVY SVET.   The New World.**   1950–
     4732 Broadway   (216) 271-1911
     Cleveland, Ohio 44127

Editor: Miloslava Hyvnar
Sponsor: Board of Directors of Novy Svet
         Publications
Language: Czech

Circulation: 1,200
Frequency: weekly
Subscription: $.20/copy

General, international, national, and local news.

192. **POSEL.   The Messenger.**   1926–
     5349 Dollo Road   (216) 341-0444
     Cleveland, Ohio 44127

Editor: Ernest Zizka
Sponsor: The Czech Catholic Union
Language: Czech

Circulation: 6,000
Frequency: quarterly
Subscription: free to members

193. **PRAVDA A SLAVNA NADEJE.   Truth and Glorious Hope.**   1919–
     316 South Park Street
     Westmont, Illinois 60559

Editor: Rev. J. P. Piroch
Sponsor: Czechoslovak Baptist Convention of
         U. S. and Canada
Language: Czech and Slovak

Circulation: 1,027
Frequency: monthly
Subscription: n.i.

194. **PROMĚNY.   Metamorphoses.**   1964–
     381 Park Avenue South, Room 1121   (212) 686-4220
     New York, New York 10016

Editor: Vratislav Busek, New York representative   Circulation: 750
        on Editorial Board   Frequency: quarterly
Sponsor: Czechoslovak Society of Arts and   Subscription: $7.50
         Sciences in America
Language: Czech and Slovak

Sections of this literary quarterly are devoted to poetry; scholarly articles on philosophy, economics, political science, history, and art; short stories; critical book reviews; and other fields in the humanities and the social sciences. The articles in *Promeny* are indexed in the *MLA International Bibliography*.

195. SOKOL TYRS NEWSLETTER.
3689 East 131st Street
Cleveland, Ohio 44120

Editor: Elsie V. Suster
Sponsor: American Sokol Gymnastic Organization
Language: Czech and English

Circulation: n.i.
Frequency: bi-monthly
Subscription: n.i.

This fraternal magazine features sports news.

196. SPJST VESTNIK. **SPJST Herald.** 1897–
P. O. Box 100 (817) 733-1575
Temple, Texas 76501

Editor: Rudy J. Sefcik
Sponsor: Slavonic Benevolent Order of the
State of Texas
Language: English and Czech

Circulation: 11,760
Frequency: weekly
Subscription: $4.50

Strictly fraternal in nature, this weekly has two parts: one in English and one in Czech. It includes newsbriefs and features on members; letters and reports from the various lodges concerning their social, cultural, and financial matters; and a section devoted to youth activities, which includes reports and letters from district youth directors, lodge youth leaders, and youth members.

197. SVOBODNE ČESKOSLOVENSKO. **Free Czechoslovakia.** 1943–
4029 West 25th Place (312) 521-0120
Chicago, Illinois 60623

Editor: Bela Kotrsal
Sponsor: Czech American National Alliance
Language: Czech

Circulation: 800
Frequency: monthly
Subscription: $2.00

This monthly is political in nature.

198. TEXASKY ROLNIK. **Texas Farmer.** 1930–
P. O. Box 426
Granger, Texas 76530

Editor: Joseph Maresh, Sr.
Sponsor: Farmers Mutual Protection
Association of Texas
Language: Czech

Circulation: n.i.
Frequency: quarterly
Subscription: free to members

199. VĚSTNIK. **Herald.** 1954–
2137 South Lombard Avenue
Cicero, Illinois 60650

Editor: Vlasta Vraz
Sponsor: Czechoslovak National Council of
America
Language: Czech

Circulation: 3,030
Frequency: monthly
Subscription: $2.00

This magazine serves as a forum of expression mainly for members of the Czechoslovak National Council of America. Contents include reports on the activities of the Czech and Slovak communities in the United States, articles on the latest events in Czechoslovakia and in the United States from the standpoint of the Czech-Slovak American citizens, and articles devoted to the Czechoslovak culture. The journal is an "anti-communist organ which stresses the importance of the struggle against Communist and other totalitarian domination" (editor's statement).

200. VĔSTNIK. Herald. 1916–
P. O. Box 85
West, Texas 76691

Editor: R. J. Sefcik
Sponsor: Slavonic Benevolent Order of Texas
Language: Czech and English

Circulation: 10,587
Frequency: weekly
Subscription: n.i.

201. ZPRAVODAJ. Reporter. 1969–

Editor: n.i.
Sponsor: Alliance of Czechoslovak Exiles in
    Chicago
Language: Czech

Circulation: n.i.
Frequency: monthly
Subscription: n.i.

**202. ZPRÁVY SVU. Bulletin of the Czechoslovak Society of Arts and
Sciences in America.** 1959–
381 Park Avenue South, Room 1121   (212) 686-4220
New York, New York 10016

Editor: Andrew Elias
Sponsor: Czechoslovak Society of Arts and
    Sciences in America
Language: Czech and Slovak

Circulation: 1,190
Frequency: monthly
Subscription: $3.00

This bulletin includes announcements of its sponsoring organization; reports on activities of
local chapters and individual members; news items of interest in the arts and sciences; book
reviews; and biographic and bibliographic items.

Czech Publications in English

203. AMERICAN BULLETIN. 1954–
2137 South Lombard Avenue
Cicero, Illinois 60650

Editor: Vlasta Vraz
Sponsor: Czechoslovak National Council of
    America
Language: English

Circulation: 3,050
Frequency: monthly
Subscription: $2.00

Carries news of interest to Americans of Czech and Slovak descent pertaining to Czechoslovakia
and to ethnic matters. "It is dedicated to the struggle for democracy and defeat of communism"
(editor's statement).

204. SOKOL AMERICKY. American Sokol. 1879–
6426 West Cermak Road   (312) 795-6671
Berwyn, Illinois 60402

Editor: George Herink
Sponsor: American Sokol Educational and
    Physical Culture Organization
Language: English

Circulation: 5,910
Frequency: monthly
Subscription: $3.00

Designed to "educate our members further through articles relating to our cultural history. We
hope to keep our gymnastic instructors informed as to current trends in worldwide gymnastic
activities" (editor's statement). A fraternal publication.

205. SOUTH OMAHA SOKOL. 1964–
5601 South 21st Street   (402) 731-1065
Omaha, Nebraska 68107

Editor: E. J. Pavoucek
Sponsor: Gymnastic Sokol Society Fuegner Tyrs
Language: English

Circulation: 900
Frequency: monthly
Subscription: $5.00

Includes articles on physical education and news about the Sokol's members.

DANISH PRESS
See also Scandinavian Press

Danish and Danish-English Publications

206. BIEN.   The Bee.   1882–
435 Duboce Avenue
San Francisco, California 94117

Editor: Sven Stribolt   Circulation: 3,500
Sponsor: Bien Publishing Company   Frequency: weekly
Language: Danish   Subscription: $7.00

This is the only Danish weekly in the United States. It includes national, international, and local news, plus coverage of group activities and events. Its main objective is to "maintain and support the Danish language and customs" (editor's statement).

207. DEN DANSKE PIONEER.   The Danish Pioneer.   1872–
36 Conti Parkway
Elmwood Park, Illinois 60635

Editor: Hjalmar Bertelsen   Circulation: 7,000
Sponsor: Bertelsen Publishing Co.   Frequency: semi-monthly
Language: Danish and English   Subscription: $10.00

This paper provides news coverage of events in Denmark and the United States. Also included are reports on the activities of Danish groups throughout the United States, and feature items on individuals and their accomplishments.

208. KIRKE OG FOLK.   Church and People.   1951–
1506 Thompson Avenue
Des Moines, Iowa 50316

Editor: Johannes Knudsen   Circulation: 1,000
Sponsor: The Danish Interest Conference of the   Frequency: semi-monthly
         Lutheran Church in America   Subscription: $5.00
Language: Danish and English

Contains articles on the Danish religious and cultural heritage, as well as poetry and Danish prose. As a special feature it publishes a special Christmas issue with articles, stories, and illustrations.

Danish Publications in English

209. THE AMERICAN DANE MAGAZINE.   1882–
3717 Harvey Street   (402) 341-5049
Omaha, Nebraska 68131

Editor: Don Eversoll   Circulation: 9,500
Sponsor: Danish Brotherhood in America   Frequency: monthly
Language: English   Subscription: $2.00

This fraternal organ features articles on the Danish-American heritage and news items on Danish Brotherhood activities.

210. THE DANA REVIEW.   1945–
2848 College Drive   (402) 426-4101
Blair, Nebraska 68008

Editor: Phillip A. Pagel   Circulation: 12,500
Sponsor: Dana College   Frequency: quarterly
Language: English   Subscription: free

Carries news of interest to Dana College alumni and to Danish Americans involved in ethnic studies and research.

211. DANISH BROTHERHOOD MAGAZINE.   1926–
3717 Harney Street   (402) 341-5049
Omaha, Nebraska 68131

Editor: Einar Danielsen   Circulation: 10,000
Sponsor: Danish Brotherhood in America   Frequency: monthly
Language: English   Subscription: $.50

212. DANISH ODD FELLOW BULLETIN.   1917–
220 East 15th Street   (212) 254-2077
New York, New York 10003

Editor: Svend A. Hansen   Circulation: 250
Sponsor: Berthel Thorvaldsen Lodge No. 530,   Frequency: bi-monthly
    IOOF, Inc.   Subscription: free/membership
Language: English

Contains material pertaining to the Lodge's activities as well as brief informative articles on
Danish organizations in the United States. Prior to 1942 it was published in Danish.

213. DANISH SISTERHOOD NEWS.   1947–
3438 North Opal Avenue   (312) 625-9031
Chicago, Illinois 60634

Editor: Virginia Christensen   Circulation: 4,500
Sponsor: Danish Sisterhood of America   Frequency: monthly
Language: English   Subscription: $.50

The purpose of this publication is to provide information concerning the activities of lodges in
the various states. Contents also include funeral benefit notices, listings of new members, and
general information pertaining to the members' duties and rights within the organization.

214. PHØEBE.   Phoebe.
Box 344   (303) 842-2861
Brush, Colorado 80723

Editor: Raymond M. Paulsen   Circulation: 1,000
Sponsor: Ebenezer Lutheran Care Center   Frequency: quarterly
Language: English   Subscription: n.i.

Carries information on the institution's various types of service.

DUTCH PRESS
Dutch and Dutch-English Publications

215. DIS MAGAZINE.   1970–
2216 Edgewood, S.E.   (616) 949-8338
Grand Rapids, Michigan 49506

Editor: Gerrit den Glollander   Circulation: 18,600
Sponsor: Dutch Immigrant Society   Frequency: quarterly
Language: Dutch and English   Subscription: $3.00

Contains information on DIS activities and its members and articles on Dutch people in the
United States and the Netherlands.

216. THE HOLLAND REPORTER.   1965–
3680 Division Street   (213) 257-2330
Los Angeles, California 90065

Editor: Marinus W. M. Van der Steen, Jr.   Circulation: 8,200
Sponsor: Marinus W. M. Van der Steen, Jr. Frequency: weekly
Language: Dutch and English   Subscription: $5.00

Family Dutch-American weekly. Includes news from Holland and from the Dutch community
in the United States.

217. DE WACHTER.　　The Watchman.　　　　　　　　　　　1868–

2850 Kalamazoo Avenue, S.E.　　　　　(616) 241-1691
Grand Rapids, Michigan 49508

Editor: Rev. William Haverkamp　　　　Circulation: 2,850
Sponsor: Christian Reformed Church　　Frequency: bi-weekly
Language: Dutch　　　　　　　　　　Subscription: $4.00

Serves as an organ of the Christian Reformed Church. Content is religious in nature. Includes articles on various aspects of the church's activities and affairs.

Dutch Publications in English

218. ATLANTIC OBSERVER-KNICKERBOCKER INTERNATIONAL.　　1938–

P. O. Box 554, Lenox Hill Station
New York, New York 10021

Editor: Albert C. Balink　　　　　　Circulation: n.i.
Sponsor: Atlantic Observer, Inc.　　　Frequency: monthly
Language: English　　　　　　　　　Subscription: $6.00

This journal primarily analyzes the economic policies and situations in Holland, stressing various types of economic cooperation between Holland other countries, particularly the United States. Its purpose is to "promote better relationships between the United States and the Netherlands in business" (editor's statement).

219. THE BANNER.　　　　　　　　　　　　　　　　　1866–

2850 Kalamazoo Avenue　　　　　　(616) 241-1691
Grand Rapids, Michigan 49506

Editor: Lester R. DeKoster　　　　　　Circulation: 45,200
Sponsor: Christian Reformed Publishing House　Frequency: weekly
Language: English　　　　　　　　　Subscription: $6.00

This is the official organ of the Christian Reformed Church. Its chief objectives are "to promote denominational activity and to provide families with religious reading relevant to today's needs" (editor's statement). Although the contents reflect the spiritual aspects of life, articles dealing with relevant topics in today's world are also included.

220. CALVINALIA.　　　　　　　　　　　　　　　　　1960–

Calvin College and Seminary
Grand Rapids, Michigan 49506

Editor: n.i.　　　　　　　　　　　　Circulation: n.i.
Sponsor: Calvin College and Seminary　Frequency: quarterly
Language: English　　　　　　　　　Subscription: free to students and
　　　　　　　　　　　　　　　　　　　　　　　　alumni

Includes news items concerning Calvin College and Seminary. Illustrated.

221. DE HALVE MAEN.　　The Half Moon.　　　　　　　　1922–

122 East 58th Street　　　　　　　　(212) 758-1675
New York, New York 10022

Editor: Richard H. Amerman　　　　Circulation: 1,500
Sponsor: Holland Society of New York　Frequency: quarterly
Language: English　　　　　　　　　Subscription: free to members

Historical in nature. Contents include articles on the history of the early Dutch settlers in America (1609-1675), their contribution to American life, and the genealogy of Dutch families from the earliest times fo date. Items on the activities of the Society and its members are also printed. In order to qualify for membership the applicant must show proof of being a descendant of a colonist who lived in New Netherland during or before 1675.

222. NEW HORIZONS. 1912–

1450 East Fulton Street (616) 459-3495
Grand Rapids, Michigan 49503

Editor: Thomas A. DeGroot   Circulation: 3,500
Sponsor: Holland Home   Frequency: monthly
Language: English   Subscription: $5.00 donation

This is primarily a public relations instrument to keep the Association members informed of activities and current events that relate to the Association and its members. The paper includes articles on a variety of topics of special interest to members and their families. Until May 1975 it was published under the title *Holland Home News*.

EAST INDIAN PRESS
See **Indian Press**

EGYPTIAN PRESS
See **Arabic Press**

ESTONIAN PRESS
Estonian Publications

223. MEIE TEE.   Our Path. 1931–

243 East 34th Street (212) 686-3356
New York, New York 10016

Editor: Harald Raudsepp   Circulation: 1,035
Sponsor: World Association of Estonians, Inc.   Frequency: bi-monthly
Language: Estonian   Subscription: $5.00

This monthly is highly political in tone, discussing cultural and political questions of interest to Estonians. Ideologically it presents a strong anti-communist view, with a pro-American leaning.

224. UUS ILM.   The New World. 1909–

Box 5342, Grand Central Station
New York, New York 10016

Editor: Michael Nukk   Circulation: 800
Sponsor: Uus Ilm Publishing Company, Inc.   Frequency: monthly
Language: Estonian   Subscription: $4.00

Official organ of the Estonian Progressive Society "Kiir." Contains items on group activities and events. Also includes articles on labor problems.

225. VABA EESTI SONA.   Free Estonian Word. 1949–

243 East 34th Street
New York, New York 10016

Editors: Erich Ernits and Harald Raudsepp   Circulation: 4,000
Sponsor: Nordic Press, Inc.   Frequency: weekly
Language: Estonian   Subscription: $13.50

General international and national news coverage.

FILIPINO PRESS
See also **Asian Press**

Filipino Publications in English

226. CABLE MASONICO.

95 Center Place
San Francisco, California 94107

CABLE MASONICO (cont'd)
Editor: Severino E. Ruste, Grand Master
Sponsor: Grand Lodge of the Gran Oriente
    Filipino
Language: English

Circulation: n.i.
Frequency: semi-annual
Subscription: free to members

227. **FILIPINO AMERICAN WORLD.**   1968–
     800 Southern Avenue, S.E., Room 408
     Washington, D. C. 20032

Editor: Elias J. Venali
Sponsor: Filipino International Community
    Newsletter, Inc.
Language: English

Circulation: 10,000
Frequency: monthly
Subscription: $3.00

This is primarily a publication for Filipino-Americans in the United States and Canada. Special features include "personality of the month"; regional headlines; a pictorial page; Philippine news; "speaking out"; poetry corner; directory; etc. Covers the educational, cultural, and political activities of the Filipino-American communities both here and abroad.

228. **FILIPINO FORUM.**   1928–
     4627 43rd Avenue South
     Seattle, Washington 98119

Editor: Martin J. Sibonga
Sponsor: n.i.
Language: English

Circulation: 2,000
Frequency: monthly
Subscription: $5.00

Contains news and articles on the Filipino-American community. "We believe, also, each minority can—and should—retain its ethnic heritage as each maintains its share in the quest for civil rights, for everyone" (editor's statement).

229. **LAGING UNA.**   **Always First.**   1949–
     3003 Future Place
     Los Angeles, California 90065

Editor: Martires M. Monosco
Sponsor: n.i.
Language: English

Circulation: 5,000
Frequency: monthly
Subscription: $2.50

Provides expatriate Filipinos in the United States with news of the Philippines. Contains editorial analyses of the socioeconomic and political problems of the Philippines, Southeast Asia, Africa, Europe, and the Americas. Ideologically, this publication leans to the left.

230. **THE MABUHAY REPUBLIC.**   1969–
     833 Market Street, Room 502
     San Francisco, California 94103

Editor: J. T. Esteva
Sponsor: Philippine Service Company
Language: English

Circulation: 3,450
Frequency: monthly
Subscription: $2.00

This publication, serving as the "voice" of the Filipino community in California, reports on the social and cultural life of the Filipino community. Includes items on the contribution of individual Filipinos.

231. **NIÑGAS-COGON.**   **Brush Fire.**   1972–
     351 West 22nd Street
     New York, New York 10011

Editor: Nelson A. Navarro
Sponsor: Lewis Nicholas Co. Inc.
Language: English

Circulation: n.i.
Frequency: monthly
Subscription: $6.00

Provides articles on Filipino life in the United States and in the Philippines. One section is devoted to a news digest. Short stories and poetry are included. Illustrated.

232. PHILIPPINE AMERICAN. 1960–
  395 Broadway, Suite 1209
  New York, New York 10013

Editor: Teddy de Nolasco   Circulation: 25,000
Sponsor: n.i.   Frequency: semi-monthly
Language: English   Subscription: $3.00

This newspaper contains news on international, national, and local affairs with frequent items about the Philippines and Filipinos in the United States. Sections are also devoted to commentaries, letters to the editor, and social events.

233. THE PHILIPPINES MAIL. 1930–
  943 Sierra Madre Drive   (408) 422-6546
  Salinas, California 93901

Editor: Delfin F. Cruz   Circulation: 5,000
Sponsor: none   Frequency: monthly
Language: English   Subscription: $5.00

News on international, national, and local affairs and events, with emphasis on the Philippines and Filipino groups in the United States. Also included are commentaries and articles on various issues and topics of special interest to the Filipino communities in this country.

FINNISH PRESS
Finnish and Finnish-English Publications

234. AMERIKAN UUTISET. American News. 1932–
  P. O. Box 125
  New York Mills, Minnesota 56567

Editor: Toivo Halonen   Circulation: 5,390
Sponsor: Northwestern Publishing Company   Frequency: semi-weekly
Language: Finnish   Subscription: $11.00

General international, national, and local news of interest to the Finnish community.

235. INDUSTRIALISTI. Industrialist. 1914–
  106 East 1st Street   (218) 722-0642
  Duluth, Minnesota 55802

Editor: Jack Ujanen   Circulation: 2,548
Sponsor: Workers Publishing Company   Frequency: weekly
Language: Finnish   Subscription: $12.00

This is a pro-labor (IWW) paper.

236. NAISTEN VIIRI. Women's Banner. 1911–
  601 Tower Avenue
  Superior, Wisconsin 54880

Editor: Helen Kruth   Circulation: 1,566
Sponsor: Tyomies Society   Frequency: weekly
Language: Finnish   Subscription: $10.00

This publication features news and articles of interest to Finnish women. Illustrated.

237. NEW YORKIN UUTISET. The Finnish New York News. 1906–
  4418-22 Eighth Avenue
  Brooklyn, New York 11220

Editor: Esa Arra   Circulation: 2,580
Sponsor: Finnish Newspaper Company, Inc.   Frequency: semi-weekly
Language: Finnish   Subscription: $15.00

Contains news of a general nature, plus items on various cultural and social activities and events among the Finnish people.

238. RAIVAAJA. Pioneer.   1905–
811 Main Street   (617) 343-3822
Fitchburg, Massachusetts 01420

Editor: Savele Syrjala   Circulation: 2,110
Sponsor: Raivaaja Publishing Co.   Frequency: weekly
Language: Finnish   Subscription: $15.00

Aims at preserving the Finnish cultural heritage in the United States. Features articles concerning Finnish cultural, religious, political, and educational affairs. Illustrated.

239. RAUHAN TERVEHDYS. Peace Greetings.   1920–
120 Amygdaloid Street
Laurium, Michigan 49913

Editors: Walter Torola and P. A. Heidman   Circulation: 750
Sponsor: Finnish Apostolic Lutheran Church of   Frequency: monthly
         America   Subscription: $1.50
Language: Finnish

Contains religious news and articles on the Finnish Lutheran Church, its parishes and parishioners.

240. SUOMI-OPISTON VIESTI. Message.   1958–
Hancock, Michigan 49930

Editor: E. Olaf Rankinen   Circulation: 6,000
Sponsor: Suomi College   Frequency: quarterly
Language: Finnish   Subscription: free

This publication is a college quarterly. All items are related to the activities, events, and affairs of Suomi College.

241. TYÖMIES-ETEENPÄIN. Workingman-Forward.   1903–
601-603 Tower Avenue
Superior, Wisconsin 54880

Editor: Timo Poropudas   Circulation: 1,725
Sponsor: Tyomies Society   Frequency: semi-weekly
Language: Finnish and English   Subscription: $15.00

Designed to promote the American-Finnish culture and to "serve the workers' and farmers' interests for world peace and coesixtence" (editor's statement). Serves the interests of American Finns in cultural and trade union fields.

Finnish Publications in English

242. FINAM NEWS LETTER.   1962–
P. O. Box 3515   (503) 227-4205
Portland, Oregon 97208

Editor: Walter Mattila   Circulation: 400
Sponsor: Finnish American Historial Society   Frequency: irregular
         of the West   Subscription: $1.50; members only
Language: English

Includes promotional literature on Finns in the West, as well as research into the various achievements of Finnish pioneers.

FLEMISH PRESS
See **Belgian-Flemish Press**

FRENCH PRESS
French and French-English Publications

**243. LE BULLETIN DE LA FÉDÉRATION FÉMININE FRANCO-
AMÉRICAINE.**   1961–
  412 Waterville
  Waterbury, Connecticut 06710

  Editor: Martha Peloquin   Circulation: 14,000
  Sponsor: Federation of French American Women   Frequency: weekly
  Language: French and English   Subscription: n.i.

Promotes the retention of French cultural heritage in the United States.

244. LE CALIFORNIEN.   The Californian.   1963–
  1603 Hyde Street
  San Francisco, California 94109

  Editor: Pierre Idiart   Circulation: 1,900
  Sponsor: Le Californien Publishing Company   Frequency: weekly
  Language: French   Subscription: $8.50

Contains news items on world affairs, political and cultural events in France, and social and cultural activities among the French-Americans in California and other states. Also included are editorials; excerpts from *Le Monde*, *Le Figaro*, *Paris Match*, etc.; and a page for women.

245. LE CANADO-AMÉRICAIN.   1900–
  52 Concord Street   (603) 625-8577
  Manchester, New Hampshire 03101

  Editor: Gerald Robert   Circulation: 15,500
  Sponsor: Association Canado-Americaine   Frequency: quarterly
  Language: French and English   Subscription: $2.00 for non-members

This official publication of a fraternal insurance benefit society includes reports on fraternal activities in its courts and villas, as well as at the home office. Covers Franco-American news as well as Canadian news of ACA interest.

246. FRANCE-AMÉRIQUE–LE COURRIER FRANÇAIS DES ÉTATS-UNIS.
The French Newspaper in the United States.   1827–
  1111 Lexington Avenue
  New York, New York 10021

  Editor: Francoise Martin-Chollet   Circulation: 35,000
  Sponsor: Trocadero Publishing Co.   Frequency: weekly
  Language: French   Subscription: $13.00

This is the oldest French language newspaper in the United States. It emphasizes news from France and news about the French in the United States. Also includes international news, comments on world events, a literary page, feature articles, interviews, reports on movies, art, theater, music, fashion, and sports, and short stories. Illustrated.

247. NOUVELLES DU MOUVEMENT SYNDICAL LIBRE.   Free Trade
Union News.   1945–
  815 16th Street, N.W.   (202) 637-5041
  Washington, D. C. 20006

  Editor: George Meany   Circulation: 15,000
  Sponsor: AFL-CIO.   Frequency: monthly
  Language: French   Subscription: free

International labor newsletter.

248. LE TRAVAILLEUR.   The Hustler.   1931–

P. O. Box 543
Linwood, Massachusetts 01525   (617) 278-2355

Editor: Wilfrid Beaulieu   Circulation: 3,900
Sponsor: Le Travailleur.   Frequency: semi-monthly
Language: French   Subscription: $7.00

Features "articles devoted to literary, cultural, educational, historical, political (but non-partisan) topics" (editor's statement), plus general information.

249. L'UNION.

1 Social Street   (401) 769-0520
Woonsocket, Rhode Island 02895

Editor: John G. Laplante   Circulation: 35,000
Sponsor: Union Saint-Jean-Baptiste   Frequency: quarterly
Language: French and English   Subscription: $1.00 for non-members

Publishes articles of interest to members of a fraternal society, such as "accounts of fraternal activities in our various Councils, articles concerning our French or Canadian heritage, religious news, etc." (editor's statement). Illustrated.

French Publications in English

250. AMERICAN SOCIETY LEGION OF HONOR MAGAZINE.   1930–

22 East 60th Street
New York, New York 10022

Editor: Sylviane Glad   Circulation: n.i.
Sponsor: American Society of the French   Frequency: 3 times/year
         Legion of Honor   Subscription: free to members of the
Language: English   Society, selected universities, and pub-
                                               lic libraries in the United States and
                                               abroad

The objective of this journal is to promote appreciation in the United States of French culture and to strengthen the friendship between the people of the United States and France. Articles are devoted to history, art, literature, music, and other subjects related to French and American culture.

251. FRENCH AMERICAN COMMERCE.   1896–

1350 Avenue of the Americas   (212) 581-4554
New York, New York 10019

Editor: Jacques Douguet   Circulation: 2,500
Sponsor: French Chamber of Commerce in   Frequency: bi-monthly
         the U. S.   Subscription: n.i.
Language: English

252. TODAY IN FRANCE.   1961–

P. O. Box 551, Cathedral Station   (212) 749-3843
New York, New York 10025

Editor: Benjamin Potter   Circulation: 1,000
Sponsor: Society for French-American Affairs   Frequency: bi-monthly
Language: English   Subscription: $4.00

Features political, cultural, and historical materials covering France and the French people. Promotes French-American friendship. Special feature: one section is devoted to the bibliography of French publications.

GEORGIAN PRESS
Georgian Publications

253. GEORGIAN OPINION.   1951–
    535 East 78th Street
    New York, New York 10021

Editor: M. Sindikeli   Circulation: 1,000
Sponsor: Georgian National Alliance   Frequency: bi-monthly
Language: Georgian   Subscription: $10.00

Provides "the opinion of immigrees of Georgian origin on historical and current events. Its purpose is to keep the hope that some day the men and women within Georgia will be able to express and enjoy individual freedom" (editor's statement).

GERMAN PRESS
German and German-English Publications

254. ABENDPOST-SONNTAGPOST. Evening Paper-Sunday Paper.   1889–
    223 West Washington Street   (312) 368-4800
    Chicago, Illinois 60606

Editor: Ludwig Gehrken   Circulation: 12,500
Sponsor: Abendpost Company   Frequency: daily
Language: German   Subscription: $22.00

"Our purpose is to provide our readers with local, national and international news with the emphasis on items of particular interest to the German and German-American community. This includes news and sports items from Germany as well as events occurring within the German-American communities in the United States" (editor's statement). Illustrated.

255. AMERICA HEROLD–LINCOLN FREIE PRESSE. America Herald
    and Lincoln Free Press.   1873–
    4614 Dodge Street
    Omaha, Nebraska 68110

Editor: William Peter   Circulation: 5,223
Sponsor: Tribune Publishing Company Frequency: weekly
Language: German   Subscription: $6.50

International, national, and local news coverage of interest to the German community.

256. AMERIKANISCHE SCHWEIZER ZEITUNG. American Swiss Gazette. 1868–
    608 5th Avenue
    New York, New York 10020

Editor: Max E. Ammon   Circulation: 2,400
Sponsor: Swiss Publishing Company   Frequency: weekly
Language: German and English   Subscription: $8.00

257. AUFBAU. Reconstruction.   1934–
    2121 Broadway
    New York, New York 10023

Editor: Hans Steinitz   Circulation: 31,000
Sponsor: New World Club, Inc.   Frequency: weekly
Language: German and English   Subscription: $10.50

This newspaper was first created to represent the interests and viewpoints of German, mostly Jewish, refugees from Hitler's Germany. Editorially it represents several major themes: the cultural German background, Jewish faith and traditions, and a loyalty to the United States.

Contents include items from special correspondents, reports on life in Germany and Israel, coverage of cultural life, literature, theater, music, etc. Special sections and supplements are devoted to such topics as life on the West Coast, the German restitution issue, book reviews, vacation and travel, etc.

258. BAHN FREI. Clear Track.   1883–
   Lexington Avenue & 85th Street
   New York, New York 10028

   Editor: Walter Pfister   Circulation: 800
   Sponsor: New York Turn Verein   Frequency: monthly
   Language: German   Subscription: $2.00

259. BALTIMORE CORRESPONDENT AND WOCHENEND-MAGAZIN.   1841–
   1211 Havenwood Road
   Baltimore, Maryland 21201

   Editor: Erwin Single   Circulation: 1,822
   Sponsor: n.i.   Frequency: weekly
   Language: German   Subscription: n.i.

This paper presents news of general interest to the German-speaking community.

260. BUFFALO VOLKSFREUND.   Buffalo People's Friend.   1868–
   947 Ellicott Square Building   (716) 855-3940
   Buffalo, New York 14203

   Editor: Burt Erickson Nelson   Circulation: 1,350
   Sponsor: Tribune Publishing Co.   Frequency: weekly
   Language: German   Subscription: $10.00

This publication provides coverage of western New York State's German-American communities, and includes articles of state, national, and international news, with an emphasis on German-speaking countries. Ads for this family newspaper are translated into German and are also accepted in English.

261. CALIFORNIA STAATS-ZEITUNG.   California State Journal.   1890–
   221 East Pico Boulevard
   Los Angeles, California 90015

   Editor: Albert Ebert   Circulation: 10,100
   Sponsor: Raymond E. Stuetz (publisher)   Frequency: weekly
   Language: German   Subscription: $3.00

262. CINCINNATI KURIER.   Cincinnati Courier.   1964–
   421 North 38th Avenue
   Omaha, Nebraska 68131

   Editor: William A. Peter   Circulation: 2,700
   Sponsor: Peter Publications   Frequency: weekly
   Language: German   Subscription: $7.50

International and national news, sports, features, and women's page. Includes literary materials. Illustrated.

263. DETROITER ABEND-POST.   Detroiter Evening Post.   1854–
   1436 Brush Street   (313) 961-3467
   Detroit, Michigan 48226

   Editor: Knuth Beth   Circulation: 12,000
   Sponsor: Detroit Abend-Post Publishing Co. Frequency: weekly
   Language: German   Subscription: $14.95

This newspaper provides political, social, cultural, sports, and other news for German-Americans. Special features include women's pages, finance and science pages.

264. DER DEUTSCH-AMERIKANER. The German-American.
4740 North Western Avenue   (312) 561-2488
Chicago, Illinois 60625

Editor: Werner Baroni   Circulation: 12,200
Sponsor: German-American National   Frequency: monthly
     Congress, Inc.   Subscription: $4.00
Language: German and English

The official organ of the German-American National Congress, this monthly presents organizational news. Its aim is to unite all German Americans and to preserve German language, culture, and customs. Includes articles on Germany and German Americans.

265. EINTRACHT. Harmony.   1923–
9456 North Lawler Avenue   (312) 677-9456
Skokie, Illinois 60076

Editor: Gottlieb Juengling   Circulation: 5,150
Sponsor: None   Frequency: weekly
Language: German   Subscription: $9.00

Contains information on German-American clubs, including cultural activities and international sports. Illustrated.

266. EVANGELIUMS POSAUNE. Gospel Trumpet.   1895–
2301 Lincoln Avenue   (402) 362-5133
York, Nebraska 68467

Editor: Fritz Friedrich   Circulation: 2,000
Sponsor: Christian Unity Press   Frequency: semi-monthly
Language: German   Subscription: $5.00

Features articles on Christian virtues and life. Also includes religious poetry and prose.

267. FLORIDA STAATS-ZEITUNG UND HEROLD.   1965–
P. O. Box 1236
North Miami, Florida 33161

Editor: Erwin A. Single   Circulation: 800
Sponsor: Staats-Herold Corporation   Frequency: weekly
Language: German   Subscription: $23.75

Special Florida edition of *New Yorker Staats Zeitung und Herold*. International, national and regional news, with particular coverage of the activities of German Americans.

268. FREIGEWERKSCHAFTLICHE NACHRICHTEN. Free Trade
Union News.   1945–
815 16th Street, N.W.   (202) 627-5041
Washington, D. C. 20006

Editor: George Meany   Circulation: 15,000
Sponsor: AFL-CIO   Frequency: monthly
Language: German   Subscription: free

International labor press.

269. DIE HAUSFRAU. The Housewife.   1904–
1517 West Fullerton Avenue   (312) 935-8780
Chicago, Illinois 60614

Editor: J. Edelmann   Circulation: 44,000
Sponsor: Die Hausfrau, Inc.   Frequency: monthly
Language: German   Subscription: $5.00

General interest magazine for the whole family.

270. HEROLD DER WAHRHEIT.   **Herald of Truth.**   1912–
Route 2, Box 252   (319) 656-2006
Kalona, Iowa 52247

Editors: Lester B. Miller and Jonas J. Beachy   Circulation: 1,325
Sponsor: Publication Board of the Amish-   Frequency: monthly
      Mennonite Publishing Association   Subscription: $2.50
Language: English and German (in Gothic script)

This is a religious monthly published in the interest of the Amish Mennonite Churches. The German section is published in Gothic script.

271. INTERNATIONAL MONTHLY.   1959–
P. O. Box 5335
San Jose, California 95100

Editor: Ute Lorenz   Circulation: 4,000
Sponsor: International Press   Frequency: monthly
Language: German and English   Subscription: $4.00

Serves German Americans and students of the German language, with circulation primarily in Western states. Publishes news from Germany, plus a local section devoted to organizations such as ethnic clubs and schools. "Covers wide variety of subjects, including politics, education, medicine, exhibitions, social changes, elections, travel, entertainment, and others" (editor's statement). Illustrated.

272. INTERNATIONALE BIBELLEKTIONEN.   **International Bible Lessons.**   1920–
4912 Northwestern Avenue
Racine, Wisconsin 53406

Editor: Rev. Fritz Lenk   Circulation: 1,200
Sponsor: Christian Unity Press   Frequency: quarterly
Language: German   Subscription: $1.00

Promotes the teachings of the Bible as understood by the Church of God. Gothic script.

273. KATHOLISCHER JUGENFREUND.   **Catholic Young People's Friend.**   1877–
2001 Devon Avenue
Chicago, Illinois 60645

Editor: John S. West   Circulation: n.i.
Sponsor: Angel Guardian Orphanage   Frequency: monthly
Language: German   Subscription: n.i.

274. KATHOLISCHES WOCHENBLATT UND DER LANDMANN.   **Catholic Weekly and the Farmer.**   1902–
2002 North 16th Street
Omaha, Nebraska 68110

Editor: William Peter   Circulation: 760
Sponsor: Tribune Publishing Company   Frequency: weekly
Language: German   Subscription: n.i.

This weekly presents Catholic and agricultural news.

275. KIRCHLICHES MONATSBLATT FUER DAS EVANGELISCH-LUTHERISCHE HAUS.   **Church Monthly for the Evangelical Lutheran Homes.**   1943–
584 East Geneva Avenue
Philadelphia, Pennsylvania 19120

Editor: Pastor Karl Schild   Circulation: 3,000
Sponsor: German Interest Conference of the   Frequency: monthly
      Lutheran Church in America   Subscription: $2.00
Language: German

KIRCHLICHES MONATSBLATT FUER DAS EVANGELISCH-LUTHERISCHE HAUS (cont'd)

Official organ of the German Interest Conference of the Lutheran Church in America. Features church news of special interest to German-speaking congregations. Missionary news, religious poetry, and devotional material.

276. KONTINENT. 1964–
 601 West 26th Street
 New York, New York 10001

Editor: J. Hartmann	Circulation: 30,000
Sponsor: Transatlantik Publishing Corp.	Frequency: monthly
Language: German	Subscription: $4.00

277. LOS ANGELES KURIER. Los Angeles Courier. 1964–
 5858 Hollywood Boulevard
 Los Angeles, California 90028

Editor: Theodore Val Peter	Circulation: 1,390
Sponsor: Tribune Publishing Company	Frequency: weekly
Language: German	Subscription: n.i.

278. DER LUTHERANER. The Lutheran. 1845–
 3550 South Jefferson
 St. Louis, Missouri 63118

Editor: Rev. Herman A. Mayer	Circulation: 4,675
Sponsor: Concordia Publishing House	Frequency: monthly
Language: German	Subscription: $2.25

Official organ of the Lutheran Church–Missouri Synod. Contains news of the activities of the church, plus doctrinal and devotional materials. Annual subscription includes the bi-weekly *Lutheran Witness Reporter*. Illustrated.

279. MILWAUKEE DEUTSCHE ZEITUNG. Milwaukee German Journal. 1890–
 223 West Washington Street
 Chicago, Illinois 60606

Editor: Werner Baroni	Circulation: 7,000
Sponsor: Apendpost Company	Frequency: daily
Language: German	Subscription: $21.00

280. MILWAUKEE HEROLD. Milwaukee Herald. 1854–
 4614 Dodge Street
 Omaha, Nebraska 68103

Editor: William A. Peter	Circulation: 1,965
Sponsor: Peter Publications	Frequency: weekly
Language: German	Subscription: $7.50

This weekly includes general and local news of interest to the German-speaking community.

281. NACHRICHTEN DER DONAUSCHWABEN IN AMERIKA. News of the Danube Swabians in America. 1955–
 4219 North Lincoln Avenue
 Chicago, Illinois 60618

Editor: Jacob Awender	Circulation: 3,200
Sponsor: Society of the Danube Swabians of	Frequency: monthly
the United States	Subscription: $2.00
Language: German	

The main objective of this monthly is "to promote the social life, culture, economy and progress of Danube Swabians" (editorial statement). Contains information on various activities of the Danube Swabians in the United States.

282. NEUE ZEITUNG.   American European Weekly.   1966–
  9471 Hidden Valley Place
  Beverly Hills, California 90210

Editor: Heinz Jurisch   Circulation: 9,950
Sponsor: German American League, Inc.   Frequency: weekly
Language: German   Subscription: $5.00

This weekly covers the highlights of European politics, and also presents articles on commerce and travel. Includes a women's page and reports on sports and local club activities.

283. NEW JERSEY FREIE ZEITUNG.   New Jersey Free Newspaper.   1856–
  70 Wolf Place
  Hillside, New Jersey 07205

Editor: Helmut Heimsch   Circulation: 2,175
Sponsor: New Jersey Freie Zeitung, Inc.   Frequency: weekly
Language: German   Subscription: $4.00

284. NEW YORKER STAATS-ZEITUNG UND HEROLD.   1835–
  36-30 37th Street   (212) 786-1110
  New York, New York 11101

Editor: Erwin A. Single   Circulation: 29,350
Sponsor: Staats-Herold Corporation   Frequency: daily
Language: German   Subscription: $36.00

This is one of the most influential German dailies in the United States. It presents international, national, and regional news, with an emphasis on German events. Special coverage is given to the German-American community. Special Florida and Philadelphia editions.

285. OSTFRIESEN ZEITUNG.   East Frisia News.   1881–
  Wall Lake, Iowa 51466

Editor: D. B. Aden   Circulation: 1,275
Sponsor: n.i.   Frequency: monthly
Language: German   Subscription: $3.00

286. PLATTDEUTSCHE POST.   Platt-German Post.   1934–
  91 New Dorp Plaza
  Staten Island, New York 10306

Editor: Herbert Stein   Circulation: 2,257
Sponsor: Plattdeutsche Post, Inc.   Frequency: weekly
Language: German   Subscription: $4.00

General and local news published in German dialect.

287. RUNDBRIEF.   1927–
  357 Tom Hunter Road   (212) 944-5497
  Fort Lee, New Jersey 07024

Editor: Gilbert Derleberg   Circulation: 500
Sponsor: n.i.   Frequency: monthly
Language: German   Subscription: $3.00

This German youth magazine includes essays, poems, short stories, and travel accounts of interest to German youth.

288. ST. JOSEPH'S BLATT.   St. Joseph's Page.   1888–
  St. Benedict, Oregon 97373

Editor: Manfred Friedrich Ellenberger   Circulation: 1,360
Sponsor: n.i.   Frequency: monthly
Language: German   Subscription: $6.00

This is a Catholic religious magazine. Illustrated.

289. SAXON NEWS VOLKSBLATT. 1911–
5393 Pearl Road   (216) 842-0333
Cleveland, Ohio 44129

Editor: Stefan Deubel   Circulation: 4,030
Sponsor: Alliance of Transylvanian Saxons   Frequency: weekly
Language: English and German   Subscription: $5.00

Contains articles on ATS and its various branches. Also includes national and international news. Fraternal publication. Illustrated.

290. DER SENDBOTE.   The Messenger. 1853–
7308 Madison Street
Forest Park, Illinois 60130

Editor: Rev. Reinhold J. Kerstan   Circulation: 3,000
Sponsor: North American Baptist General   Frequency: monthly
           Conference (Roger Williams Press)   Subscription: $3.50
Language: German

Monthly magazine of North American Baptists. Contains religious materials and denominational news. Subjects covered include race relations, war and peace, poverty, pornography, etc. Illustrated.

291. SIEBENBUERGISCH-AMERIKANISCHES VOLKSBLATT.   Transylvanian-
American People's Letter. 1905–
1436 Brush Street
Detroit, Michigan 48226

Editor: Berthold Vogt   Circulation: 3,850
Sponsor: Central Verband der Siebenbuerger   Frequency: weekly
           Sachsen of the U. S.   Subscription: $3.25
Language: German

292. SONNTAGSPOST.   Sunday Post. 1873–
223 Washington Street
Chicago, Illinois 60606

Editor: William Peter   Circulation: 4,180
Sponsor: Abendpost Company   Frequency: weekly
Language: German   Subscription: $6.50

This is an independent weekly featuring general and local news.

293. DER STAATS-ANZEIGER.   State Advertiser. 1906–
622 12th Street
Bismarck, North Dakota 58501

Editor: Phillip Wall   Circulation: 789
Sponsor: Tribune Publishing Company   Frequency: weekly
Language: German   Subscription: $6.50

294. THE SWISS AMERICAN.
603 Forest Avenue
Paramus, New Jersey 07652

Editor: Anton Haemmerle   Circulation: n.i.
Sponsor: North American Swiss Alliance   Frequency: monthly
Language: German   Subscription: n.i.

See also Swiss Press.

295. TÄGLICHE ANDACHTEN.   Daily Devotions. 1937–
3558 South Jefferson Avenue
St. Louis, Missouri 63118

TÄGLICHE ANDACHTEN (cont'd)

Editor: Rudolph F. Norden
Sponsor: The Lutheran Church–Missouri Synod
Language: German

Circulation: 28,880
Frequency: bi-monthly
Subscription: $1.25

This bi-monthly publication contains daily devotions consisting of Biblical text. The authors are, for the most part, retired pastors.

296. **VOLKSZEITUNG TRIBUNE.** People's Journal and Tribune. 1875–
4614 Dodge Street
Omaha, Nebraska 68132

Editor: William Peter
Sponsor: Tribune Publishing Company
Language: German

Circulation: 1,770
Frequency: weekly
Subscription: $6.50

This independent weekly contains general news of interest to the German community.

297. **WAECHTER UND ANZEIGER.** Observer and Announcer. 1852–
4164 Lorain Avenue
Cleveland, Ohio 44113

(216) 281-7636 l

Editor: Stefan Deubel
Sponsor: Waechter and Anzeiger Publishing Co.
Language: German

Circulation: 3,550
Frequency: weekly
Subscription: $7.00

This weekly publishes mostly international, society, and local news.

298. **WASHINGTON JOURNAL.** 1859–
844 National Press Building
Washington, D. C. 20004

Editor: Gerald R. Kainz
Sponsor: Washington Journal, Inc.
Language: German

Circulation: n.i.
Frequency: weekly
Subscription: $9.50

International, national, and local news. Includes feature articles on Germany and news items on the activities of German Americans. Illustrated.

299. **DIE WELT POST.** The World Post. 1916–
4614 Dodge Street
Omaha, Nebraska 68103

Editor: William Peter
Sponsor: n.i.
Language: German

Circulation: 527
Frequency: weekly
Subscription: $6.50

German Publications in English

300. **THE BLACK AND RED.** 1897–
Northwestern College
Watertown, Wisconsin 53094

Editor: Lloyd H. Lemke
Sponsor: Students of Northwestern College
Language: English

Circulation: 850
Frequency: monthly
Subscription: $2.50

This is a student paper whose objective is "to encourage students in preparation for the Lutheran ministry in the Wisconsin Evangelical Lutheran Synod (WELS)" (editor's statement).

301. **THE BULLETIN OF THE HOME FOR AGED LUTHERANS.** 1959–
7500 West North Avenue
Wauwatosa, Wisconsin 53213

THE BULLETIN OF THE HOME FOR AGED LUTHERANS (cont'd)

Editor: Rev. William T. Baaess

Sponsor: Home for Aged Lutherans

Language: English

Circulation: 10,000

Frequency: quarterly

Subscription: n.i.

Contains news items concerning the Home of Aged Lutherans. Illustrated.

302. CATHOLIC WOMAN'S JOURNAL. 1921–

3835 Westminster Place   (314) 371-1653

St. Louis, Missouri 63108

Editor: Harvey J. Johnson

Sponsor: National Catholic Woman's Union

Language: English

Circulation: 1,331

Frequency: 10/year

Subscription: $1.50

A general magazine of Catholic orientation for Catholic women and for members of the National Catholic Woman's Union.

303. G.B.U. REPORTER. 1892–

4254 Clairton Boulevard

Pittsburgh, Pennsylvania 15227

Editor: Karl Filsinger

Sponsor: Greater Beneficial Union of Pittsburgh

Language: English

Circulation: 20,150

Frequency: monthly

Subscription: n.i.

A fraternal magazine.

304. GERMAN AMERICAN TRADE NEWS. 1946–

666 Fifth Avenue   (212) 582-7788

New York, New York 10019

Editor: n.i.

Sponsor: German American Chamber of

          Commerce

Language: English

Circulation: 15,000

Frequency: monthly

Subscription: $5.00

This monthly provides economic and financial information, with a special section on U.S.-German business.

305. THE MENNONITE. 1885–

722 Main Street, Box 347   (316) 283-5100

Newton, Kansas 67114

Editor: Larry Kehler

Sponsor: General Conference Mennonite Church

Language: English

Circulation: 15,700

Frequency: weekly

Subscription: $7.00

Features news, comment, and discussion on church and world affairs of interest to Mennonites.

306. NINTH MANHATTAN MASONIC NEWS. 1937–

220 East 15th Street

New York, New York 10003

Editor: Marvin Goldsmith

Sponsor: Ninth Manhattan District, German

          Masonic Home Corporation

Language: English

Circulation: n.i.

Frequency: semi-monthly

Subscription: n.i.

A fraternal magazine.

307. PENNSYLVANIA DUTCH NEWS AND VIEWS. 1965–

Lenhartsville, Pennsylvania   (215) 562-4803

Editors: Florence Baver and Helen Buck

Sponsor: Pennsylvania Dutch Folk Culture

          Society, Inc.

Language: English

Circulation: 250

Frequency: bi-annually

Subscription: $1.00

PENNSYLVANIA DUTCH NEWS AND VIEWS (cont'd)
The main objective is to "foster the preservation of the homelife, dialect, and customs" (editor's statement) of the Pennsylvania Germans. Illustrated.

308. SAENGER-ZEITUNG.   Journal for Singers.   1924–
   1832 Hillsdale Avenue   (513) 275-5460
   Dayton, Ohio 45414

   Editor: Walter Hoops   Circulation: 600
   Sponsor: Federation of Workers' Singing   Frequency: bi-monthly
         Societies of America   Subscription: free/membership
   Language: English

Publishes reports of the activities of affiliated singing societies and promotes district and national song festivals. It also publishes articles about choral singing and biographical information about composers.

309. THE SCHWENKFELDIAN.   1903–
   1 Seminary Street   (215) 679-7175
   Pennsburg, Pennsylvania 18073

   Editor: Jack R. Rothenberger   Circulation: 1,600
   Sponsor: Board of Publication of the   Frequency: quarterly
         Schwenkfelder Church   Subscription: $3.00
   Language: English

"Serves as the voice of our five churches and as an official record of significant events in our churches. Used as a means to circulate the writings of Caspar Schwenkfeld von Oseig in English and to inform the reader about the teachings of the Schwenkfelder Church. Contains general purpose editorial material concerning contemporary church related issues" (editor's statement).

310. SOLIDARITY.   1906–
   714 Seneca Avenue
   Brooklyn, New York 11227

   Editor: Jack Hengerson   Circulation: 23,000
   Sponsor: Workmen's Benefit Fund   Frequency: 9/year
   Language: English   Subscription: membership fee

"It shall be the policy of *Solidarity* to emphasize the democratic way of life of the American people and to disseminate the spirit of fraternalism for purposes of mutual help and protection" (editor's statement). Articles deal with questions of health, economic security, social problems, and international affairs. The German edition was discontinued after the December 1968 issue.

311. THE STEUBEN NEWS.
   369 Lexington Avenue, Suite 2003   (212) 867-1646
   New York, New York 10017

   Editor: Henry F. Heinlein   Circulation: n.i.
   Sponsor: The Steuben News   Frequency: monthly
   Language: English   Subscription: $3.00

General national and local news and news of the Steuben Society. Features articles about world affairs written by various correspondents.

312. VOICE OF AMERICANS OF GERMAN DESCENT.   1949–
   59-17 Palmetto Street
   Ridgewood, New York 11227

   Editor: Gertrude J. B. Barron   Circulation: n.i.
   Sponsor: German-American National Congress   Frequency: monthly
   Language: English   Subscription: $4.00

Features articles on German Americans and Germany. Its main objective is "to secure an Atlantic Charter Peace for Germany; to make people aware of anti-German defamation in the media; to help promote German culture" (editor's statement).

313. THE WANDERER. 1867–
128 East 10th Street
St. Paul, Minnesota 55101

Editor: Walter Matt   Circulation: 34,000
Sponsor: Wanderer Printing Company   Frequency: weekly
Language: English   Subscription: $7.00

This Catholic magazine covers various topics of interest to the German Catholic community.

GREEK PRESS
Greek and Greek-English Publications

314. APOLLON. 1930–
401 South Garfield Street   (703) 892-2424
Arlington, Virginia 22204

Editor: E. S. Athanas   Circulation: 2,500
Sponsor: Pan-Rhodian Society of America Inc.   Frequency: quarterly
Language: Greek   Subscription: $2.00

This fraternal and educational magazine promotes the preservation of the Greek Orthodox religion and of customs and traditions pecular to Rhodes. It is aimed primarily at Greeks and their descendants from the Rhodes area.

315. ATHENAI.   Detroit Athens. 1928–
520 Monroe Avenue
Detroit, Michigan 48226

Editor: Basil Lukos   Circulation: 4,030
Sponsor: Eagle Printing and Publishing Company   Frequency: weekly
Language: Greek   Subscription: $6.00

Oriented toward the interests of all Greek readers in the area. International, national, and local news coverage.

316. ELLENIKOS-ASTER.   The Greek Star. 1904–
4731 North Western
Chicago, Illinois 60625

Editor: Nicholas Philippidis   Circulation: 7,500
Sponsor: Lerner Newspapers   Frequency: weekly
Language: English and Greek   Subscription: $5.00

Provides general news of interest to the Greek community. Currently ninety per cent of the newspaper is published in English.

317. ELLENIKOS TYPOS.   The Greek Press. 1911–
509 North LaSalle Street
Chicago, Illinois 60610

Editor: Aris Angelopoulos   Circulation: 15,250
Sponsor: The Greek Press, Inc.   Frequency: monthly
Language: Greek and English   Subscription: $10.00

Covers "all aspects of the news that affect the Greek community including news from Greece, political, social, cultural, educational" (editor's statement).

318. O ELLENISMOS TES AMERIKIS.   Hellenism in America. 1969–
400 South Orange Street   (215) 565-5861
Media, Pennsylvania 19063

Editor: Constantine N. Tsirpanlis   Circulation: 4,000
Sponsor: C. N. Tsirpanlis   Frequency: monthly
Language: Greek   Subscription: $10.00

O ELLENISMOS TES AMERIKIS (cont'd)
Promotes "ethnic, commercial, cultural and social relations of the Greek communities in the United States with Greece" (editor's statement). Prints comprehensive reports on the origins, activities; and contributions of Greek immigrants in the United States.

319. ELLENOAMERIKANOS. The Greek-American. 1969–
    251 West 42nd Street
    New York, New York 10036

Editor: Michael E. Halkias	Circulation: 12,000
Sponsor: Grekam Publications, Inc.	Frequency: semi-monthly
Language: English and Greek	Subscription: $5.00

Emphasis is on Greek activities in the United States; general and local news coverage is also provided.

320. ETHNIKOS KERIX. The National Herald. 1915–
    134-140 West 26th Street   (212) 929-4200
    New York, New York 10001

Editor: B. J. Marketos	Circulation: 18,942
Sponsor: The Nation Herald, Inc.	Frequency: daily
Language: Greek and English	Subscription: $36.00

International, national, and local news coverage. Special English section in Sunday edition.

321. KAMPANA. Bell. 1917–
    360 West 36th Street   (212) 736-0892
    New York, New York 10018

Editor: Costas Athanasiades	Circulation: 8,200
Sponsor: Campana Printing Co.	Frequency: semi-monthly
Language: Greek	Subscription: $8.00

Its purpose is to enlighten the Greek communities of the United States and Canada about their responsibilities to Greek and American social, economic, and political affairs. Contains materials on Greeks in the United States and their organized life.

322. KYPIAKATIKA NEA. Greek Sunday News. 1954–
    231 Harrison Avenue   (617) 426-1948
    Boston, Massachusetts 02111

Editor: William A. Harris	Circulation: 18,500
Sponsor: William A. Harris	Frequency: weekly
Language: Greek and English	Subscription: $5.00

Features general and local news covering Greeks in the United States and Greece.

323. MAKEDONIA. Macedonia. 1953–
    246 Eighth Avenue
    New York, New York 10011

Editor: V. T. Daniels	Circulation: 3,000
Sponsor: Pan-Macedonian Association	Frequency: bi-monthly
Language: Greek and English	Subscription: $5.00

Includes national and local Greek news. Its main objective is to "advance friendly relations between Greece and the Americans, to support religious and educational causes and to distribute information on the land and people of Macedonia, Greece" (editor's statement).

324. NATIONAL GREEK TRIBUNE. 1920–
    1215 Brush
    Detroit, Michigan 48226

Editor: James Lagos	Circulation: 9,845
Sponsor: n.i.	Frequency: weekly
Language: Greek and English	Subscription: $10.00

NATIONAL GREEK TRIBUNE (cont'd)
Most of the paper is in Greek, with only a few columns in English. Contains articles on Greek culture and politics as well as Greek Americans. Illustrated.

325.   THE NEW CALIFORNIA.   Nea California.   1907–
     1666 Market Street
     San Francisco, California 94102

     Editor: N. S. Dallas   Circulation: 3,000
     Sponsor: Acropolis Publishing Corporation   Frequency: weekly
     Language: Greek and English   Subscription: $8.00

Provides general, national, and local news coverage.

326.   NEW YORK HELLENIC NEWS.   Ellenika Nea.   1963–
     117 West 57th Street
     New York, New York 10019

     Editor: Spyros Triantafyllou   Circulation: 5,338
     Sponsor: Hellenic News, Inc.   Frequency: weekly
     Language: Greek and English   Subscription: n.i.

Contains general news of interest to the Greek community.

327.   I PHONI TOU EVANGELIOU.   The Voice of the Gospel.   1949–
     801 Broad Avenue   (201) 943-4733
     Ridgefield, New Jersey 07657

     Editor: Rev. Spiros Zodhiates   Circulation: 6,000
     Sponsor: AMG International   Frequency: monthly
     Language: Greek   Subscription: $5.00

This is a religious monthly containing "Biblical exposition, sermons, missionary news–chiefly for the spiritual education of Greek Evangelicals" (editor's statement).

328.   ORTHODOX OBSERVER.   1934–
     8 East 79th Street   (212) 628-2590
     New York, New York 10021

     Editors: P. J. Gazouleas and J. G. Couchell   Circulation: 83,739
     Sponsor: Greek Orthodox Archdiocese Press   Frequency: bi-weekly
     Language: English and Greek   Subscription: $8.00

The periodical is published for the Greek Orthodox Archdiocese of North and South America. It features primarily news of the Greek Orthodox Church in the Americas, with some coverage of other Orthodox Churches (Russian, Syrian, Serbian, etc.) and of Orthodoxy worldwide, and some general religious news. Has regular columns of book reviews, film reviews, parish news, and "spiritual guidance." Some coverage of news from Greece. Has a monthly four-page Youth Supplement, and there are occasional features on topics of special interest (e.g., Greek monasteries, contraception).

329.   ROUMELIOTIKOS TYPOS.   Roumeli Press.   1964–
     2412 Broadway   (212) 937-4072
     New York, New York

     Editor: Efthimios Thomopoulos   Circulation: 2,000
     Sponsor: Roumeli Press Co.   Frequency: monthly
     Language: Greek and English   Subscription: $6.00

330.   THE TRIBUNE OF G.A.P.A.
     3600 Fifth Avenue   (412) 621-4676
     Pittsburgh, Pennsylvania 15213

THE TRIBUNE OF G.A.P.A. (cont'd)
Editor: Editorial Committee
Sponsor: Greek-American Progressive Association
Language: Greek and English

Circulation: n.i.
Frequency: 5 times/year
Subscription: n.i.

A fraternal publication.

Greek Publications in English

331. THE AHEPA MESSENGER. 1931–
409 West 44th Street
New York, New York 10036

Editor: Angelos G. Chaoush
Sponsor: Metropolitan Chapter of AHEPA
Language: English

Circulation: 2,000
Frequency: monthly
Subscription: membership dues

Published by the American Hellenic Educational Progressive Association, this monthly is a fraternal publication.

332. THE AHEPAN. 1927–
1422 K Street, N. W. (202) 628-4974
Washington, D. C. 20005

Editor: Charles J. Drewes
Sponsor: Order of AHEPA
Language: English

Circulation: 27,500
Frequency: bi-monthly
Subscription: $3.00

"Primarily news articles of activities of Ahepa Chapters and Auxiliary chapters in U.S.A. and Canada—and matters concerning Americans of Greek descent" (editor's statement). Official organ of the strongest Greek fraternal organization, the American Hellenic Educational Progressive Association (AHEPA); its aim is to preserve Greek culture and to encourage the study of Greek classics. Illustrated.

333. THE BULLETIN OF THE MODERN GREEK STUDIES ASSOCIATION. 1968–
185 Nassau Street
Princeton, New Jersey 08540

Editor: Julia Loomis
Sponsor: Modern Greek Studies Association
Language: English

Circulation: 375
Frequency: bi-annually
Subscription: free/membership

Contains materials concerning the status of Greek studies in the United States.

334. THE CHICAGO PNYX. 1939–
P. O. Box 67
Glenview, Illinois 60025

Editor: Peter N. Mantzoros
Sponsor: PNYX Publishing Company
Language: English

Circulation: 2,000
Frequency: semi-monthly
Subscription: $5.00

National and local news coverage, plus informative materials on Greece. Special feature: news items on the Order of Ahepa.

335. THE GREEK ORTHODOX THEOLOGICAL REVIEW. 1954–
50 Goddard Avenue (617) 232-4544
Brookline, Massachusetts 02146

Editor: Rev. Dr. Nomikos Michael Vaporis
Sponsor: Holy Cross Orthodox Press
Language: English

Circulation: 1,200
Frequency: quarterly
Subscription: $10.00

A journal of contemporary Orthodox theological thought featuring scholarly papers and reviews in the fields of Biblical studies, Orthodox theology, and Byzantine and church history.

336. THE HELLENIC CHRONICLE.   1950–
        324 Newbury Street
        Boston, Massachusetts 02115

Editor: James Anagnostos   Circulation: 32,717
Sponsor: Hellenic Publishing Corporation   Frequency: weekly
Language: English   Subscription: $5.00

Provides international, national, and local news of interest to the Greek community.

337. OLOGOS.   Orthodox Lore of the Gospel of Our Saviour.   1950–
        P. O. Box 5333   (314) 533-7755
        St. Louis, Missouri 63115

Editor: Rev. George Mastrantonis   Circulation: 2,600
Sponsor: n.i.   Frequency: bi-monthly
Language: English   Subscription: $2.00

Subjects cover the teachings of the Orthodox Church, meditation, saints, events in Christ's life, social problems, the Bible, and other topics.

HEBREW PRESS
See Jewish Press

HUNGARIAN PRESS
Hungarian and Hungarian-English Publications

338. AMERIKAI MAGYAR ELET.   American Hungarian Life.   1958–
        3636 North Paris Avenue   (312) 625-8774
        Chicago, Illinois 60634

Editor: Louis H. Adam   Circulation: 14,850
Sponsor: American Hungarian Life Enterprises   Frequency: weekly
Language: Hungarian   Subscription: $15.00

Features political articles related to the present situation in Hungary. Its main objective is "to promote and enhance the recognition of the plight of the Hungarian nation now under Soviet domination" (editor's statement).

**339. AMERIKAI MAGYAR NEPSZAVA.   American Hungarian People's
        Voice.**   1899–
        1736 East 22nd Street
        Cleveland, Ohio 44114

Editor: Zoltan Gombos   Circulation: 10,830
Sponsor: Liberty Publishing Company   Frequency: daily
Language: Hungarian   Subscription: $30.00

This newspaper prints special news and events of interest to Hungarian readers. Included are general news items about domestic and foreign affairs, sports, arts, theater, and news of local events. Sections are also devoted to reports from foreign correspondents, novels, essays, and poetry. The "publication is politically independent" (editor's statement).

340. AMERIKAI MAGYAR SZEMLE.   The American Hungarian Review.   1963–
        5410 Kerth Road
        St. Louis, Missouri 63128

Editor: Leslie Konnyu   Circulation: 1,000
Sponsor: The American Hungarian Review   Frequency: quarterly
Language: English and Hungarian   Subscription: $5.00

This magazine focuses on the arts, sciences, and humanities. American-Hungarian historical and cultural relations are also explored.

341. AMERIKAI MAGYAR SZÓ. **Hungarian Word.** 1902–
130 East 16th Street (212) 254-0397
New York, New York 10003

Editor: James Lustig Circulation: 3,200
Sponsor: American Hungarian Word, Inc. Frequency: weekly
Language: Hungarian Subscription: $12.50

Contains news of domestic and foreign affairs, editorials, comments on various societal problems, reports on international sports events, humor, and short items on various personalities. Illustrated.

342. AMERIKAI MAGYAR VILAG. **American Hungarian World.** 1964–
1736 East 22nd Street (216) 241-5905
Cleveland, Ohio 44114

Editor: Zoltan Gombos Circulation: 9,019
Sponsor: Associated Hungarian Press, Inc. Frequency: weekly
Language: Hungarian Subscription: $12.00

343. CHICAGO ES KORNYEKE. **Chicago and Vicinity.** 1906–
1541 West Touhy Avenue
Chicago, Illinois 60626

Editor: Julius Hovany Circulation: 2,301
Sponsor: n.i. Frequency: weekly
Language: Hungarian Subscription: $8.00

This weekly provides general international, national, and local news coverage.

344. DETROITI MAGYAR UJSAG. **Detroit Hungarian News.** 1911–
1580 Oak Street
Wyondotte, Michigan 48192

Editor: Amelia Fodor Circulation: 1,600
Sponsor: Amelia Fodor Frequency: weekly
Language: Hungarian and English Subscription: $10.00

Contains general news and materials concerning Hungarian life in the United States.

345. EVANGÉLIUMI HIRNÖK. **Gospel Messenger.** 1908–
750 Fordham Road (305) 724-1580
Palm Bay, Florida 32905

Editor: Bela Udvarnoki Circulation: 600
Sponsor: Hungarian Baptist Union of America Frequency: semi-monthly
Language: Hungarian Subscription: $6.00

This is the official publication of the Hungarian Baptist Union of America. Contains inspirational and doctrinal articles, with coverage of church activities and events.

346. HIRADO. **Herald.** 1921–
303 Maple Street
Perth Amboy, New Jersey 08861

Editor: L. I. Dienes Circulation: 3,950
Sponsor: L. I. Dienes Frequency: weekly
Language: Hungarian Subscription: $8.00

General national and local news of interest to Hungarian community.

347. KATOLIKUS MAGYAROK VASARNAPJA. **Catholic Hungarians'**
Sunday. 1894–
517 South Belle Vista Avenue (216) 799-1888
Youngstown, Ohio 44509

KATOLIKUS MAGYAROK VASARNAPJA (cont'd)

Editor: Fr. Nicholas G. Dengl O.F.M.
Sponsor: Commissariat of St. Stephen's
      Franciscan Province
Language: Hungarian

Circulation: 3,400
Frequency: weekly
Subscription: $12.00

This newspaper contains information regarding the state of the Church in Hungary as well as in other countries with Hungarian populations. Also included are news items dealing with various aspects of Hungarian cultural, social, and political activities and events in various countries. Contains "political essays opposing all kinds of totalitarian systems as opposed to human and religious freedom" (editor's statement).

348. **KEPES MAGYAR VILAGHIRADO.** **Illustrated Hungarian World Review.** 1971–
P. O. Box 332
Twinsburg, Ohio 44087
(216) 562-7239

Editor: Judith Petres Ewendt
Sponsor: Maksymilian Ewendt
Language: Hungarian

Circulation: 1,358
Frequency: monthly
Subscription: $10.00

Features "pictorial reports of the various cultural and social affairs of the Hungarian groups and societies" (editor's statement). Contains poetry and short stories written by Hungarian authors in exile.

349. **LITERARY HERALD.** **Irodalmi Hirado.** 1955–
323 East 79th Street
New York, New York 10021

Editor: Samuel Weiss
Sponsor: New York First Hungarian Literary
      Society
Language: Hungarian and English

Circulation: 2,500
Frequency: monthly
Subscription: $2.00

350. **LORAIN ES VIDEKE.** **Lorain & Vicinity.** 1913–
1826 East 28th Street
Lorain, Ohio 44055

Editor: Louis P. Bodnar
Sponsor: Bodnar Printing Company
Language: Hungarian

Circulation: 648
Frequency: semi-monthly
Subscription: $5.00

This publication is directed toward the Hungarian population in Lorain, Ohio, and its nearby communities. News items deal primarily with church, lodge, and social activities of interest to Hungarians in this area. At times, it includes news dealing with national affairs and events in Hungary.

351. **MAGYAR CSERKESZ.** **Hungarian Scout Magazine.** 1951–
247 Lanza Avenue
Garfield, New Jersey 07026
(201) 772-8810

Editor: Ferenc Koreh
Sponsor: Hungarian Scouts Association
Language: Hungarian

Circulation: 1,500
Frequency: quarterly
Subscription: $4.00

Contains news about Hungarian scout activities. Illustrated.

352. **MAGYAR EGYHAZ.** **Magyar Church.** 1922–
1657 Centerview Drive
Akron, Ohio 44321
(216) 666-4600

Editor: Rev. Tibor Domotor
Sponsor: Magyar Egyhaz Publishing Co.
Language: Hungarian and English

Circulation: 4,500
Frequency: monthly
Subscription: $3.00

MAGYAR EGYHAZ (cont'd)

This is the official organ of the Hungarian Reformed Church in America. Its main objective is "to inform members of the denomination about events in the ecclesiastical world—the denomination, the United States, and the world, with special emphasis on events concerning the Reformed and Presbyterian Churches" (editor's statement). Material includes devotional and doctrinal articles. Each issue contains a section on "News from the Congregations" in both Hungarian and English.

353. MAGYAR HIRADO.   Magyar Herald.   1909–
    222 Amboy Avenue   (202) 548-1369
    Metuchen, New Jersey 08840

    Editor: Laszlo I. Dienes   Circulation: 4,940
    Sponsor: Associated Hungarian Press, Inc.   Frequency: weekly
    Language: Hungarian   Subscription: $15.00

This weekly contains news of general interest for Hungarian groups, including items on world and domestic events, activities within Hungarian communities, and news from Hungary. Much space is devoted to articles by individual writers on a variety of topics.

354. MAGYARSAG.   Hungarian People.   1925–
    200 Johnston Avenue
    Pittsburgh, Pennsylvania 15207

    Editor: Jeno Szebedinszky   Circulation: 3,840
    Sponsor: Jeno Szebedinszky   Frequency: weekly
    Language: Hungarian   Subscription: $8.00

355. NEMZETVEDELMI TAJEKOZTATO.   Information about Defense of
    Nation.   1967–
    P. O. Box 38031
    Hollywood, California 90038

    Editor: Geza Gorgenyi   Circulation: n.i.
    Sponsor: Hungarian World Federation of the   Frequency: monthly
        Defense of Nation   Subscription: $6.00
    Language: Hungarian

Orientation is political and historical. Ideologically, this publication takes an anti-communist stand.

356. PATRIA.   1973–
    2046 Bunts Road   (216) 521-2005
    Lakewood, Ohio 44107

    Editor: Dennis Frigyes   Circulation: 4,500
    Sponsor: Patria Civic Society   Frequency: quarterly
    Language: Hungarian and English   Subscription: free

Features articles on the Hungarian contribution to American political and cultural life, preservation of Hungarian culture in the United States, and other materials relevant to the Hungarian community. Designed for younger Hungarian Americans.

357. ST. LOUIS ES VIDEKE.   St. Louis and Vicinity.   1913–
    5535 Alcott Avenue
    St. Louis, Missouri 63120

    Editor: Louis B. Denes   Circulation: 10,000
    Sponsor: n.i.   Frequency: bi-weekly
    Language: Hungarian   Subscription: $6.00

358. THE SOUTHWEST JOURNAL. Délnyngati Ujság.   1914–
8502 West Jefferson Avenue
Detroit, Michigan 48217

Editor: Mrs. Ernest Palos   Circulation: 12,505
Sponsor: n.i.   Frequency: weekly
Language: Hungarian and English   Subscription: $2.00

This weekly journal provides general, national, and local news coverage.

359. SZABADSAG. Liberty.   1801–
1736 East 22nd Street   (216) 241-5905
Cleveland, Ohio 44114

Editor: Zoltan Gombos   Circulation: 5,325
Sponsor: Liberty Publishing Company   Frequency: weekly
Language: Hungarian   Subscription: $12.00

Covers general foreign and domestic news and events of interest to Hungarian readers. Also includes literature (novels, poetry, essays).

360. SZABADSÁGHARCOS HIRADÓ. Freedom Fighter News.   1971–
P. O. Box 34705   (213) 839-1895
Los Angeles, California 90034

Editor: Julius Bogar   Circulation: 1,500
Sponsor: Hungarian Freedom Fighters   Frequency: monthly
    Federation of California Inc.   Subscription: $2.00
Language: Hungarian

Contains historical and political articles covering the Hungarian Revolution of 1956, as well as information concerning the Hungarian community and its activities in the United States.

361. A SZIV. The Heart.   1915–
76 Locust Hill Avenue
Yonkers, New York 10701

Editor: Rev. Rochus Radany   Circulation: 2,800
Sponsor: Hungarian Jesuit Fathers   Frequency: monthly
Language: Hungarian   Subscription: $3.00

This Roman Catholic devotional publication deals with various subjects relevant to contemporary Roman Catholic life.

362. TESTVERISEG. Fraternity.   1923–
3216 New Mexico Avenue, N. W.
Washington, D. C. 20016

Editor: Rt. Rev. Dr. Zoltan Beky   Circulation: 16,786
Sponsor: Hungarian Reformed Federation of   Frequency: monthly
    America   Subscription: free to members
Language: English and Hungarian

363. AZ UJSAG. The Hungarian News.   1921–
1017 Fairfield Avenue   (216) 696-3635
Cleveland, Ohio 44102

Editor: Zoltan Kotai   Circulation: 1,260
Sponsor: Karpat Publishing Company   Frequency: weekly
Language: Hungarian   Subscription: $10.00

364. VEZETŐK LAPJA.   **Leaders Magazine.**   1951–
247 Lanza Avenue   (201) 772-8810
Garfield, New Jersey 07026

Editor: Rev. Dr. John Ádám   Circulation: 1,500
Sponsor: Hungarian Scouts Association   Frequency: quarterly
Language: Hungarian   Subscription: $4.00

Covers the activities of the Hungarian Scouts Association, with articles also on education, recreation, outdoor life, and other topics of interest to Hungarian Scouts. Illustrated.

365. VIRRASZTÓ.   **Awakener.**   1970–
45-54 41st Street   (212) 784-2791
Long Island City, New York 11104

Editor: V. Erdélyi István   Circulation: 1,000
Sponsor: Virraszto Research Committee   Frequency: irregular
Language: Hungarian   Subscription: $5.00 (4 issues)

Virraszto is the successor of the *Larmafa*, which was published and edited in Austria between 1959 and 1968. *Virraszto* publishes historical and political essays and documents dealing with the Carpathian territory. The aim of this publication is "to nullify the Trianon Peace Treaty of 1920 and to restore the political unity of the Carpathian basin" (editor's statement).

366. WILLIAM PENN LIFE.   1965–
429 Forbes Avenue   (412) 281-8950
Pittsburgh, Pennsylvania 15219

Editor: Elmer Charles   Circulation: 33,000
Sponsor: William Penn Association   Frequency: quarterly
Language: Hungarian and English   Subscription: free to members

This fraternal publication contains news of the activities of the WPA. Illustrated.

367. "WISCONSINI MAGYARSA'G" HUNGARIAN NEWSPAPER.   **Wisconsin**
Hungarians.   1924–
609 North Plankinton Avenue, Room 508
Milwaukee, Wisconsin 53203

Editor: Charles Klein   Circulation: 18,700
Sponsor: n.i.   Frequency: weekly
Language: Hungarian   Subscription: $5.00

This publication, established for the Hu ngarians residing in the state of Wisconsin, contains news items on various group activities and events as well as articles dealing with topics of special interest to Hungarian groups.

Hungarian Publications in English

368. FRATERNITY.
3216 New Mexico Avenue, N. W.
Washington, D. C. 20016

Editor: Rt. Rev. Dr. Zoltan Beky   Circulation: 32,000
Sponsor: Rt. Rev. Dr. Zoltan Beky   Frequency: quarterly
Language: English   Subscription: n.i.

369. HUNGARIAN STUDIES NEWSLETTER.   1973–
177 Somerset Street   (201) 846-5777
New Brunswick, New Jersey 08903

Editor: Bela C. Maday   Circulation: n.i.
Sponsor: Hungarian Research Center, American   Frequency: 3 times a year
            Hungarian Foundation   Subscription: $3.00
Language: English

HUNGARIAN STUDIES NEWSLETTER (cont'd)

A major portion of this publication is devoted to reviews of books related to Hungarian history, politics, economy, culture, and other areas. Also includes "miscellaneous news" section and research in progress. "The *HSN* is the only English language periodical to report on scholarly activities related to Hungary and Hungarians" (editor's statement).

INDIAN PRESS

See also Asian Press

Indian Publications in English

370. BHARAT DARSHAN.   1970–
106 East Hall, Columbia University
New York, New York 10027

Editors: Rajiv Sinha and Murau Nair	Circulation: 5,000
Sponsor: India Club of Columbia University	Frequency: irregular
Language: English	Subscription: free

Contains brief articles on East Indians in the United States, especially in the New York area.

371. INDIA ABROAD.   1970–
60 East 42nd Street   (212) 490-1770
New York, New York 10017

Editor: Gopal Raju	Circulation: 11,000
Sponsor: India Abroad Publications Inc.	Frequency: weekly
Language: English	Subscription: $10.00

Its aim is to promote a better Indo-U. S. understanding. Besides news of major Indian events each week, the paper also reports news from the Indian states; events of interest to Indians in America; and matters of Indo-U. S. concern. It carries "articles and in-depth features that put the news in perspective; book and film reviews; sports news; as well as a column on immigration questions" (editor's statement). Illustrated.

372. INDIA NEWS.   1970–
2107 Massachusetts Avenue, N. W.
Washington, D. C. 20008

Editor: n.i.	Circulation: n.i.
Sponsor: Embassy of India	Frequency: weekly
Language: English	Subscription: free

Provides important news about and from India, and job information for Indians living in the United States. Summarizes the news about new developments in India.

IRANIAN PRESS

Iranian and Iranian-English Publications

373. THE IRAN TIMES.   1970–
1917 Eye Street, N. W.
Washington, D. C. 20006

Editor: Javad Khakbaz	Circulation: n.i.
Sponsor: Iran Times, Inc.	Frequency: n.i.
Language: Persian and English	Subscription: $15.00

IRISH PRESS

Irish Publications in English

374. THE BULLETIN OF THE AMERICAN IRISH HISTORICAL SOCIETY.   1973–
991 Fifth Avenue   (212) 288-2263
New York, New York 10028

THE BULLETIN OF THE AMERICAN IRISH HISTORICAL SOCIETY (cont'd)
Editor: n.i.   Circulation: n.i.
Sponsor: American Irish Historical Society   Frequency: semi-annual
Language: English   Subscription: n.i.

Contains news on the activities of American Irish Historical Society, whose aim is to preserve the Irish heritage in America.

375. EIRE–IRELAND.   1966–
683 Osceola   (612) 647-5678
St. Paul, Minnesota 55105

Editor: Eoin McKiernan   Circulation: 5,200
Sponsor: Irish American Cultural Institute   Frequency: quarterly
Language: English   Subscription: $15.00

Features articles on Irish history, culture, arts, and creative writing, with a special book review section. The magazine's main objective is to promote the study of Irish civilization, with an emphasis on the interrelationships between Irish and American culture.

376. THE IRISH ADVOCATE.   1893–
15 Park Row   (212) 233-4672
New York, New York 10038

Editor: James N. O'Connor   Circulation: 27,500
Sponsor: James N. O'Connor   Frequency: weekly
Language: English   Subscription: $7.00

This weekly newspaper is devoted to Irish news and to the business, social, political, and athletic activities of Irish Americans in Greater New York and the United States; it also provides news from Ireland. According to the editor the newspaper is "non-sectarian, pro-labor, and liberal." Illustrated.

377. IRISH ECHO.   1928–
3 East 28th Street   (212) 889-4070
New York, New York 10016

Editor: John Thornton   Circulation: 29,950
Sponsor: Irish Echo Newspaper Corp.   Frequency: weekly
Language: English   Subscription: $7.50

Includes news from the Irish-American community in the United States, particularly the social and sports scenes in New York City and environs. Weekly features include columns by Bob Considine and Jack O'Brian, chosen and edited for Irish interest. "Other weekly features are columns from Ireland: Investing in Ireland, written by a banker in Dublin, and Dublin Report, a commentary on the political and socio-economic scene in Ireland, including the North (editor's statement). Illustrated.

378. IRISH HERALD.   1962–
2123 Market Street   (415) 621-2200
San Francisco, California 94114

Editor: John Whooley   Circulation: 5,300
Sponsor: Irish Heritage Center   Frequency: n.i.
Language: English   Subscription: $5.00

Covers topics of interest to Irish Americans.

379. IRISH WORLD AND GAELIC AMERICAN.   1870–
84-90 Fifth Avenue
New York, New York 10011

Editor: M. P. Ford   Circulation: n.i.
Sponsor: M. P. Ford   Frequency: weekly
Language: English   Subscription: $5.00

Features articles and news on Irish-American life in the United States.

ITALIAN PRESS
Italian and Italian-English Publications

380. L'ADUNATA DEI REFRATTARI.   The Call of the 'Refractaires.'   1922–
216 West 18th Street
New York, New York 10011

Editor: Owen Agostinelli   Circulation: 3,990
Sponsor: n.i.   Frequency: bi-weekly
Language: Italian   Subscription: $3.00

This publication features general and political articles.

381. THE AMERICAN CITIZEN.   1923–
1134 North 17th Street   (402) 345-9158
Omaha, Nebraska 68102

Editor: Victor Failla   Circulation: 541
Sponsor: The American Citizen   Frequency: semi-monthly
Language: Italian   Subscription: $3.00

Provides coverage of international, national, and local news of special interest to Italian Americans. Illustrated.

382. BOLLETTINO DELLA FEDERAZIONE CATTOLICA ITALIANA.
Bulletin of the Italian Catholic Federation.   1924–
678 Green Street   (415) 421-7993
San Francisco, California 94133

Editor: Mario J. Cugia   Circulation: 20,825
Sponsor: Central Council of the Italian Frequency: monthly
         Catholic Federation   Subscription: $1.00
Language: English and Italian

The official organ of the Italian Catholic Federation, this monthly contains news items on activities of the various branches composing the Federation. Also includes articles on travel, comments on religious matters, and book reviews.

383. THE BULLETIN OF ITALIAN CHAMBER OF COMMERCE OF
CHICAGO.   1907–
712 Rosedale   (312) 427-3014
Glenview, Illinois 60025

Editor: Benny G. Zucchini   Circulation: 1,600
Sponsor: Italian Chamber of Commerce of Frequency: bi-monthly
         Chicago   Subscription: n.i.
Language: English and Italian

The aim of this publication is to "strengthen and increase relations between members of the Italian Chamber of Commerce by providing information on firms in the United States. It also provides information on customs regulations, foreign trade rules, and governmental controls.

384. CONNECTICUT ITALIAN BULLETIN.   1950–
P. O. Box 1264
Hartford, Connecticut 06105

Editor: unknown   Circulation: 5,000
Sponsor: Connecticut Italian Publishing Frequency: bi-weekly
         Company, Inc.   Subscription: free
Language: Italian and English

385. IL CORRIERE DEL BERKSHIRE. The Berkshire Courier. 1930–
45 Thomson Place
Pittsfield, Massachusetts 01202

Editor: Enzo Marinare Circulation: 3,600
Sponsor: n.i. Frequency: weekly
Language: Italian Subscription: $1.00

This is a political magazine.

386. THE ECHO. 1896–
243 Atwells Avenue (401) 521-5760
Providence, Rhode Island 02903

Editor: Dean Whitten Circulation: 29,000
Sponsor: PR Associates Frequency: weekly
Language: English and Italian Subscription: $7.00

This family-oriented weekly promotes "Italo-American lifestyles, accomplishments and heritage" (editor's statement). Covers international, national, and local news, with special sections on the arts, education, and sports. Illustrated.

387. L'ECO D'ITALIA. Echo of Italy. 1966–
709 Union Street
San Francisco, California 94133

Editor: Pierino Mori Circulation: 3,000
Sponsor: Pierino Mori Frequency: weekly
Language: Italian Subscription: $6.00

Features community news, news from Italy, and national news. Its main objective is to "inform the Italo-American community of events of the day, locally as well as in Italy; to record for posterity, the events of the Italo-American community; to preserve our Italian heritage" (editor's statement). Illustrated.

388. LA FOLLIA DI NEW YORK. The New York Folly. 1893–
125 East 95th Street (212) 722-6409
New York, New York 10028

Editor: Michael Sisca Circulation: 4,500
Sponsor: The Italian National Magazine Co., Inc. Frequency: monthly
Language: Italian and English Subscription: $10.00

Publishes cultural, political, historical, musical, scientific, and medical articles of interest to the Italian community. Illustrated.

389. FORUM ITALICUM. Italian Forum. 1967–
221 Crosby Hall
Buffalo, New York 14214

Editor: M. Ricciardelli Circulation: 600
Sponsor: State University of New York Frequency: quarterly
at Buffalo Subscription: $4.00
Language: English and Italian

This publication serves as a forum for the views of scholars and teachers on the language, culture, and literature of Italy and of other countries in relation to Italy. Contains sections on poetry, creative essays, reviews, and news.

390. GIUSTIZIA. Justice. 1918–
1710 Broadway
New York, New York 10019

Editor: Lino Manocchia Circulation: 51,000
Sponsor: International Ladies Garment Frequency: monthly
Workers Union Subscription: $2.00
Language: Italian

GIUSTIZIA (cont'd)
This is the official organ of the Ladies Garment Workers Union. It is primarily devoted to news of Union activities and politics, although it also contains general news on women's fashions.

391. THE ITALIAN BULLETIN.   1949–
P. O. Box 1264
Hartford, Connecticut 06105

Editor: Ven Sequenzia
Sponsor: Connecticut Publishing Company–
    European Cultural Bureau
Language: Italian and English

Circulation: 3,500
Frequency: bi-weekly
Subscription: n.i.

392. ITALIAN NEWS.   1921–
Box 94, Hanover Station
Boston, Massachusetts 02113

Editor: Varoujan Samuelian
Sponsor: Italian News Publishing Company, Inc.
Language: Italian

Circulation: 2,705
Frequency: weekly
Subscription: $3.00

393. ITALICA.   1924–
Department of Italian
Columbia University
New York, New York 10027

Editor: Olga Ragusa
Sponsor: American Association of Teachers
    of Italian
Language: Italian and English

Circulation: 1,820
Frequency: quarterly
Subscription: $6.00

The principal objective of this publication is to promote the study of the Italian language and literature in both the United States and Canada.

394. L'ITALO AMERICANO DI LOS ANGELES. Los Angeles Italian
American.   1908–
1035 North Broadway
Los Angeles, California 90012

Editors: Cleto M. Baroni and Mario Trecco
Sponsor: n.i.
Language: Italian

Circulation: 4,400
Frequency: weekly
Subscription: $2.00

395. IL LEONE. The Lion.   1931–
5051 Mission Street
San Francisco, California 94112

Editor: Roland G. DeRocili
Sponsor: Grand Lodge of California, Order of
    Sons of Italy in America
Language: Italian

Circulation: 12,007
Frequency: monthly
Subscription: $3.00

Features fraternal news.

396. IL MESSAGGERO. The Messenger.   1925–
544 Wabash   (816) 241-7738
Kansas City, Missouri 62124

Editor: J. B. Bisceglia
Sponsor: The Italian Mission
Language: Italian and English

Circulation: 800
Frequency: monthly
Subscription: n.i.

The contents of this publication are religious and educational in nature. It is intended primarily for Italian-Americans residing in Kansas City.

397. MIDDLETOWN BULLETIN. 1948–
790 Ridge Road
Middletown, Connecticut 06457

Editor: Max B. Corvo
Sponsor: Middletown Bulletin, Inc.
Language: English and Italian

Circulation: 1,335
Frequency: weekly
Subscription: $2.00

Provides general, national, and local news coverage.

398. IL MONDO LIBERO. The Free World. 1956–
2844 Syracuse Street
Dearborn, Michigan 48124

Editor: G. Oberdam Rizzo
Sponsor: Free World International Academy, Inc.
Language: Italian and English

Circulation: 2,300
Frequency: monthly
Subscription: $5.00

This publication, basically cultural in nature, includes poetry, literature, science, the arts, commentaries, and coverage of current events.

399. THE NATIONAL ITALIAN-AMERICAN NEWS. 1970–
26 Court Street
Brooklyn, New York 11242

Editor: Joseph Preite
Sponsor: The Italian American News, Inc.
Language: English and Italian

Circulation: 11,310
Frequency: weekly
Subscription: $9.00

The main objective of the publication is to keep the community "informed of all that happens within the community in the United States and major events in Italy" (editor's statement). Contains articles on Italy and Italians in the United States. Aims at participation of Italian Americans in political and social activities, as well as community involvement. Illustrated.

400. LA NOTIZIA. The News. 1916–
30-34 Battery Street
G. P. O. Box 1870
Boston, Massachusetts 02109

Editor: G. N. Longarini
Sponsor: n.i.
Language: Italian

Circulation: 24,600
Frequency: weekly
Subscription: $5.00

Provides coverage of national, international, and local news, plus information about public and private institutions. Serves as an aid for the Italian-speaking population in "adjusting to the new environment" (editor's statement).

401. LA NUOVA AURORA. The New Dawn. 1903–
314 Richfield Road (215) 352-2396
Upper Darby, Pennsylvania 19082

Editor: The Rev. Dr. Anthony F. Vasquez
Sponsor: The Italian Baptist Association of
America
Language: English and Italian

Circulation: 1,500
Frequency: quarterly
Subscription: $3.00

Contains international and informational articles in the field of religion, for Americans of Italian background.

402. LA NUOVA CAPITALE. The New Capital. 1929–
681 South Broad Street
Trenton, New Jersey 08611

Editor: Maurice Perilli
Sponsor: n.i.
Language: Italian

Circulation: 2,595
Frequency: monthly
Subscription: $2.00

403. OSIA NEWS. 1946–
41 Austin Street
Worcester, Massachusetts 01609

Editor: Albert A. Maino   Circulation: 32,000
Sponsor: Order of Sons of Italy in America   Frequency: monthly
Language: English and Italian   Subscription: n.i.

"Publication is of and for the members of the organization, its interests in matters concerning immigration and naturalization, and its many and varied national programs, such as culture, Italian language, birth defects" (editor's statement). Illustrated.

404. LA PAROLA DEL POPOLO.   The Word of the People.   1908–
6740 West Diversey Avenue   (312) 637-5523
Chicago, Illinois 60635

Editor: E. Clemente   Circulation: 5,000
Sponsor: La Parola del Popolo Pub. Assn. Frequency: bi-monthly
Language: Italian   Subscription: $6.00

A pro-labor, Democratic Socialist publication recognized by the Socialist Labor International. Contains news and commentaries on economic, social, and political affairs of Italy and the United States.

405. IL PENSIERO.   The Thought. 1904–
2126 Marconi   (314) 771-6769
St. Louis, Missouri 63110

Editors: Antonino Lombardo and Anthony   Circulation: 5,000
              Gandolfo   Frequency: semi-monthly
Sponsor: Antonino Lombardo and Anthony   Subscription: $3.00
              Gandolfo
Language: Italian and English

Provides coverage of news events in Italy as well as activities within Italian communities in the United States.

406. IL POPOLO ITALIANO.   The Italian People. 1935–
4203 Ventnor Avenue   (609) 348-2032
Atlantic City, New Jersey 08401

Editor: Arnold R. Orsatti   Circulation: 7,578
Sponsor: Italian Community Publishing Co. Frequency: monthly
Language: Italian and English   Subscription: $2.00

Features news and articles on Italian-American life and activities, Italian organizations, and international, national, and local news of interest to the Italian community. Illustrated.

407. IL PROGRESSO ITALO-AMERICANO.   Italian-American Progress.   1880–
260 Audubon Avenue
New York, New York 10033

Editor: Fortune Pope   Circulation: 69,735
Sponsor: Il Progresso Italo-Americano   Frequency: daily
              Publishing Company, Inc.   Subscription: $40.00
Language: Italian

The objective of this publication is "to provide Italian readers with international, national, and local news" (editor's statement). News coverage of events in Italy is stressed. The only Italian daily in the United States.

408. IL RINNOVAMENTO. The Renewal. 1933–
117 North Broadway
Nyack, New York 10960

Editor: Rev. J. Jerry Cardo
Sponsor: Italian Evangelical Publication Society
Language: Italian

Circulation: 300
Frequency: bi-monthly
Subscription: n.i.

409. NOTIZIA DI FIGLI DI ITALIA. Sons of Italy News. 1928–
126 Cambridge Street   (617) 227-4838
Boston, Massachusetts 02114

Editor: Ralph Ferruzzi
Sponsor: Grand Lodge of Massachusetts, Order
of Sons of Italy in America
Language: English and Italian

Circulation: 18,500
Frequency: monthly
Subscription: $2.00

This is a news medium "for over 135 lodges representing well over 20,000 members in the state of Massachusetts. This news concerns the activities of these lodges and activities of their members, socially, civicly, professionally, charitably, or fraternally" (editor's statement).

410. SONS OF ITALY TIMES. 1936–
Broad and Federal Streets
Philadelphia, Pennsylvania 19146

Editor: Joseph L. Monte
Sponsor: Grand Lodge of Pennsylvania, Order
of Sons of Italy in America
Language: English and Italian

Circulation: 29,000
Frequency: weekly
Subscription: $2.00

This fraternal newspaper contains news concerning the 300 lodges throughout Pennsylvania. Also contains editorials on topics such as education, law, pollution, politics, etc.

411. LA TRIBUNA ITALIANA D'AMERICA. Italian Tribune of America. 1909–
13517 Gratiot Avenue
Detroit, Michigan 48205

Editor: Ferrucio Serdoz
Sponsor: Giuliano Travel, Inc.
Language: Italian

Circulation: 1,600
Frequency: weekly
Subscription: $6.00

412. UNIONE. Union. 1890–
1719 Liberty Avenue
Pittsburgh, Pennsylvania 15222

Editor: Victor Frediani
Sponsor: Order of Italian Sons and Daughters
of America
Language: Italian

Circulation: 13,287
Frequency: weekly
Subscription: $2.50

A fraternal magazine.

413. LA VOCE DEL POPOLO. Voice of the People. 1910–
7050 Pinehurst
Dearborn, Michigan 48126

Editor: Victor Viberti
Sponsor: Pious Society of St. Paul
Language: Italian and English

Circulation: 2,000
Frequency: weekly
Subscription: n.i.

414. LA VOCE ITALIANA.   **The Italian Voice.**   1934–
    77-79 Mill Street
    Paterson, New Jersey 07501

Editor: Emilio Augusto   Circulation: 4,764
Sponsor: n.i.   Frequency: weekly
Language: Italian   Subscription: $3.50

This weekly provides general, national, and local news coverage.

Italian Publications in English

415. ACIM DISPATCH.   1953–
    9 East 35th Street   (212) 679-4650
    New York, New York 10016

Editor: Rev. Joseph A. Cogo   Circulation: 32,000
Sponsor: American Committee on Italian   Frequency: irregular
        Migration   Subscription: $5.00
Language: English

Promotes "fair immigration policies" (editor's statement).

416. AMERICA-ITALY NEWSLETTER.
    22 East 60th Street   (212) 838-1560
    New York, New York 10022

Editor: Hedy Giusti-Lanham   Circulation: 1,600
Sponsor: America-Italy Society, Inc.   Frequency: irregular
Language: English   Subscription: $7.50 (membership
                                       dues)

This organ of the American-Italy Society provides news on events and activities sponsored by the Society.

417. COLORADO LEADER.   1923–
    3630 Osage Street   (303) 477-0768
    Denver, Colorado 80211

Editor: J. L. Eitzen   Circulation: 2,200
Sponsor: None   Frequency: weekly
Language: English   Subscription: $3.00

Originally *Colorado*, this publication merged with *Denver Leader* to become *Colorado Leader*. Although it is not specifically ethnic, there is a one-page section in English aimed at the Italians of Denver and Colorado.

418. COLUMBUS PRESS.   1933–
    315 Larimer Avenue
    Pittsburgh, Pennsylvania 15206

Editor: n.i.   Circulation: n.i.
Sponsor: Federation of Sons of Columbus   Frequency: semi-monthly
        of America   Subscription: n.i.
Language: English

419. ITALIAN AMERICANA.   1974–
    State University College at Buffalo
    1300 Elmwood Avenue
    Buffalo, New York 14222

Editors: Ernest S. Falbo and Richard Gambino   Circulation: 700
Sponsor: Queens College of the City University   Frequency: semi-annually
       of New York, State University   Subscription: $10.00
       College at Buffalo, New York
Language: English

ITALIAN AMERICANA (cont'd)
The first academic journal devoted to the Italian experience in the United States. The journal "encompasses all dimensions of the Italian participation in American civilization, both historical and contemporary, including studies and commentary in the humanities and social sciences, fiction, poetry, bibliographies and reviews of significant books, films, plays and art" (editor's statement).

420. ITALIAN QUARTERLY. 1957–
Harbor Campus (617) 287-1900
Boston, Massachusetts 02125

Editor: Spencer Di Scala Circulation: 550
Sponsor: University of Massachusetts Frequency: quarterly
Language: English Subscription: $8.00

Articles on Italy and Italian culture. Topics covered include literature, economics, art, education, music, politics, and cinema.

421. THE ITALIAN TRIBUNE NEWS. 1931–
427 Bloomfield Avenue (201) 485-6000
Newark, New Jersey 07107

Editor: Joan Alagna Circulation: 20,000
Sponsor: Ace Alagna Publication Frequency: weekly
Language: English Subscription: $8.00

"The main objective of the paper is to provide insight into the Italian people and culture of their native land. We provide special features weekly – Italian language lessons weekly – a series on Italian Heritage men and women called "We Italians," also a special centerfold on early Italian settlers in America sent in by our readers" (editor's statement). Illustrated.

422. ITALO-AMERICAN TIMES. 1964–
Box 1492, Baychester Station
The Bronx, New York, New York 10469

Editor: Rudy Damonte Circulation: 10,000
Sponsor: Italo-American Times Publishing Frequency: bi-monthly
Company Subscription: $1.00
Language: English

This publication provides news of special interest for the Italian-American community of Bronx County, plus coverage of international, national, and local events. It also contains reports on developments in Italy, and analyses of topics of special concern to Americans of Italian descent.

423. THE NATIONAL ITALIAN-AMERICAN NEWS. 1969–
26 Court Street (212) 875-0580
Brooklyn, New York 11242

Editor: Joseph Preite Circulation: n.i.
Sponsor: The Italian-American News, Inc. Frequency: monthly
Language: English Subscription: $4.00

Features articles and news on Italians in the United States and their activities. Illustrated.

424. NEWSLETTER OF THE ISTITUTO ITALIANO DI CULTURA OF
NEW YORK. 1968–
686 Park Avenue (212) 879-4242
New York, New York 10021

Editor: Giuseppe Cardillo Circulation: 6,800
Sponsor: Italian Cultural Institute Frequency: quarterly
Language: English Subscription: free

NEWSLETTER OF THE ISTITUTO ITALIANO DI CULTURA OF NEW YORK
(cont'd)

Covers cultural events in Italy as well as Italian-American cultural activity in the United States. Also includes section on books recently published in Italy and publications of Italian-American interest.

425. POST-GAZETTE. 1896–
5 Prince Street
Boston, Massachusetts 02113

Editor: Caesar Donnaruma	Circulation: 14,900
Sponsor: n.i.	Frequency: weekly
Language: English	Subscription: $7.50

This weekly provides general international, national, and local news coverage.

426. STAR BULLETIN. 1959–
77-79 Mill Street
Paterson, New Jersey 07501

Editor: Emilio Augusto	Circulation: 134
Sponsor: n.i.	Frequency: weekly
Language: English	Subscription: n.i.

Covers local events of interest to the Italian community in New Jersey.

427. UNICO MAGAZINE. 1948–
72 Burroughs Place   (201) 748-9144
Bloomfield, New Jersey 07003

Editor: Hugo W. Senerchia	Circulation: 12,000
Sponsor: Unico National	Frequency: monthly
Language: English	Subscription: $5.00

Features articles on the Italian contribution to America as well as materials related to education and social problems in Italy and the United States.

JAPANESE PRESS
See also Asian Press

Japanese and Japanese-English Publications

428. THE CHICAGO SHIMPO. Chicago News. 1945–
3744 North Clark Street
Chicago, Illinois 60613

Editor: Ryeichi Fujii	Circulation: 3,020
Sponsor: The Chicago Shimpo, Inc.	Frequency: semi-weekly
Language: Japanese and English	Subscription: $10.00

Provides general coverage, including international, national, and local news. Also presents news concerning the Japanese community in the United States.

429. HAWAII HOCHI. Hawaii Herald. 1912–
917 Kokea Street   (808) 845-2255
Honolulu, Hawaii 96817

Editor: Don Takeshi Fujikawa	Circulation: 12,603
Sponsor: Hawaii Hochi Ltd.	Frequency: daily
Language: Japanese and English	Subscription: $39.50

This daily provides general international, national, and local news to the Japanese-speaking community in the state of Hawaii. There is heavy emphasis on news from Japan and local activities of the Japanese community – Buddhist Churches, businesses, clubs and societies, and visiting Japanese cultural and entertainment groups.

430. HAWAII TIMES. 1895–
P. O. Box 1230
Honolulu, Hawaii 96817

Editor: Ryokin Toyomira
Sponsor: Hawaii Times, Ltd.
Language: English and Japanese

Circulation: 12,475
Frequency: daily
Subscription: $36.50

431. HOKUBEI-HOCHI. 1946–
517 South Main Street (206) 623-0100
Seattle, Washington 98104

Editor: Takami Hibiya
Sponsor: The North American Post, Inc.
Language: Japanese and English

Circulation: 2,050
Frequency: daily
Subscription: n.i.

Provides coverage of international, national, regional, and local news of interest to Japanese Americans, with heavy emphasis on news from Japan.

432. HOKUBEI MAINICHI. North American Daily. 1948–
1737 Sutter Street
San Francisco, California 94115

Editor: Iwao Shimizu
Sponsor: Hokubei Mainichi, Inc.
Language: Japanese and English

Circulation: 7,000
Frequency: daily
Subscription: $30.00

433. JAPAN-AMERICA SOCIETY BULLETIN. 1957–
1755 Massachusetts Avenue, N. W., No. 308 (202) 265-0777
Washington, D. C. 20036

Editor: Ann F. Rushforth
Sponsor: Japan-American Society of Washington
Language: English and Japanese

Circulation: 1,100
Frequency: monthly
Subscription: $10.00

"A publication designed to help bring the peoples of the United States and Japan closer together in their appreciation and understanding of each other and each other's way of life" (editor's statement). Special features include a calendar of events and information about new books on Japan.

434. KASHU MAINICHI. California Daily News. 1931–
346 East First Street
Los Angeles, California 90012

Editor: Haruo Murokana
Sponsor: n.i.
Language: English and Japanese

Circulation: 5,610
Frequency: daily
Subscription: $17.00

This daily presents international, national, and local news, emphasizing articles of general interest to Japanese Americans. Published daily except Sundays and holidays.

435. THE NEW YORK NICHIBEI. New York Japanese American. 1945–
260 West Broadway
New York, New York 10013

Editor: Isaku Kida
Sponsor: Japanese American News Corporation
Language: Japanese and English

Circulation: 1,066
Frequency: weekly
Subscription: $6.00

436. RAFU SHIMPO.   Los Angeles Japanese Daily News.   1903–
242 South San Pedro Street
Los Angeles, California 90012

Editors: Teiho Hashida (Japanese) and   Circulation: 19,669
    Ellen Kayano (English)   Frequency: daily
Sponsor: Los Angeles News Publishing Company   Subscription: $17.00
Language: Japanese and English

This daily consists of two sections: Japanese and English. It is "an ethnic-oriented newspaper specializing in news concerning or involving persons of Japanese descent with emphasis on the Japanese American community in Southern California" (editor's statement). The Japanese section also highlights international and national news and includes a few popular serial novels.

437. ROCKY MOUNTAIN JIHO.   Rocky Mountain Times.   1962–
28 East 20th Avenue   (303) 534-7070
Denver, Colorado 80202

Editor: M. Tsubokawa   Circulation: 1,000
Sponsor: n.i.   Frequency: weekly
Language: English and Japanese   Subscription: $12.00

This weekly provides local news about the Japanese-American community, aiming especially at the non-English-speaking first generation of Japanese Americans.

438. THE UTAH NIPPO.
52 North Ninth West Street
Salt Lake City, Utah 84116

Editor: Terumasa Adachi   Circulation: 910
Sponsor: n.i.   Frequency: 3 times/week
Language: Japanese and English   Subscription: $7.00

Japanese Publications in English

439. BULLETIN OF THE JAPAN-AMERICA SOCIETY.   1957–
1785 Massachusetts Avenue, N. W.   (202) 265-0777
Washington, D. C. 10036

Editor: Scott F. Runkle   Circulation: 770
Sponsor: Japan-American Society of Washington   Frequency: monthly
Language: English   Subscription: free/membership

Presents news items dealing with various aspects of American-Japanese relationships, covering news from Japan as well as from Japanese-American communities.

440. JAPAN HOUSE NEWSLETTER.   1970–
333 East 47th Street   (212) 832-1155
New York, New York 10017

Editor: Sandra Faux   Circulation: 3,000
Sponsor: Japan Society, Inc.   Frequency: monthly
Language: English   Subscription: free/membership

The aim is "to provide a medium through which each nation may learn from the experiences and accomplishments of the other" (editor's statement). The newsletter includes articles on Japan-related subjects written by noted authors and specialists and provides a list of important Japanese cultural and educational events occurring in the United States, Japan, and Europe. Also highlights the activities of the Japan Society.

441. JOURNAL OF THE ASSOCIATION OF TEACHERS OF JAPANESE. 1963–
Department of Far Eastern Languages, (312) 753-2628
University of Chicago
Chicago, Illinois 60637

Editor: Eric W. Johnson   Circulation: 425
Sponsor: The Association of Teachers of   Frequency: 3/year
         Japanese   Subscription: $9.00
Language: English

Professional in nature, the journal includes articles on the teaching of Japanese, as well as on literature and linguistics.

442. PACIFIC CITIZEN. 1930–
125 Weller Street (213) 626-6936
Los Angeles, California 90012

Editor: Harry K. Honda   Circulation: 22,250
Sponsor: Japanese American Citizens League   Frequency: weekly
Language: English   Subscription: $7.00

This official publication of the Japanese American Citizens League, a public relations medium, reports the achievements, contributions, problems, and issues affecting persons of Japanese ancestry.

JEWISH PRESS
Jewish Publications in Hebrew and Hebrew-English

443. HADOAR HEBREW WEEKLY. The Mail. 1921–
120 West 16th Street (212) 879-2232
New York, New York 10011

Editor: David Epstein   Circulation: 5,100
Sponsor: Histadruth Ivrith of America   Frequency: weekly
Language: Hebrew   Subscription: $20.00

"From its earliest beginning the *Hadoar* encouraged the creative work of Hebrew writers, poets, scholars, and thinkers in this country to create in Hebrew" (editor's statement). Includes articles, news, and book reviews of interest to Jews.

444. HAPARDES. Orchard. 1926–
4809 14th Avenue
Brooklyn, New York 11219

Editor: Rabbi S. Elberg   Circulation: 1,950
Sponsor: n.i.   Frequency: monthly
Language: Hebrew   Subscription: n.i.

This is a religious monthly.

445. IGERET. Newsletter. 1960–
515 Park Avenue (212) 752-2986
New York, New York 10022

Editor: Yariv Ben-Eliezer   Circulation: 6,000
Sponsor: Israeli Students Organization in the   Frequency: bi-monthly
         United States   Subscription: free
Language: Hebrew

Covers topics of interest to Israeli students in the United States and Canada.

446. JEWISH HERITAGE.   1957–
1640 Rhode Island Avenue, N. W.   (203) 393-5284
Washington, D. C. 20036

Editor: Lily Edelman   Circulation: 8,100
Sponsor: B'nai B'rith Commission on Adult   Frequency: quarterly
        Jewish Education   Subscription: $3.00
Language: Hebrew and English

This family-oriented magazine is devoted to all aspects of Jewish life. Also published in Spanish, Portuguese, and English.

447. LAMATCHIL.   Easy Hebrew Paper.   1960–
515 Park Avenue   (212) 371-7750
New York, New York 10022

Editor: Rachel Enver   Circulation: 4,500
Sponsor: Jewish Agency for Israel–American   Frequency: weekly
        Section   Subscription: $5.00
Language: Hebrew

Middle-Eastern and world news in Hebrew (made simpler by the inclusion of vowel markings).

448. PIONEER WOMAN.   1926–
315 Fifth Avenue   (212) 725-8010
New York, New York 10016

Editor: Ruth Levine   Circulation: 30,000
Sponsor: Pioneer Women, the Women's Labor   Frequency: monthly
        Zionist Organization of America,   Subscription: $2.00
        Inc.
Language: Hebrew, Yiddish, and English

449. TALPIOTH.   1943–
Amsterdam Avenue and 186th Street
New York, New York 10033

Editor: Editorial Board   Circulation: 850
Sponsor: Yeshiva University   Frequency: irregular
Language: Hebrew   Subscription: $6.50/copy

This publication is dedicated to Hebrew philosophy, law, and ethics.

Jewish Publications in Yiddish and Yiddish-English

450. BIALYSTOKER STIMME.   Voice of Bialystok.
228 East Broadway
New York, New York 10002

Editor: Rabbi Azriel Weissman   Circulation: 4,000
Sponsor: Bialystoker Center and Home for   Frequency: semi-annually
        the Aged   Subscription: free
Language: Yiddish and English

This house organ, designed for aged Jewish people, includes news concerning the Bialystoker Center activities.

451. B'NAI YIDDISH.   B'nai Yiddish Magazine.   1968–
22 East 17th Street
New York, New York 10003

Editor: Itzik Koslovsky   Circulation: 1,500
Sponsor: B'nai Yiddish Society   Frequency: bi-monthly
Language: Yiddish and English   Subscription: $3.50

B'NAI YIDDISH (cont'd)

Contains articles on Jewish culture and Jewish history, plus an analysis of the news. "The main objective is to check assimilation, to perpetuate the Yiddish language and Yiddish culture as a barrier to keep assimilation and assimilationist leadership out of the Jewish community" (editor's statement).

452. FARBAND NEWS.　　　　　　　　　　　　　　　　　　　1912–

575 Sixth Avenue　　　　　　　　　(212) 989-0300
New York, New York 10011

Editor: Jacob Katzman　　　　　　　Circulation: 25,000
Sponsor: Farband-Labor Zionist Order　　Frequency: irregular
Language: Yiddish and English　　　　Subscription: n.i.

453. FREIE ARBEITER STIMME. Free Voice of Labor.　　　1890–

33 Union Square West, Room 808　　(212) 929-3799
New York, New York 10003

Editor: P. Constan　　　　　　　　Circulation: 1,700
Sponsor: Free Voice of Labor Association　Frequency: monthly
Language: Yiddish　　　　　　　　Subscription: $7.00

"Propagation of libertarian socialist ideas. Exposure of anarchist philosophy in American traditional political and social thinking, as well as in its history. Critical comments from the anarchist point of view on current events. Support of organized labor in its economic struggles. Reviews of books on economics and finance. Support of Yiddish language, Yiddish theater, poetry, art, literature. Helping to keep alive the memory of six million Jews, murdered in the Holocaust" (editor's statement). Anti-communist orientation.

454. FREIHEIT. Freedom.　　　　　　　　　　　　　　1922–

35 East 12th Street
New York, New York 10003

Editor: P. Novick　　　　　　　　Circulation: 6,091
Sponsor: Morgen Freiheit Publishing Company　Frequency: daily
Language: Yiddish　　　　　　　　Subscription: $23.00

455. KINDER JOURNAL. Children Magazine.　　　　　　1919–

22 East 17th Street　　　　　　　(212) 257-7140
New York, New York 10003

Editor: Saul Goodman　　　　　　Circulation: 1,200
Sponsor: Sholem Aleichem Folk Institute　Frequency: bi-monthly
Language: Yiddish　　　　　　　　Subscription: $2.00

The main objective of this publication is "to acquaint children with Jewish culture—particularly Yiddish literature, poetry, and folklore" (editor's statement).

456. MIZRACHI WOMAN.　　　　　　　　　　　　　　1935–

250 Park Avenue South　　　　　　(212) 477-4720
New York, New York 10003

Editor: Gabriel Levenson　　　　　Circulation: 26,000
Sponsor: Mizrachi Women's Organization　Frequency: monthly
Language: Yiddish and English　　　Subscription: free to members

Provides general information on Jewish life in the world, especially in the United States and Isarel, with special emphasis on education and social topics. Promotes Zionism.

457. MORGEN FREIHEIT. Morning Freedom. 1922–
    35 East 12th Street
    New York, New York 10003

    Editor: Paul Novick   Circulation: 7,000
    Sponsor: n.i.   Frequency: daily
    Language: Yiddish   Subscription: $25.00

Provides general international, national, and local news.

**458. SHMUESSEN MIT KINDER UN YUGNT. Talks with Children and
Youths.** 1942–
    770 Eastern Parkway
    Brooklyn, New York 11213

    Editor: Nissan Mindel   Circulation: 4,500
    Sponsor: Merkos L'Inyonei Chinuch, Inc.   Frequency: monthly
    Language: Yiddish   Subscription: $1.50

Published simultaneously in separate English and Yiddish pamphlets. General articles on
Jewish life and history, with a column devoted to "do's" and "don'ts" for upcoming
Jewish holidays.

459. UNSER TSAIT. Our Time. 1941–
    25 East 78th Street   (212) 535-0850
    New York, New York 10021

    Editor: Emanuel Scherer   Circulation: 5,500
    Sponsor: International Jewish Labor Bund   Frequency: monthly
    Language: Yiddish   Subscription: n.i.

"Covers topics of general and Jewish political, social, and cultural character, reflecting Bund's
ideals of democratic internationalistic socialism. Is against both assimilation and Zionism, but
for maintaining national Jewish identity" (editor's statement). Critical attitude toward the
state of Israel.

460. YEDIES FUN YIVO. News of the YIVO. 1925–
    1048 Fifth Avenue   (212) 535-6700
    New York, New York 10028

    Editor: Shmuel Lapin   Circulation: 5,000
    Sponsor: YIVO Institute for Jewish Research   Frequency: quarterly
    Language: Yiddish and English   Subscription: membership dues

461. DER YID. The Jew. 1951–
    134 Broadway
    Brooklyn, New York 11211

    Editor: Sender Deutsch   Circulation: 7,250
    Sponsor: Der Yid Publishing Association   Frequency: semi-monthly
    Language: Yiddish   Subscription: $5.00

General and local news of interest to the Jewish community in the greater New York area.
Includes book reviews and illustrations.

462. DI YIDDISHE HEIM. The Jewish Home. 1959–
    770 Eastern Parkway
    Brooklyn, New York 11213

    Editors: Tema Gurary (Yiddish) and Rachel   Circulation: 5,000
            Altein (English)   Frequency: quarterly
    Sponsor: Lubavitch Women's Organization   Subscription: $2.00
    Language: Yiddish and English

General articles on Judaism, essentially from the Hassidic viewpoint. Specifically geared to
the interests of the Jewish woman.

463. YIDDISHE KULTUR.   **Yiddish Culture.**   1938–
80 Fifth Avenue   (212) 477-9084
New York, New York 10011

Editor: I. Goldberg   Circulation: 3,900
Sponsor: Yiddisher Kultur Farband, Inc.   Frequency: monthly
Language: Yiddish   Subscription: $10.00

Middle-Eastern, American, and world news, with analyses and a few general articles on Jewish personalities, literature, and culture.

464. DOS YIDDISHE VORT.   **The Yiddish Word.**
5 Beekman Street
New York, New York 10038

Editor: Joseph Friedenson   Circulation: 11,000
Sponsor: Agudath Israel of America   Frequency: monthly
Language: Yiddish   Subscription: $7.00

Features articles on Jewish culture and life in general, with the aim of presenting "the Orthodox Jewish viewpoint on current issure of Jewish interest in the United States" (editor's statement).

465. YIDDISHER KEMFER.   **The Jewish Combatant.**   1906–
575 Sixth Avenue   (212) 741-2404
New York, New York 10011

Editor: Mordecai Shtrigler   Circulation: 3,500
Sponsor: Labor Zionist Letters, Inc.   Frequency: weekly
Language: Yiddish   Subscription: $15.00

Articles on labor, Zionism, Jewish affairs, the Middle East, world news, and literature.

466. DER YIDDISHER KWAL.   **Jewish Well.**   1967–
82 Lee Avenue   (212) 963-9260
Brooklyn, New York 11211

Editor: Sender Deutsch   Circulation: 7,500
Sponsor: United Talmudical Company   Frequency: weekly
Language: Yiddish   Subscription: $10.00

Features educational and religious articles and Chassidic tales.

467. YIDISHE SHPRAKH.   **Jewish Language.**   1941–
1048 Fifth Avenue   (212) 535-6700
New York, New York 10028

Editor: Mordkhe Schaechter   Circulation: 3,500
Sponsor: YIVO Institute for Jewish Research   Frequency: 3 times/year
Language: Yiddish   Subscription: membership dues

468. YIVO BLETER.   1931–
1048 Fifth Avenue   (212) 535-6700
New York, New York 10028

Editor: Shlomo Noble   Circulation: 3,000
Sponsor: YIVO Institute for Jewish Research   Frequency: irregular
Language: Yiddish   Subscription: membership dues

"Provides a forum for the researcher in Jewish social sciences and humanities" (editor's statement). Emphasis is on the Eastern European Jewish experience, as well as on problems of acculturation, bilingualism, etc.

469. YUGNTRUF.   Call of Youth.   1964–
    3328 Bainbridge Avenue
    Bronx, New York 10467

Editor: Shimke Levine   Circulation: 2,500
Sponsor: YUGNTRUF–Youth for Yiddish, Inc.   Frequency: quarterly
Language: Yiddish   Subscription: $4.00

Most articles deal with Jewish history and culture, as well as with contemporary Jewish issues. Regular columns include "The Young Jokester," "In the Movement," "For the Beginner." The objective is to stimulate Yiddish creativity among the younger generation.

470. ZAMLUNGEN.   Gatherings.   1954–
    35 East 12th Street
    New York, New York 10003

Editor: Ber Green   Circulation: 1,100
Sponsor: Yiddish Writers Organization at the   Frequency: quarterly
       YKUF   Subscription: $4.00
Language: Yiddish

Dedicated to Yiddish literature and Jewish culture.

471. ZEIN.   To Be.   1954–
    144 West 73rd Street
    New York, New York 10023

Editor: L. Rosof   Circulation: 1,400
Sponsor: n.i.   Frequency: quarterly
Language: Yiddish   Subscription: $5.00

Includes general articles, stories, and poetry.

472. THE ZUKUNFT.   The Future.   1892–
    25 East 78th Street   (212) 879-2232
    New York, New York 10021
    Editors: Morris Crysta, Hyman Bass, and   Circulation: 4,000
       Eliezer Greenberg   Frequency: monthly
    Sponsor: Congress for Jewish Culture   Subscription: $7.00
    Language: Yiddish
Covers all aspects of Jewish cultural and social life in the United States as well as in the world.

Jewish Publications in German

473. AUFBAU.   Reconstruction.   1934–
    2121 Broadway
    New York, New York 10023

Editor: Hans Steinitz   Circulation: 31,000
Sponsor: New World Club, Inc.   Frequency: weekly
Language: German   Subscription: $12.50

This newspaper was first created to represent the interests and viewpoints of German, mostly Jewish, refugees from Hitler's Germany. Editorially it represents several major themes: the cultural German background, Jewish faith and traditions, and a loyalty to the United States. Contents include special correspondents, reports on life in Germany and Israel, coverage of cultural life, literature, theater, music, etc. Special sections and supplements are devoted to such topics as life on the West Coast, the German restitution issue, book reviews, vacation and travel, etc.

Jewish Publications in English

474. THE ALBANY JEWISH WORLD. 1965–
416 Smith Street (518) 370-5483
Schenectady, New York 72305

Editor: Sam S. Clevenson Circulation: 8,800
Sponsor: Sam S. Clevenson Frequency: weekly
Language: English Subscription: $7.00

This community-oriented weekly provides coverage of Jewish civic, organizational, and synagogue activities in the Albany, Troy, Poughkeepsie, and Schenectady areas. It also includes articles on Judaism and Jewish events around the world.

475. AMERICAN ISRAELITE. 1854–
906 Main Street (513) 621-3145
Cincinnati, Ohio 45202

Editor: Henry C. Segal Circulation: 8,381
Sponsor: n.i. Frequency: weekly
Language: English Subscription: $6.00

A community-oriented publication, it provides coverage of Jewish organizations and religious institutions in the Cincinnati area, as well as news coverage of events in Israel and national and international issues of special interest to Jews. Believed to be the oldest American-Jewish newspaper in the country.

476. AMERICAN JEWISH HISTORICAL QUARTERLY. 1893–
2 Thornton Road (617) 891-8110
Waltham, Massachusetts 02154

Editor: Nathan M. Kaganoff Circulation: 3,150
Sponsor: American Jewish Historical Society Frequency: quarterly
Language: English Subscription: $15.00

Contains research articles devoted to the broad analysis of American Jewish history (European background, immigration, assimilation, and adjustments in the United States, and impact of the Jewish community on the United States and abroad). Also features book reviews, bibliography notes and documents, and historical news.

477. AMERICAN-JEWISH LIFE. 1958–
701 South Broad Street (609) 883-0031
Trenton, New Jersey 08618

Editor: Kent H. Jacobs Circulation: 18,000
Sponsor: n.i. Frequency: monthly
Language: English Subscription: $3.00

Emphasis is on Israel and the Middle East, with coverage also of national, local, and group affairs of importance to the Jewish people. Includes items on the activities of community leaders, plus commentaries and opinions.

478. AMERICAN JEWISH TIMES–OUTLOOK. 1933–
P. O. Box 10674 (704) 376-3405
Charlotte, North Carolina 28234

Editor: Janet Hough Scarboro Circulation: 5,000
Sponsor: American Jewish Times–Outlook Frequency: monthly
Language: English Subscription: $5.00

The purpose of this regional publication is "to keep alive Jewish consciousness and provide a forum for American Jewish thought and opinions. It seeks to encourage a dialogue between the various components of the Jewish community over significant contemporary challenges. The magazine is devoted to the intellectual and spiritual growth of the individual while promoting better religious relations between the area communities" (editor's statement). Illustrated.

479. AMERICAN POST.   1954–
    349 East 36th Street
    Paterson, New Jersey 07504

Editor: Reuben Kaufman   Circulation: 1,381
Sponsor: American Post, Inc.   Frequency: weekly
Language: English   Subscription: $5.00

Covers local, national, and international news with emphasis on Israel and Jewish communities. It includes editorial comments on Jewish problems, congregational announcements, social news, Biblical quotations and interpretations, announcements from various Jewish organizations, book reviews, youth features, entertainment, etc.

480. THE AMERICAN SEPHARDI.   1964–
    500 West 185th Street   (212) 568-8400
    New York, New York 10033

Editor: Herman P. Salomon   Circulation: 5,000
Sponsor: Sephardic Studies Program, Yeshiva   Frequency: annual
          University   Subscription: $5.00
Language: English

Features popular articles on Sephardic history for the general reader.

481. AMERICAN ZIONIST.   1910–
    145 East 32nd Street   (212) 683-9200
    New York, New York 10016

Editor: Elias Cooper   Circulation: 50,000
Sponsor: Zionist Organization of America   Frequency: monthly
Language: English   Subscription: $4.00

Articles on Jewish, Israeli, and Zionist issues, with emphasis on the Zionist movement. Special features include editorial commentary, book reviews, and the American Zionist Forum.

482. ARIZONA POST.   1943–
    102 North Plumer   (602) 792-3641
    Tucson, Arizona 85719

Editor: Mrs. Samuel Rothman   Circulation: 3,000
Sponsor: Tucson Jewish Community Council   Frequency: bi-weekly
Language: English   Subscription: $4.00

This publication is community oriented, although local and national news of special interest to Jews is also included. Provides coverage of activities by Jewish organizations and communities in Arizona, with special features for youth.

483. BALTIMORE JEWISH TIMES.   1918–
    2104 North Charles Street   (301) 752-3504
    Baltimore, Maryland 21218

Editor: Gary Rosenblatt   Circulation: 18,150
Sponsor: Susan Alter Patchen and Charles   Frequency: weekly
        Alter Buerger (Co-publishers)   Subscription: $6.50; $8.50
Language: English   out of state

Provides "coverage and analysis of international, national and local news of special interest to the Jewish population. Emphasis on Israel and Judaism. Includes sections devoted to the media, entertainment, youth, travel, sports and food" (editor's statement).

484. B'NAI B'RITH MESSENGER.   1897–
    2510 West 7th Street
    Los Angeles, California 90057

Editor: Joseph J. Cummins   Circulation: 49,994
Sponsor: n.i.   Frequency: weekly
Language: English   Subscription: $6.00

Coverage of international, national, and local news of special interest to the Jewish population in Southern California. Includes sections on book reviews, business, future social events, and items of interest to women.

485. BROTHERHOOD.   1967–
    838 Fifth Avenue   (212) 249-0100
    New York, New York 10021

Editor: Sylvan Lebow   Circulation: 70,000
Sponsor: National Federation of Temple   Frequency: quarterly
           Brotherhoods   Subscription: $1.00
Language: English

A magazine of general interest to the members of Reform temple families. Emphasizing religious and educational topics, it includes articles, book reviews, and a youth section. Illustrated.

486. BUFFALO JEWISH REVIEW.   1918–
    110 Pearl Street   (716) 854-2192
    Buffalo, New York 14202

Editor: Elias R. Jacobs   Circulation: 13,000
Sponsor: n.i.   Frequency: weekly
Language: English   Subscription: $5.00

Provides coverage of various activities within Jewish communities in the Buffalo area, but also includes national and international news. Sections cover editorials, youth items, book reviews, and coming events.

487. CALIFORNIA JEWISH RECORD.   1943–
    P. O. Box 983   (415) 776-5350
    San Francisco, California 94101

Editor: David Reznek   Circulation: 10,000
Sponsor: Orot, Inc.   Frequency: n.i.
Language: English   Subscription: $4.00

Provides coverage of Jewish communities in northern and central California, but also includes national and international news of interest to the Jewish people. There are sections devoted to youth features, music, entertainment, and book reviews.

488. COMMENTARY.   1945–
    165 East 56th Street   (212) 751-4000
    New York, New York 10022

Editor: Norman Podhoretz   Circulation: 60,500
Sponsor: American Jewish Committee   Frequency: monthly
Language: English   Subscription: $10.00

Contains analytical articles on political and social issues for the purpose of clarification and understanding. Also includes book reviews and letters to the editor.

489. CONGRESS MONTHLY.   1934–
    15 East 84th Street   (212) 879-4500
    New York, New York 10028

Editor: Herbert Poster   Circulation: 42,091
Sponsor: American Jewish Congress   Frequency: monthly
Language: English   Subscription: $5.00

CONGRESS MONTHLY (cont'd)
This is a magazine of "liberal opinion concerned with human rights, Jewish life at home and abroad and books, art and music dealing with Jewish themes or by Jewish artists. We publish topical articles, factual or opinion, on issues of interest to liberal Jewish readers—international relations, civil rights, civil liberties, Middle East, Israel, Jewish education, culture, communal affairs, politics, life abroad and personal essays" (editor's statement).

490. CONNECTICUT JEWISH LEDGER.   1929–
P. O. Box 1107   (203) 249-8428
Hartford, Connecticut 06101

Editor: Rabbi A. J. Feldman   Circulation: 22,895
Sponsor: n.i.   Frequency: weekly
Language: English   Subscription: $5.00

News coverage of international, national, and local events of special interest to the Jewish population, including news of financial matters and announcements of forthcoming events.

491. CONSERVATIVE JUDAISM.   1945–
3080 Broadway   (212) 749-8000
New York, New York 10027

Editor: Stephen C. Lerner   Circulation: 3,000
Sponsor: The Rabbinical Assembly and the   Frequency: quarterly
        Jewish Theological Seminary   Subscription: $5.00
        of America
Language: English

"Study of Judaica in terms of its theology, philosophy and education. Examination of the philosophical stance of Conservative Judaism in the United States. Also includes articles on the problems of the Jewish community in the United States and abroad, Israel and politics of the Middle East. Reviews of books with Jewish content" (editor's statement).

492. DAVKA.   The Convert.   1970–
900 Hilgard Avenue   (213) 474-7717
Los Angeles, California 90024

Editor: Aron Hirt-Manheimer   Circulation: 5,000
Sponsor: Hillel Council at UCLA   Frequency: quarterly
Language: English   Subscription: $3.50

Features religious, historical, and cultural articles, with the objective of raising "Jewish consciousness in North America and abroad by raising issues of Jewish concern" (editor's statement). Illustrated.

493. DAYTON JEWISH CHRONICLE.   1965–
118 Salem Avenue   (513) 222-0783
Dayton, Ohio 45406

Editor: Anne M. Hammerman   Circulation: 1,450
Sponsor: Dayton Jewish Chronicle, Inc.   Frequency: weekly
Language: English   Subscription: $4.50

National and international news of special interest to the Jewish reader, plus coverage of local Jewish social and other events.

494. THE DETROIT JEWISH NEWS.   1942–
17515 West Nine Mile Road, Suite 865   (313) 424-8833
Southfield, Michigan 48075

Editor: Philip Slomovitz   Circulation: 17,900
Sponsor: The Jewish News Publishing Co.   Frequency: weekly
Language: English   Subscription: $10.00

THE DETROIT JEWISH NEWS (cont'd)
Emphasizes coverage of Jewish communities in Michigan and Windsor, Ontario but also includes international and national news of special interest to the Jewish people. Sections are devoted to special features such as commentaries on important issues, business news, social affairs, club and organizational news, coming events, and book reviews.

495. DIMENSIONS IN AMERICAN JUDAISM. 1966–
838 Fifth Avenue (212) 249-0100
New York, New York 10021

Editor: Myrna Pollak Circulation: 10,000
Sponsor: Union of American Hebrew Frequency: quarterly
       Congregations Subscription: $3.00
Language: English

This religious publication also includes articles dealing with various social, philosophical, and political issues. Features sections on the arts and book reviews.

496. HADASSAH MAGAZINE. 1925–
65 East 52nd Street (212) 255-7900
New York, New York 10022

Editor: Miriam K. Freund Circulation: 350,000
Sponsor: Hadassah, Women's Zionist Frequency: monthly
       Organization of America Subscription: n.i.
Language: English

Articles on various social issues in the Middle East, with emphasis on cultural, educational, and philanthropic activities of Jewish groups both in the United States and in Israel. Includes book reviews.

497. HEBREW WATCHMAN. 1925–
277 Jefferson Avenue
Memphis, Tennessee 38103

Editor: Herman I. Goldberger Circulation: 2,196
Sponsor: n.i. Frequency: weekly
Language: English Subscription: $6.00

Coverage of international, national, and local news of special interest to the Jewish community in Tennessee.

498. HEIGHTS SUN PRESS.
2156 Lee Road
Cleveland Heights, Ohio 44118

Editor: Harry Volk Circulation: 44,000
Sponsor: Comcorp Newspapers Frequency: weekly
Language: English Subscription: $5.00

Community-oriented newspaper covering social, organizational, and club news of the Jewish people in Cleveland. Also features book reviews, letters to the editor, and entertainment.

499. HERITAGE-SOUTHWEST JEWISH PRESS. 1954–
2130 South Vermont Avenue (213) 939-1133
Los Angeles, California 90007

Editor: Herb Brin Circulation: 10,800
Sponsor: Heritage Publishing Company Frequency: weekly
Language: English Subscription: $7.50

Heritage-Southwest Jewish Press (Los Angeles) is one of four papers published by the Heritage Publishing Company. In addition to this newspaper, the Heritage Publishing Company also publishes *Southwest Jewish Press-Heritage*, which originally began in 1914

HERITAGE-SOUTHWEST JEWISH PRESS (cont'd)
as the *Southwest Jewish Press* but which was taken over by Heritage in 1958 (San Diego, weekly, circulation 4,600); *Orange County Jewish Heritage* (Orange County, monthly, circulation 2,300); and *Central Valley Jewish Heritage* (Fresno, monthly, circulation 1,500). All four publications are edited by Herb Brin. Coverage includes national and international news of special interest to the Jewish community. There is heavy emphasis on Jewish local events, organizations, and individual personalities. Book reviews are also featured.

500. HILLCREST SUN MESSENGER.
2156 Lee Road   (216) 932-3300
Cleveland Heights, Ohio 44118

Editor: Harry Volk   Circulation: 23,000
Sponsor: Comcorp Newspapers   Frequency: weekly
Language: English   Subscription: $5.00

Community-oriented publication with extensive coverage of organizations, temple events, social activities, and clubs in the Cleveland area.

501. HISTADRUT FOTO NEWS.   Federation Foto News.   1948–
33 East 67th Street   (212) 628-1000
New York, New York 10021

Editor: Nahum Guttman   Circulation: 24,000
Sponsor: National Committee for Labor Israel   Frequency: 7 months/year
Language: English   Subscription: $2.50

Publishes information on the various activities and programs of the Committee related to the works of Histadrut, the Israeli labor organization. "Seeks to promote financial aid for the health and social welfare programs of Histadrut in Israel" (editor's statement).

502. INTERMOUNTAIN JEWISH NEWS.   1913–
1275 Sherman Street, Suite 215-217   (303) 825-3271
Denver, Colorado 80203

Editor: Mrs. Max Goldberg   Circulation: 7,000
Sponsor: n.i.   Frequency: weekly
Language: English   Subscription: $15.00

Intensive Rocky Mountain coverage, emphasizing local, national, international, and Israel news. Features include human interest stories and news on cultural, business, and amusement topics. Includes book review section.

503. ISRAEL DIGEST.   1950–
515 Park Avenue   (212) 775-7400
New York, New York 10022

Editor: Dan Leon   Circulation: 8,000
Sponsor: Jewish Agency for Israel–American   Frequency: semi-monthly
       Section   Subscription: $3.00
Language: English

Presents items on various activities and events in Israel, with the aim of keeping the American Jewish population informed on Israeli affairs.

504. ISRAEL INVESTOR'S REPORT.   1961–
c/o Israel Communications Inc.   (212) 421-5547
110 East 59th Street
New York, New York 10022

Editor: Aryeh Greenfield   Circulation: 10,100
Sponsor: A. G. Publications Ltd.   Frequency: monthly
Language: English   Subscription: $20.00

ISRAEL INVESTOR'S REPORT (cont'd)
Although this paper is published in Israel, its audience is the Jewish population primarily in the
United States, and to some extent in Canada. It includes reports and articles on all aspects of
Israeli economy (economic trends, industrial achievements, financial activities, investments, new
projects, etc.) of special interest to American and Canadian Jews holding various investments in
Israel.

505. ISRAEL MAGAZINE. 1968–
110 East 59th Street
New York, New York 10022

Editor: Nahum Sirotsky Circulation: 56,000
Sponsor: Israel Publishing Company Frequency: monthly
Language: English Subscription: $15.00

This illustrated magazine presents an overview of life in Israel. Each issue usually spotlights a
given theme, and regular features include tourism, book reviews, art, and literature.

506. JWB CIRCLE. 1947–
15 East 26th Street (212) 898-0850
New York, New York 10010

Editor: Lionel Koppman Circulation: 14,000
Sponsor: JWB, The Association of Jewish Frequency: monthly
    Community Centers Subscription: $3.00
Language: English

Features articles on Jewish community centers and their services. Its aim is to enrich Jewish and
American cultures.

507. JEWISH ADVOCATE. 1902–
251 Causeway Street (617) 227-5130
Boston, Massachusetts 02114

Editor: Joseph G. Weisberg Circulation: 24,300
Sponsor: Jewish Advocate Publishing Frequency: weekly
    Corporation Subscription: $7.50
Language: English

This newspaper is "dedicated to Americanism, Judaism, and social justice" (editor's statement).
It publishes comprehensive local, national, international, and Israeli news of special interest
to the Jewish people. Features heavy coverage of the Jewish community in Boston, book
reviews, political commentary, financial news, entertainment, and society news.

508. JEWISH BOOKLAND. 1945–
15 East 26th Street (212) 532-4949
New York, New York 10010

Editor: A. Alan Steinbach Circulation: 19,000
Sponsor: Jewish Book Council of National Frequency: 7 times/year
    Welfare Board Subscription: $3.00
Language: English

Devoted entirely to book reviews, this periodical's aim is "to evaluate books of Jewish interest
and to stimulate their sale and reading" (editor's statement).

509. JEWISH CHRONICLE. 1962–
315 Bellefield Avenue (412) 687-1000
Pittsburgh, Pennsylvania 15213

Editor: Albert W. Bloom Circulation: 15,000
Sponsor: Pittsburgh Jewish Publication and Frequency: weekly
    Education Foundation Subscription: $8.00
Language: English

JEWISH CHRONICLE (cont'd)

National, international, and Jewish community news, with an emphasis on the Middle East, Israel, and Jewish activities and affairs in the United States.

510. JEWISH CIVIC LEADER.   1923—
11 Norwich Street   (617) 791-0953
Worcester, Massachusetts 01608

Editor: Conrad H. Isenberg   Circulation: 16,302
Sponsor: Worcester Leader Publishing Company   Frequency: weekly
Language: English   Subscription: $5.00

The main purpose of this publication is "to disseminate news of Jewish content on the local, national, and international scene" (editor's statement). It also includes news on current Jewish organizational and religious activities, and special announcements, such as births, engagements, marraiges, and social events. Occasionally editorials and book reviews are featured.

511. THE JEWISH CIVIC PRESS.   1965—
5529 Magazine, P. O. Box 15500   (504) 895-8784
New Orleans, Louisiana 70175

Editor: Alan M. Wexler   Circulation: 2,550
Sponsor: Alan M. Wexler   Frequency: monthly
Language: English   Subscription: $3.00

This community-oriented newspaper emphasizes the various activities within the Jewish community of New Orleans, but it is also the major source of international and national news pertinent to the Jewish community. Includes international news and features that do not appear in the local press as well as editorials and opinions.

512. JEWISH COMMUNITY REPORTER.   1949—
999 Lower Ferry Road
Trenton, New Jersey 06818

Editor: Arnold Ropeik   Circulation: 2,900
Sponsor: Jewish Federation of Trenton   Frequency: monthly
Language: English   Subscription: free

A community-oriented publication with coverage of local and international news.

513. JEWISH CURRENTS.   1946—
22 East 17th Street, Suite 601   (212) 924-5740
New York, New York 10003

Editor: Morris U. Schappes   Circulation: 4,445
Sponsor: Jewish Currents, Inc.   Frequency: monthly
Language: English   Subscription: $7.50

Provides coverage of various current issues such as Israeli affairs, the black movement, Black-Jewish relations, Jewish culture, Jews in Eastern Europe, and American Jewish organizational life. The publication is "pro Israel but non-Zionist" (editor's statement).

514. JEWISH DIGEST.   1955—
1363 Fairfield Avenue   (203) 384-2284
Bridgeport, Connecticut 06605

Editor: Bernard Postal   Circulation: 14,800
Sponsor: Jewish Digest Association   Frequency: monthly
Language: English   Subscription: $10.00

Presents condensations of materials from newspapers, magazines, books, reports, documents, etc., on every phase of Jewish life, history, and problems of the past and present.

515. JEWISH EXPONENT. 1887–
1513 Walnut Street (215) 459-4100
Philadelphia, Pennsylvania 19102

Editor: Frank F. Wundohl Circulation: 69,000
Sponsor: The Federation of Jewish Agencies of Frequency: weekly
          Greater Philadelphia Subscription: $7.50
Language: English

Provides coverage of news and opinions pertaining to or of interest to the Jewish community, including local, national, and international news, with heavy emphasis on organizational activity and Israel. Also featured are book reviews, a food column, sports, and financial news.

516. THE JEWISH FLORIDIAN. 1928–
P. O. Box 01-2973 (305) 373-4605
Miami, Florida 33101

Editor: Fred K. Shochet Circulation: 22,000
Sponsor: Fred K. Shochet Frequency: weekly
Language: English Subscription: $10.00

National and international news, with emphasis on Israel and the various activities of the Jewish community in the greater Miami area.

517. THE JEWISH FRONTIER. 1934–
515 Sixth Avenue (212) 989-0300
New York, New York 10011

Editor: Judah J. Shapiro Circulation: 6,350
Sponsor: Labor Zionist Letters Frequency: monthly
Language: English Subscription: $6.00

This is the official organ of the Labor Zionist Movement in the United States. It is concerned primarily with commentary, with the purpose of "interpreting Zionism and Israel from the viewpoint of Labor Zionist ideology" (editor's statement). It presents articles on American social, political, and economic developments; the situation of world Jewry; and the Middle East. Its periodic supplement, "Israel Seen From Within," gives information about Israel's current problems; it is prepared by Israelis. The publication features letters to the editor and book reviews.

518. JEWISH HERITAGE. 1957–
1640 Rhode Island Avenue, N. W.
Washington, D. C. 20036

Editor: Lily Edelman Circulation: 10,000
Sponsor: B'nai B'rith Frequency: quarterly
Language: English Subscription: $3.00

This quarterly publication offers articles on all aspects of Jewish life, past and present.

519. JEWISH HOMEMAKER. 1968–
105 Hudson Street (212) 851-6428
New York, New York 10013

Editor: Rabbi Bernard Levy Circulation: 40,000
Sponsor: O. K. Laboratories Frequency: bi-monthly
Language: English Subscription: $2.50

This home-oriented magazine is aimed at the Jewish housewife. Contains articles pertaining to the observance of traditional Judaism in the home, in education, in child psychology and child raising, in recipes, in decorating, and in book reviews.

520. JEWISH HORIZON.   1937–
    200 Park Avenue South   (212) 673-8100
    New York, New York 10003

    Editor: Rabbi William Herskowitz   Circulation: 10,000
    Sponsor: Religious Zionists of America   Frequency: quarterly
    Language: English   Subscription: $1.50

Contains articles, editorials, short stories, and poems relating to Zionism, Israel, and Judaica. Social and religious issues in the United States are also covered.

521. JEWISH LEDGER.   1926–
    721 Monroe Avenue   (617) 275-9090
    Rochester, New York 14607

    Editor: Donald Wolin   Circulation: 8,000
    Sponsor: n.i.   Frequency: weekly
    Language: English   Subscription: $4.00

National, international, and local news coverage. Emphasis is on the community activities of the Jewish population in the Rochester area. Features book reviews, by-lined columns on Israel, and business news.

522. THE JEWISH MONITOR.   1948–
    P. O. Box 9155, Crestline Station   (205) 879-0362
    Birmingham, Alabama 35213

    Editor: J. S. Gallinger   Circulation: 4,090
    Sponsor: Jewish Monitor   Frequency: monthly
    Language: English   Subscription: $3.00

Covers a broad scope of issues affecting Judaism both in the United States and abroad, along with news of Jewish activities in the Mississippi and Alabama region.

523. THE JEWISH NEWS.   1947–
    220 South Harrison Street   (201) 678-4955
    East Orange, New Jersey 07018

    Editor: Harry Weingast   Circulation: 26,800
    Sponsor: Jewish Community Federation of   Frequency: weekly
             Metropolitan New Jersey   Subscription: $5.00
    Language: English

"This newspaper seeks to be an informational and educational medium carrying news and feature material about Jewish events and activities at home and overseas" (editor's statement). Features news on Israel, Jews in the United States, and the metropolitan New Jersey area.

524. THE JEWISH OBSERVER.   1963–
    5 Beekman Street   (212) 964-1620
    New York, New York 10038

    Editor: Rabbi Nisson Wolpin   Circulation: 13,000
    Sponsor: Agudath Israel of America   Frequency: monthly
    Language: English   Subscription: $6.50

Examines national and international events, and current issues and problems from an Orthodox Jewish perspective. "Also reviews historical events and key personalities in terms of modern-day implications" (editor's statement). Illustrated.

525. JEWISH POST AND OPINION.   1931–
    611 North Park Avenue   (317) 634-1307
    Indianapolis, Indiana 46204

    Editor: Gabriel Cohen   Circulation: 22,600
    Sponsor: National Jewish Post, Inc.   Frequency: weekly
    Language: English   Subscription: $10.00

JEWISH POST AND OPINION (cont'd)
This publication provides national and international news coverage of special interest to Jews.
It also features opinions, commentaries, and book reviews.

526. **JEWISH PRESS.** 1921–
333 South 132nd Street (402) 334-8200
Omaha, Nebraska 68154

Editor: Richard B. Pearl Circulation: 4,514
Sponsor: Jewish Federation of Omaha, Inc. Frequency: weekly
Language: English Subscription: $7.50

This weekly "serves as the informational link between its Nebraska and Iowa Jewish readers and
between them and the national and international Jewish communities by providing local, national
and world news of Jewish interest. Provides editorial columns on controversial issues, reader opinion forum and book reviews in addition to regular objective news coverage" (editor's statement).

527. **JEWISH RECORD.** 1939–
1537 Atlantic Avenue (609) 344-5119
Atlantic City, New Jersey 08401

Editor: Martin Korik Circulation: 3,337
Sponsor: n.i. Frequency: weekly
Language: English Subscription: $3.50

Local, national, and international news of significance to the Jewish communities of southern
New Jersey. The objective of the publication is to "sustain a Jewish awareness" (editor's
statement).

528. **JEWISH SOCIAL STUDIES.** 1939–
2929 Broadway (212) 663-2886
New York, New York 10025

Editor: Bertram E. Schwarzbach Circulation: 1,500
Sponsor: Conference on Jewish Social Frequency: quarterly
Studies, Inc. Subscription: $20.00
Language: English

Covers contemporary and historical aspects of Jewish life, publishing scholarly articles and
book reviews of Jewish issues in the various social science fields.

529. **JEWISH SPECTATOR.** 1935–
250 West 57th Street (212) 255-1937
New York, New York 10019

Editor: Trude Weiss-Rosmarin Circulation: 19,000
Sponsor: Jewish Spectator Frequency: monthly
Language: English Subscription: $6.00

This is a journal of "Jewish opinion on Jewish affairs and letters" (editor's statement). Israel
and the American Jewish community are principal subject areas. Also features short stories
and book reviews. Its objective is to "inform and bring the insights of the Jewish tradition to
bear upon and illuminate current problems and issues" (editor's statement).

530. **THE JEWISH STANDARD.** 1931–
40 Journal Square (201) 653-6330
Jersey City, New Jersey 07306

Editor: Morris J. Janoff Circulation: 12,555
Sponsor: Morris J. Janoff Frequency: weekly
Language: English Subscription: $6.00

THE JEWISH STANDARD (cont'd)
Presents national and international news coverage of special interest to the Jewish population, emphasizing Jewish community news in Jersey City. Features include book reviews, entertainment, youth news, and a food column.

531. JEWISH STAR.   1951–
    693 Mission Street, Suite 305   (415) 421-4874
    San Francisco, California 94105

Editor: Alfred Berger   Circulation: 2,000
Sponsor: n.i.   Frequency: bi-monthly
Language: English   Subscription: $3.00

National and international news, with an emphasis on Israel.

532. THE JEWISH TIMES.   1945–
    118 Cypress Street   (617) 566-7710
    Brookline, Massachusetts 02146

Editor: James Kahn   Circulation: 10,500
Sponsor: Jewish Times Publishing Company   Frequency: weekly
Language: English   Subscription: $3.00

This weekly publishes local, national, and international news of interest to the Jewish people, providing coverage of Jewish organizational activities on the local (Boston and New England) and national levels. It also includes youth features, book reviews, and business news.

533. JEWISH TRANSCRIPT.   1924–
    614 Securities Building   (206) 624-0136
    Seattle, Washington 98101

Editor: Colin Shellshear   Circulation: 5,500
Sponsor: Jewish Federation and Council of   Frequency: semi-monthly
        Seattle   Subscription: $3.00
Language: English

Features articles on topics of special interest to the Jewish people in the Seattle area, including reports from Israel, national news as it relates to Jews, and local news items of the Jewish community.

534. THE JEWISH VETERAN.   1896–
    1712 New Hampshire Avenue, N. W.   (202) 265-6280
    Washington, D. C. 20009

Editor: Albert Schlossberg   Circulation: 100,000
Sponsor: Jewish War Veterans of the United   Frequency: monthly
        States   Subscription: $2.00
Language: English

This organizational journal covers the various events, activities, and affairs of the Jewish War Veterans of the United States, on both the national and the local level.

535. THE JEWISH VOICE.   1940–
    701 Shipley Road   (302) 656-8555
    Wilmington, Delaware 19801

Editor: Morton Schlossman   Circulation: 3,125
Sponsor: The Jewish Federation of Delaware   Frequency: semi-monthly
Language: English   Subscription: $5.00

Provides general news on issues of special interest to the Jewish people in Delaware.

536. JEWISH WEEK AND AMERICAN EXAMINER. 1857–
3 East 40th Street
New York, New York 10016

Editor: Philip Hochstein
Sponsor: American Examiner, Inc.
Language: English

Circulation: 85,000
Frequency: weekly
Subscription: $10.00

This weekly publishes news, editorials, features, and articles about the Jewish world, both here and abroad. A column on the United Nations is also included.

537. JEWISH WEEKLY NEWS. 1945–
P. O. Box 1569 (413) 739-4771
Springfield, Massachusetts 01101

Editor: Leslie Bennett Kahn
Sponsor: Bennett-Scott Publishing Corp.
Language: English

Circulation: 8,459
Frequency: weekly
Subscription: $4.00

Provides in-depth coverage of international, national, and local news of special interest to the Jewish population, stressing Jewish events. Also includes book reviews.

538. JUDAISM. 1952–
15 East 84th Street (212) 751-4000
New York, New York 10028

Editor: Robert Gordis
Sponsor: American Jewish Congress
Language: English

Circulation: 2,800
Frequency: quarterly
Subscription: $8.00

The purpose of this publication is "to stimulate an informed awareness of Jewish affairs, encourage Jewish scholarship and adequate opportunities for Jewish education, and generally foster the affirmation of Jewish religious, cultural, and historic identity" (editor's statement). It features articles on the religious, moral, and philosophical concepts of Judaism and their relationship to modern society. Also includes book reviews.

539. KANSAS CITY JEWISH CHRONICLE. 1920–
P. O. Box 8709 (913) 648-4620
Kansas City, Missouri 64114

Editor: Milton Firestone
Sponsor: Kansas City Jewish Chronicle Company
Language: English

Circulation: 12,500
Frequency: weekly
Subscription: $8.00

This weekly, whose audience is the Jewish public of western Missouri and eastern Kansas, covers social, religious, cultural, national, international, and local news events.

540. KEEPING POSTED. 1955–
838 Fifth Avenue
New York, New York 10021

Editor: Edith Samuel
Sponsor: Union of American Hebrew
Congregations
Language: English

Circulation: 22,000
Frequency: monthly (October
to May)
Subscription: $3.50

This magazine is aimed at the Jewish youth attending grades 8 through 12 of Jewish religious schools, college youth and adults. It is used as reading, study, and discussion material in schools, educational camps, study circles, etc. Each issue deals with a specific Jewish theme, value, or concept. A Teacher's Edition of each issue provides eight additional pages of background, bibliography, ideas for class projects, discussions, and debates. Included in the Teacher's Edition is a "Parent's Guide to K. P."

541. LAS VEGAS ISRAELITE. 1964–
P. O. Box 14096 (702) 876-1255
Las Vegas, Nevada 14096

Editor: Jack Tell Circulation: 10,000
Sponsor: n.i. Frequency: weekly
Language: English Subscription: $7.00

This comprehensive, in-depth weekly reports news of interest to the Jewish community of Las Vegas and to Jewish tourists.

542. LILITH MAGAZINE. 1976–
500 East 63rd Street (212) 838-0467
New York, New York 10021

Editor: Susan Weidman Schneider Circulation: 1,000
Sponsor: Lilith Publications, Inc. Frequency: quarterly
Language: English Subscription: $5.00

The main objective of the magazine is "to provide a forum for the exploration of Jewish women's changing self-awareness" (editor's statement). In addition to articles, it includes brief book reviews, letters, and bibliographies.

543. LONG ISLAND JEWISH PRESS. 1945–
95-20 63rd Road (212) 886-7400
Rego Park, New York 11374

Editor: Rabbi Abraham Shoulson Circulation: 28,000
Sponsor: Zionist Region in Long Island Frequency: monthly
Language: English Subscription: $2.00

This community-oriented monthly publishes news on events within the Jewish local communities. It also reports on national and international news of special interest to the Jewish population. Book reviews are included.

544. MIDSTREAM–A MONTHLY JEWISH REVIEW. 1955–
515 Park Avenue (212) 752-0600, ext. 261
New York, New York 10023

Editor: Joel Carmichael Circulation: 10,000
Sponsor: Theodor Herzl Foundation Frequency: monthly
Language: English Subscription: $8.00

This Zionist publication covers topics of interest to the Jewish people and others, including by-lined articles that interpret issues such as social problems, ethnicity, the Middle East, and current important political events. Features book reviews.

545. NASSAU HERALD. 1924–
379 Central Avenue (516) 239-1240
Lawrence, New York 11559

Editor: Robert Richner Circulation: 11,000
Sponsor: Bi-County Publishers, Inc. Frequency: weekly
Language: English Subscription: $4.00

Heavy coverage of Jewish local community activities such as organizations, clubs, charity drives, schools, and local personalities. Features a women's column and book reviews.

546. THE NATIONAL JEWISH MONTHLY. 1885–
1640 Rhode Island Avenue, N. W. (202) 393-5284
Washington, D. C. 20036

Editor: Charles Fenyvesi Circulation: 195,819
Sponsor: The B'nai B'rith Frequency: monthly
Language: English Subscription: $5.00

THE NATIONAL JEWISH MONTHLY (cont'd)

The purpose of this monthly is to provide information on world affairs as they relate to the Jewish American family, to discuss the problems of our world society as they relate to the Jewish American family, to review the Jewish cultural heritage and contemporary literary and artistic achievement as these relate to an intelligent, educated, Jewish American family. Contains stories on contemporary art, books, history, and selected fictional items.

547. PHILADELPHIA JEWISH TIMES.   1925–
   1530 Spruce Street   (215) 545-8300
   Philadelphia, Pennsylvania 19102

   Editor: Arthur Klein   Circulation: 34,220
   Sponsor: n.i.   Frequency: weekly
   Language: English   Subscription: $4.00

Provides coverage of national and local news, with emphasis on the activities within the Jewish community in Philadelphia.

548. THE PHOENIX JEWISH NEWS.   1947–
   1530 West Thomas Road   (602) 264-0536
   Phoenix, Arizona 85015

   Editor: Pearl R. Newmark   Circulation: 3,100
   Sponsor: Cecil B. Newmark, Publisher Frequency: bi-weekly
   Language: English   Subscription: $5.75

Emphasizes Jewish fraternal, congregational, and social activities in the Phoenix area; however, reports on national and international events are also included.

549. PRESENT TENSE.   1973–
   165 East 56th Street   (212) 751-4000
   New York, New York 10022

   Editor: Murray Polner   Circulation: 19,600
   Sponsor: American Jewish Committee   Frequency: quarterly
   Language: English   Subscription: $9.00

Its main objective is "to broaden American Jewry's understanding of the condition of world Jewry" (editor's statement). Features historical, cultural, political, and other articles related to Jewish affairs, plus a book review section.

550. RECONSTRUCTIONIST.   1935–
   15 West 86th Street   (212) 787-1500
   New York, New York 10024

   Editor: Rabbi Ira Eisenstein   Circulation: 6,400
   Sponsor: Jewish Reconstructionist Foundation Frequency: monthly
   Language: English   Subscription: $10.00

This monthly contains "articles and editorials dealing with religious. ethical, social, and philosophical questions; events in the Jewish communities in the United States and abroad, cultural developments among the Jewish people; and editorial comments on national and international events" (editor's statement). Includes book reviews.

551. RHODE ISLAND JEWISH HERALD.   1929–
   99 Webster Street   (401) 724-0200
   Pawtucket, Rhode Island 02861

   Editor: Celia Zuckerberg   Circulation: 13,100
   Sponsor: Jewish Press Publishing Company Frequency: weekly
   Language: English   Subscription: $6.00

Emphasizes Jewish activities in Rhode Island, but also publishes general news.

552. RHODE ISLAND JEWISH HISTORICAL NOTES.   1954–
    209 Angell Street
    Providence, Rhode Island 02906

Editor: Seebert J. Goldowsky   Circulation: 400
Sponsor: Rhode Island Jewish Historical   Frequency: annual
        Association   Subscription: $5.00
Language: English

The main objective of this publication is to "record materials relating to the history of Jews in Rhode Island" (editor's statement). It includes historical narratives, reprints of records, bibliographical material, research reports, and pictures.

553. ROCKAWAY JOURNAL.   1883–
    379 Central Avenue   (516) 239-1240
    Lawrence, New York 11559

Editor: Robert Richner   Circulation: 7,000
Sponsor: Bi-County Publishers   Frequency: weekly
Language: English   Subscription: $4.00

This community-oriented weekly emphasizes all types of Jewish activities–individual, group, and organizational–in the Rockaway community. Features society news and book reviews.

554. ST. LOUIS JEWISH LIGHT.   1947–
    1347 Railway Exchange Building   (314) 241-4943
    611 Olive Street
    St. Louis, Missouri 63101

Editor: Robert A. Cohn   Circulation: 16,000
Sponsor: Jewish Federation of St. Louis   Frequency: semi-monthly
Language: English   Subscription: $3.50

Provides comprehensive coverage of news relating to local, national, and world events of interest to the Jewish community. Also publishes editorials, book reviews, and youth features.

555. SAVANNAH JEWISH NEWS.   1949–
    P. O. Box 6546   (912) 355-8111
    Savannah, Georgia 31405

Editor: Irwin B. Giffen   Circulation: 1,350
Sponsor: Savannah Jewish Council   Frequency: monthly
Language: English   Subscription: $2.50

Provides coverage of local Jewish organizational activities in Savannah, news of the Savannah Jewish Council, and Jewish affairs on the national and international forum.

556. THE SENTINEL.   1911–
    216 Jackson Boulevard   (312) 332-1133
    Chicago, Illinois 60606

Editor: Jack I. Fishbein   Circulation: 44,806
Sponsor: Sentinel Publishing Co.   Frequency: weekly
Language: English   Subscription: $13.50

This weekly publishes news articles and commentaries on all aspects of Jewish life on local, national, and international levels, plus news about Israel. Other features are news of social activities, book reviews, and articles on culture, art, and travel.

557. SEPHARDIC SCHOLAR.   1972–
    185 Street and Amsterdam Avenue   (212) 568-8400
    New York, New York 10033

Editor: Rachel Dalven   Circulation: 1,000
Sponsor: American Society of Sephardic Studies   Frequency: annual
Language: English   Subscription: $5.00

SEPHARDIC SCHOLAR (cont'd)
The main objective is "to advance Sephardic heritage and history through academic research" (editor's statement).

558. THE SHOFAR.   The Call.   1925–
1640 Rhode Island Avenue, N. W.   (202) 393-5284
Washington, D. C. 20036

Editor: Harvey D. Berk   Circulation: 35,000
Sponsor: B'nai B'rith Youth Organization   Frequency: 8 times/year
Language: English   Subscription: $5.00 or free with
                                                        membership

Covers educational topics of interest to Jewish high school youth, as well as news events within the B'nai B'rith Youth Organization.

559. SOUTH SHORE RECORD.   1953–
Station Plaza   (516) 374-9200
Hewlett, New York 11557

Editor: Florence Schwartzberg   Circulation: 9,128
Sponsor: n.i.   Frequency: weekly
Language: English   Subscription: $4.00

General news coverage, with an emphasis on local activities. Includes book reviews, educational news, youth features, and entertainment.

560. THE SOUTHERN ISRAELITE.   1925–
390 Courtland Street, N. E.   (404) 876-8249
Atlanta, Georgia 30303

Editor: Adolph Rosenberg   Circulation: 6,300
Sponsor: Southern Newspapers Enterprise, Inc.   Frequency: weekly
Language: English   Subscription: $10.50

Provides some coverage of national and international news, but emphasis is on news of Jewish communities in Georgia.

561. SOUTHERN JEWISH WEEKLY.   1924–
P. O. Box 3297   (904) 355-3459
Jacksonville, Florida 32206

Editor: Isadore Moscovitz   Circulation: 28,500
Sponsor: n.i.   Frequency: weekly
Language: English   Subscription: $3.00

This weekly emphasizes activities of the Jewish communities in Florida, but it also includes general news of special interest to the Jewish population.

562. THE SOUTHWEST JEWISH CHRONICLE.   1929–
324 North Robinson Street, No. 313   (405) 236-4226
Oklahoma City, Oklahoma 73102

Editor: Mrs. Samuel D. Friedman   Circulation: n.i.
Sponsor: n.i.   Frequency: quarterly
Language: English   Subscription: $3.00

Emphasis is on the various Jewish individual and organizational activities, events, and affairs in the Southwest.

563. STARK JEWISH NEWS.   1921–
P. O. Box 529
Canton, Ohio 44701

Editor: Leonard J. Leopold   Circulation: 1,200
Sponsor: n.i.   Frequency: monthly
Language: English   Subscription: $4.00

STARK JEWISH NEWS (cont'd)
This community-oriented monthly covers Jewish events within the Canton area, including announcements on births, deaths, social news, and individuals. Also features a cooking column.

564. SYNAGOGUE LIGHT.   1933–
47 Beekman Street   (212) 227-7800
New York, New York 10002

Editor: Rabbi Meyer Hager   Circulation: 17,000
Sponsor: Union of Chassidic Rabbis   Frequency: monthly
Language: English   Subscription: $5.00

Contains articles and commentaries on Judaism and the Jewish faith. Outstanding individuals of the Jewish religion are profiled in each issue.

565. SYNAGOGUE SCHOOL.   1942–
218 East 70th Street
New York, New York 10021

Editor: Morton Siegel   Circulation: 1,170
Sponsor: United Synagogue Commission on   Frequency: quarterly
         Jewish Education   Subscription: $2.50
Language: English

The main objective of this publication is "to provide a readership in the Jewish educational constituency with both theoretical and practical discussion of the needs of Jewish education as viewed from the vantage point of the Conservative Movement in Judaism" (editor's statement).

566. TEXAS JEWISH POST.   1947–
P. O. Box 742   (817) 927-2831
Fort Worth, Texas 76101

Editor: Jimmy Wisch   Circulation: 7,000
Sponsor: n.i.   Frequency: weekly
Language: English   Subscription: $7.00

General news on international, national, and local affairs of interest to the Jewish population.

567. TOLEDO JEWISH NEWS.   1957–
515 Monroe   (419) 531-2479
Toledo, Ohio 43623

Editor: Burt Silverman   Circulation: 2,611
Sponsor: Jewish Welfare Federation   Frequency: monthly
Language: English   Subscription: $4.00

Coverage of local, national, and international news of special interest to the Jewish community, and of the activities of the United Jewish Fund. Illustrated.

568. THE TORCH.   1941–
3080 Broadway   (212) 749-8000
New York, New York 10027

Editor: Mannye London   Circulation: 46,000
Sponsor: National Federation of Jewish   Frequency: quarterly
         Men's Clubs, Inc.   Subscription: $8.00
Language: English

"Contains by-lined articles on a variety of topics related to Judaism and Jewish issues as well as editorials, letters to the editor and a small amount of report on the National Federation of Jewish Men's Clubs" (editor's statement).

569. TRADITION.   1958–

220 Park Avenue, South   (212) 260-0700
New York, New York 10003

Editor: Rabbi Walter S. Wurzburger   Circulation: 4,000
Sponsor: Rabbinical Council of America   Frequency: quarterly
Language: English   Subscription: $5.00

This quarterly presents an analysis of traditional Judaism on current theological, philosophical, political, and social issues.

570. UNITED SYNAGOGUE REVIEW.   1957–

3080 Broadway   (212) 749-8000
New York, New York 10027

Editor: Rabbi Alvin Kass   Circulation: 250,000
Sponsor: United Synagogue of America   Frequency: quarterly
Language: English   Subscription: $2.00

Contains articles of Jewish interest, "from the perspective of and emphasizing Conservative Judaism. Stresses important events of the United Synagogue of America" (editor's statement).

571. VOICE.   1941–

2395 West Marlton Pike
Cherry Hill, New Jersey 08034

Editor: Bernard Dubin   Circulation: 5,800
Sponsor: Jewish Federation of Camden County   Frequency: semi-monthly
Language: English   Subscription: $2.00

Presents news of the activities of the Jewish Federation of Camden County, plus national and international news with the emphasis on Israel. Also included are articles and editorials on issues that are significant to the Jewish community.

572. WESTCHESTER JEWISH TRIBUNE.   1945–

95-20 63rd Road   (212) 896-7400
Rego Park, New York 11374

Editor: Rabbi Abraham Shoulson   Circulation: 7,800
Sponsor: Zionist Region in Westchester   Frequency: monthly
Language: English   Subscription: $2.00

This monthly publishes national and international news of special interest to the Jewish people, with the emphasis on local Jewish community activities and events. Coverage includes by-lined articles on various issues, youth features, and book reviews.

573. WESTERN STATES JEWISH HISTORICAL QUARTERLY.   1968–

2429 23rd Street   (213) 399-3585
Santa Monica, California 90405

Editor: Norton B. Stern   Circulation: n.i.
Sponsor: Southern California Jewish Historical   Frequency: quarterly
      Society   Subscription: $9.00
Language: English

Features scholarly articles on Western Jewish history, including Mexico, Alaska, and Hawaii.

574. WISCONSIN JEWISH CHRONICLE.   1921–

1360 North Prospect Avenue   (414) 271-2992
Milwaukee, Wisconsin 53202

Editor: Lawrence R. Tarnoff   Circulation: 8,000
Sponsor: Wisconsin Jewish Publications   Frequency: weekly
      Foundation, Inc.   Subscription: $8.50
Language: English

WISCONSIN JEWISH CHRONICLE (cont'd)
Provides coverage of local, national, and international Jewish news, with editorials and by-lined articles on a variety of Jewish issues. Includes coverage of organizations and personalities, plus entertainment, travel, and other features.

575. WOMEN'S AMERICAN ORT REPORTER. 1949–
1250 Broadway (212) 594-8500
New York, New York 10001

Editor: Elie Faust-Lévy Circulation: 130,000
Sponsor: Women's American Organization for Frequency: bi-monthly
    Rehabilitation through Training Subscription: $1.00
Language: English

Reports on the activities of ORT sponsored schools. Provides coverage of Jewish communities, plus national and international news of special interest to the Jewish population.

576. WOMEN'S LEAGUE OUTLOOK. 1930–
48 East 74th Street (212) 628-1600
New York, New York 10021

Editor: Mrs. Harry I. Kiesler Circulation: 171,500
Sponsor: Women's League for Conservative Frequency: quarterly
    Judaism Subscription: $2.00
Language: English

Dedicated to the preservation of Conservative Judaism, this quarterly presents articles dealing with the Jewish past and conservatism. Included are reports on the activities of the Sisterhoods (800) of the Conservative Movement of Judaism; articles on education, homemaking, art, and travel; and book reviews.

577. WOMEN'S WORLD. 1951–
1640 Rhode Island Avenue, N. W. (202) 393-5284
Washington, D. C. 20036

Editor: Helene Page Circulation: 150,000
Sponsor: B'nai B'rith Women Frequency: monthly
Language: English Subscription: free/membership

This monthly provides comprehensive reports on the activities of chapter, district, national, and international levels of the organization. Includes articles on current subjects of interest in the areas of public affairs and Jewish education.

578. WORLD OVER. 1940–
426 West 58th Street
New York, New York 10019

Editors: Ezekiel Schloss and Morris Epstein Circulation: 100,000
Sponsor: Board of Jewish Education, Inc. Frequency: n.i.
Language: English Subscription: $3.50

Aimed at the 9- to 13-year-old Jewish school child, this publication "attempts to present a portrait of Jewish life, past and present, in text, art, and photos" (editor's statement). Principal objective is to foster an appreciation of the Jewish cultural and religious heritage and contribution.

579. YONKERS JEWISH CHRONICLE. 1969–
122 South Broadway (914) 963-8457
Yonkers, New York 10702

Editor: Carolyn Weiner Circulation: 7,500
Sponsor: Jewish Council of Yonkers Frequency: weekly
Language: English Subscription: $2.00

YONKERS JEWISH CHRONICLE (cont'd)
"This newspaper . . . is published by the Jewish Council of Yonkers, the umbrella organization for forty-nine Jewish organizations. It covers news that affects Yonkers residents, whether it be local, national or international. The newspaper is also read by non-Jews and articles are sometimes written to build community relationships" (editor's statement).

580. YOUNG ISRAEL VIEWPOINT. 1952–
3 West 16th Street   (212) 929-1525
New York, New York 10011

Editor: Joel Saibel   Circulation: 31,500
Sponsor: National Council of Young Israel   Frequency: monthly
Language: English   Subscription: $2.50

This house organ of the NCYI covers activities of the organization and students, and Jewish activities worldwide.

581. YOUNGSTOWN JEWISH TIMES. 1935–
P. O. Box 777   (216) 746-6192
Youngstown, Ohio 44501

Editor: Harry Alter   Circulation: 8,975
Sponsor: n.i.   Frequency: bi-weekly
Language: English   Subscription: $3.00

Provides coverage of Jewish activities on a local, national, and international level.

582. YOUR CHILD. 1968–
218 East 70th Street
New York, New York 10021

Editor: Rabbi Chaim Rozwaski   Circulation: 2,100
Sponsor: United Synagogue Commission on   Frequency: quarterly
    Jewish Education   Subscription: $1.75
Language: English

Aimed at the Jewish parent of students of all ages and levels, this quarterly provides information on developments in Jewish education.

583. YOUTH AND NATION. 1968–
150 Fifth Avenue, Room 709   (212) 929-4955
New York, New York 10071

Editor: Edward Anzel   Circulation: 2,500
Sponsor: Hashomer Hatzair Socialist Zionist   Frequency: bi-monthly
    Youth Movement   Subscription: $1.50
Language: English

This is a journal of opinion on various Jewish issues, with a socialist orientation.

KOREAN PRESS
See also **Asian Press**

Korean and Korean-English Publications

584. GONG GAE PYUN JI.   **Korean Open Letter.** 1942–
351 Newman Drive
South San Francisco, California 94080

Editor: Young Han Choo   Circulation: 2,800
Sponsor: Young Han Choo   Frequency: bi-monthly
Language: Korean   Subscription: n.i.

GONG GAE PYUN JI (cont'd)
The successor to the "Min On" weekly, this publication is designed "to promote the reunification sentiment and spirit among the Koreans" (editor's statement). It contains international, national, and local news of interest to Koreans. Besides being distributed in the United States, the publication is mailed to Koreans in Europe, Asia, Africa, and South America.

585.   HAE OE HAN MIN BO.   Overseas Korean Journal.
        47-48 Springfield Boulevard
        Bayside, New York 11361

Editor: Jung Kyun Suh   Circulation: n.i.
Sponsor: Jung Kyun Suh   Frequency: semi-monthly
Language: Korean   Subscription: $7.00

Covers only news from the Korean communities in the United States, with an emphasis on democratic political movements among the Koreans. "Refusing the Korean dictatorial government, which oppresses the people, it struggles for the independent peaceful reunification of Korea, and tries to teach Koreans in the United States the ideas of democracy" (editor's statement). Anti-communist in outlook, it also opposes the present Korean government.

586.   THE HANKOOK ILBO.   The Korea Times.   1965–
        3418 West First Street
        Los Angeles, California 90004

Editor: Jae Ku Chang   Circulation: 2,500
Sponsor: n.i.   Frequency: daily
Language: Korean   Subscription: $44.00

This publication, the only Korean daily in the United States, carries international, national, and local news of interest to the Korean community. Illustrated. Many of the news items are reprinted in Los Angeles after being received from Seoul.

587.   HANKOOK-SHINMOON.   The Korean Newspaper.   1973–
        1750 Pennsylvania Avenue, N. W.
        Washington, D. C. 20006

Editor: Kwang-Nyun Han   Circulation: n.i.
Sponsor: Pan Asia Press   Frequency: weekly
Language: Korean   Subscription: $5.00

This weekly newspaper, edited primarily for Koreans residing in the United States, includes news relating to the Korean communities in America. Also includes some news from the Republic of Korea, especially as it affects the Korean community. A general newspaper.

588.   JOONG-ANG IL BO.   The Joong-Ang Daily.   1965–
        1116 West Olympic Boulevard
        Los Angeles, California 90015

Editor: Jin Ki Hong   Circulation: n.i.
Sponsor: The Joong Ang Il Bo Mass   Frequency: daily
        Communication Center   Subscription: $30.00
Language: Korean

The main office for this daily is located in Seoul, but the newspaper is re-edited in California in order to serve the needs of American-Koreans. General in nature, the news covers world, American, and Korean affairs, especially as they affect Korean interests. Two pages of this newspaper are devoted to activities taking place in Korean communities in the United States. Advertisers are Korean-run businesses in the United States.

589. THE KOREAN PACIFIC WEEKLY. 1913–
Box 1573
Honolulu, Hawaii 96817

Editor: Donald Chung Won Kim
Sponsor: Korean Dongji Hoi
Language: Korean and English

Circulation: 120
Frequency: weekly
Subscription: $10.00

590. THE NEW KOREA. 1905–
1368 West Jefferson Boulevard (213) 735-0424
Los Angeles, California 90007

Editor: Lee K. Park
Sponsor: Korean National Association
Language: Korean and English

Circulation: 494
Frequency: bi-weekly
Subscription: $15.00

Korean Publications in English

591. KOREA WEEK. 1968–
757 National Press Building
14th and F Streets, N. W.
Washington, D. C. 20045

Editor: Po Sung Philip Kim
Sponsor: n.i.
Language: English

Circulation: 1,200
Frequency: semi-monthly
Subscription: $9.00

"Covers developments in Korea, news in the United States related to Korea, and the Korean community in the United States" (editor's statement). Also includes news from Japan related to Korea. Among the special features are historical articles dealing with political, diplomatic, and commercial topics. Special emphasis is placed on United States-Korea relations. Illustrated.

LATVIAN PRESS
Latvian Publications

592. AGLONA VĒSTIS. Message from Aglona. 1958–
2543 West Wabansia Avenue (312) 276-9566
Chicago, Illinois 60647

Editor: Rev. Boleslavs Boginskis
Sponsor: Our Lady of Aglona Parish
Language: Latvian

Circulation: 760
Frequency: monthly
Subscription: $5.00

"The main objective of the publication is to inform the members of the Latvian Catholic community in the United States and Canada about the social, political and religious activities as they occur in the different Latvian colonies" (editor's statement). Besides carrying news items regarding the activities of the Latvian Catholic Association, it also features the writing of Latvian Catholic poets and authors.

593. AKADĒMISKĀ DZĪVE. Academic Life. 1958–
1 Vincent Avenue South
Minneapolis, Minnesota 55409

Editors: Magdalēne Rozentāls, Aivars Zaķis,
and Gunta Rozentāls
Sponsor: Association of Latvian Academic
Societies
Language: Latvian

Circulation: 1,200
Frequency: yearly
Subscription: $4.00

"Established as a forum for Latvian scientific thought in social sciences, history, political sciences, art, literary criticism and linguistics" (editor's statement). The publication's objective is to inform the Latvian community of research in these fields. As a special feature, there is a chronicle that surveys the activities of supporting academic organizations and that provides short biographical data of their members.

594. AMERIKAS LATVIETIS.   American Latvian. 1905–
Box 23
Roxbury, Massachusetts 02119

Editor: Edward Maurin   Circulation: 500
Sponsor: Baltica Publishing Company   Frequency: semi-monthly
Language: Latvian   Subscription: $3.00

Covering political, cultural, and other activities of Latvians in the United States, it also includes poetry and fiction by Latvian authors. Illustrated.

595. BITĪTE.   Little Bee. 1913–
1468 Hemlock Street   (707) 252-1809
Napa, California 94558

Editor: Eduards Putnins, Pastor   Circulation: 1,800
Sponsor: Latvian Evangelical Lutheran Church Frequency: monthly
         in Exile   Subscription: $1.50
Language: Latvian

Printed for Latvian-speaking children, this four page monthly includes meditations, stories, illustrations, and information on Latvian folklore, history, traditions, etc.

596. CELA BIEDRS.   Companion. 1956–
P. O. Box 7253   (612) 825-0909
Minneapolis, Minnesota 55407

Editor: John V. Strautnieks, Pastor   Circulation: 4,400
Sponsor: Latvian Evangelical Lutheran Church Frequency: 10 times/year
         in America   Subscription: $6.00
Language: Latvian

The major goal of this religious paper is "to communicate a Christian perspective" (editor's statement) to its Latvian readers.

597. KEGUMS. 1953–
1206 West Boulevard   (313) 547-4395
Berkley, Michigan 48072

Editors: Raimonds Caks and Mrs. G. Davidsons Circulation: 500
Sponsor: The Latvian Boy Scouts and Latvian   Frequency: semi-annual
         Girl Guides in Exile   Subscription: $2.00
Language: Latvian

The magazine serves as a guideline and forum for the exchange of ideas for Latvian Guides and Scouts. Articles explain the methods and ideology of Latvian Scouting.

598. LAIKS.   Time. 1949–
7307 Third Avenue   (212) 836-6382
Brooklyn, New York 11209

Editor: Arturs Strautmanis   Circulation: 12,380
Sponsor: Helmars Rudzitis and Lotars Rudzitis Frequency: semi-weekly
Language: Latvian   Subscription: $25.00

News items cover national, international, and local issues of interest to Latvians in the United States. Much of the coverage is political.

**599. LATVIEŠU SKAUTU PRIEKŠNIEKA APKĀRTRAKSTS.   Chief of the
Latvian Boy Scouts in Exile Letter to Latvian Scouts.** 1917–
1206 West Boulevard   (313) 547-4395
Berkley, Michigan 48072

Editor: Fricis Sipols   Circulation: 250
Sponsor: The Latvian Boy Scout Movement   Frequency: semi-annually
Language: Latvian   Subscription: free/membership dues

LATVIEŠU SKAUTU PRIEKŠNIEKA APKĀRTRAKSTS (cont'd)

Provides information on the guidelines, regulations, activities, and state of affairs of the organization.

600. LATVJU MŪZIKA.   Latvian Music.   1968–
4538 West 156th Street   (216) 433-4495
Cleveland, Ohio 44135

Editor: Valentins Bērzkalns   Circulation: 1,300
Sponsor: The Latvian Choir Association of   Frequency: annual
    the United States, Inc.   Subscription: $3.00
Language: Latvian

Serves primarily as a forum for documenting the developments in Latvian music as they occur in Latvian communities outside Latvia. International coverage.

601. MAZPUTNINŠ.   Little Bird.   1959–
314 Hilldale Avenue
Ann Arbor, Michigan 48105

Editors: Laimonis Streips and Liga K. Streips   Circulation: 1,050
Sponsor: Latvian Youth Publishing Society   Frequency: monthly
    Celinieks   Subscription: $12.00
Language: Latvian

This children's magazine "publishes reading material for the various ages, including classical Latvian children's literature, original stories, translations, Latvian folklore" (editor's statement).

602. MEZA VESTIS.   Forestry News.   1945–
2037 Bradford N. E.   (616) 774-0567
Grand Rapids, Michigan 49505

Editor: Rudolfs Markus   Circulation: 230
Sponsor: Latvian Association of Foresters in the   Frequency: quarterly
    United States   Subscription: $6.00
Language: Latvian

This illustrated journal prints articles dealing with new concepts in forestry as reflected in both Latvian and American literatures. Also includes news items on the Association's activities.

603. TREJI VĀRTI.   Three Gates.   1973–
317 South Beechtree Street   (616) 842-8841
Grand Haven, Michigan 49417

Editor: Alberts Rieksts   Circulation: 570
Sponsor: Raven Printing Inc.   Frequency: bi-monthly
Language: Latvian   Subscription: $14.00

Contains articles on such subjects as political science, history, literature, and Baltic culture in general.

604. ZIEMELKALIFORNIJAS APSKATS.   Review of Northern California.   1959–
962 Westmont Court   (408) 246-9993
San Jose, California 95117

Editor: Ojars Celle   Circulation: 600
Sponsor: Northern California Latvian   Frequency: monthly
    Association   Subscription: contributions
Language: Latvian

Serves the Northern California Latvian community by providing coverage of social, cultural, and other community activities. Also features articles on political, economic, cultural, social, and other topics. Includes a special discussion forum for readers.

LEBANESE PRESS
See **Arabic Press**

LITHUANIAN PRESS
Lithuanian and Lithuanian-English Publications

605. AIDAI. Echoes. 1950–
c/o Franciscan Fathers
361 Highland Boulevard
Brooklyn, New York 11207

Editor: Juozas Girnius   Circulation: 1,900
Sponsor: Franciscan Fathers   Frequency: monthly
Language: Lithuanian   Subscription: $7.00

This cultural magazine which deals with all aspects of Lithuanian arts and science, includes book reviews and information on Lithuanian activities in various countries.

606. AKIRAČIAI. Horizons. 1968–
6821 South Maplewood
Chicago, Illinois 60629

Editor: T. Remeikis   Circulation: 1,350
Sponsor: Viewpoint Press, Inc.   Frequency: monthly
Language: Lithuanian   Subscription: $6.00

Provides non-partisan coverage of social, cultural, economic, and political life under Soviet rule, as well as reports on the activities of Lithuanians abroad.

607. ATEITIS. The Future. 1911–
10316 Kenneth Avenue   (312) 425-1255
Oak Lawn, Illinois 60453

Editor: Rev. Dr. Kestutis A. Trimakas   Circulation: 1,250
Sponsor: Lithuanian Catholic Federation   Frequency: monthly
         ATEITIS   Subscription: $7.00
Language: Lithuanian

Initially established in Lithuania, this journal served as the ideological and cultural forum for the Lithuanian Catholic youth movement. Presently, in the United States, it retains its Catholic-Lithuanian orientation but also provides young intellectuals with a forum for screening a cross-current of ideas.

608. DARBININKAS. Worker. 1915–
361 Highland Boulevard
Brooklyn, New York 11207

Editor: Rev. Dr. Cornelius Bučmys   Circulation: 17,000
Sponsor: Franciscan Fathers   Frequency: semi-weekly
Language: Lithuanian   Subscription: $8.00

This Catholic-oriented publication covers general, international, national, and local news. Information on Lithuanian activities in the United States and other countries is also provided.

609. DIRVA. The Field. 1915–
P. O. Box 03206   (216) 321-4751
Cleveland, Ohio 44103

Editor: Vytautas Gedgaudas   Circulation: 3,450
Sponsor: "Viltis" Association   Frequency: weekly
Language: Lithuanian   Subscription: $13.00

Provides coverage of international, national, and local news of special interest to Lithuanian Americans.

610. DRAUGAS. The Friend. 1909–
4545 West 63rd Street (312) 585-9500
Chicago, Illinois 60629

Editor: F. Garsva Circulation: 13,000
Sponsor: Lithuanian Catholic Press Society Frequency: daily
Language: Lithuanian Subscription: $23.00

This daily provides general news coverage and features articles on the Lithuanian community in the United States and throughout the world. A book review section is also included. "Combating communism everywhere" (editor's statement) is its aim. The Saturday issue contains a separate section on art and literature.

611. EGLUTĖ. The Little Fir. 1950–
Immaculate Conception Convent (203) 928-5828
Putnam, Connecticut 06260

Editor: Sister Ann Mikaila Circulation: 1,000
Sponsor: Sisters of the Immaculate Conception Frequency: monthly
Language: Lithuanian Subscription: $7.00

Published exclusively for children from the ages of 5 through 11, this monthly contains stories, poems, and plays written by Lithuanian authors. The specific objective is to acquaint children with the Lithuanian cultural heritage.

612. ELTOS INFORMACIJOS. Elta Information Service. 1945–
29 West 57th Street (212) 752-0099
New York, New York 10019

Editor: Juozas Audėnas Circulation: 525
Sponsor: Supreme Committee for the Frequency: weekly
Liberation of Lithuania Subscription: minimum $25.00
Language: Lithuanian donation

The objective is to inform the public, especially Lithuanians living outside their homeland, about present-day Lithuania and the efforts being made to liberate it. The news is mostly of a political nature. Also attempts to serve as the news center for Lithuanian immigrants and exiles. A special feature is the inclusion of excerpts from recent issues of the underground publication *Chronicle of the Lithuanian Catholic Church*. Also published in English, Portuguese, Spanish, French, and Italian.

613. GARSAS. The Echo. 1917–
71-73 South Washington Street (717) 823-8876
Wilkes-Barre, Pennsylvania 18703

Editor: Matas Zujus Circulation: 7,950
Sponsor: Lithuanian R. Catholic Alliance Frequency: bi-monthly
of America Subscription: $2.00
Language: Lithuanian and English

Contains "articles and news about Lithuanian religious, national, cultural, social, and fraternal activities in the United States and other countries; news from Soviet occupied Lithuania; and general news" (editor's statement). Catholic fraternal publication.

614. GIRIOS AIDAS. Echo of the Forest. 1950–
2740 West 43rd Street
Chicago, Illinois 60632

Editor: J. Kuprionis Circulation: 200
Sponsor: Association of Lithuanian Foresters Frequency: bi-annual
in Chicago Subscription: $6.00
Language: Lithuanian

Lithuanian forestry journal. In 1975 the publication of the journal ceased temporarily and for that year a book on forestry was published in its place.

615. I LAISVE. Toward Freedom.   1941–
36 Crést Drive, Dune Acres   (219) 787-9220
Chesterton, Indiana 46304

Editor: Juozas Kojelis   Circulation: 1,000
Sponsor: Friends of the Lithuanian Front   Frequency: 3 times/year
Language: Lithuanian   Subscription: $7.00

Analyzes questions on Lithuania and Lithuanian emigration as they relate to changing international politics. Presents updated information on events occurring in Soviet-occupied Lithuania
as well as the resistance activities. Cultural, historical, and political in nature.

616. KARYS. Warrior.   1950–
341 Highland Boulevard
Brooklyn, New York 11207

Editor: Z. Raulinaitis   Circulation: 1,350
Sponsor: Association of Lithuanian Veterans   Frequency: monthly
Language: Lithuanian   Subscription: $7.00

Features articles on Lithuanian history, military history, and veterans' news.

617. KELEIVIS. Traveler.   1905–
636 Broadway   (617) 268-3071
South Boston, Massachusetts 02127

Editor: Jackus Sonda   Circulation: 2,340
Sponsor: Keleivis Publishing Company   Frequency: weekly
Language: Lithuanian   Subscription: $7.00

This weekly, sponsored by the Lithuanian Socialist Union, covers international, national, and
local news.

618. LAIŠKAI LIETUVIAMS. Letters to Lithuanians.   1950–
2345 West 56th Street   (312) 737-8400
Chicago, Illinois 60636

Editor: Joseph Vaišnys   Circulation: 3,262
Sponsor: Lithuanian Jesuit Fathers   Frequency: monthly
Language: Lithuanian   Subscription: $6.00

Includes articles on religious, educational, political, and youth topics. The main objective is "to
help Lithuanian immigrants to solve their problems in foreign countries" (editor's statement).

619. LAISVE. Liberty.   1911–
102-02 Liberty Avenue
Ozone Park, Long Island, New York 11417

Editor: Anthony Bimba   Circulation: n.i.
Sponsor: The Lithuanian Cooperative Publishing Frequency: semi-weekly
        Society, Inc.   Subscription: $9.00
Language: Lithuanian

Provides general news with a communist orientation.

620. LAISVOJI LIETUVA. Free Lithuania.   1946–
2618 West 71st Street   (312) 476-3371
Chicago, Illinois 60629

Editor: V. Šimkus   Circulation: 1,985
Sponsor: Lithuanian Regeneration Association Frequency: semi-monthly
Language: Lithuanian   Subscription: $8.00

Anti-communist in nature. Includes many articles on Lithuanian history, plus coverage of
international, national, and local events of particular interest to Lithuanian Americans.
Illustrated.

621. LAIVAS.   The Ship.   1921–
     4545 West 63rd Street
     Chicago, Illinois 60629

     Editor: Rev. J. Vaskas   Circulation: 5,000
     Sponsor: Marian Fathers   Frequency: semi-monthly
     Language: Lithuanian   Subscription: $5.00

Catholic magazine for the Lithuanians in the United States.

622. LIETUVIŲ DIENOS.   Lithuanian Days.   1950–
     4364 Sunset Boulevard   (213) 664-2919
     Los Angeles, California 90029

     Editor: Editorial Committee   Circulation: 3,000
     Sponsor: Anthony F. Skirius   Frequency: monthly
     Language: English and Lithuanian Subscription: $10.00

Highlights Lithuanian cultural activities throughout the world.

623. LITHUANIAN MUSEUM REVIEW.   1966–
     4012 South Archer Avenue   (312) 847-2441
     Chicago, Illinois 60632

     Editor: Rita Striegel   . Circulation: 5,500
     Sponsor: Balzekas Museum of Lithuanian Culture Frequency: bi-monthly
     Language: English and Lithuanian Subscription: $10.00

Covers the humanities, politics, culture, education, and history from the Lithuanian perspective, providing information on the activities of the Balzekas Museum.

624. METMENYS.   Patterns.   1959–
     3308 West 62nd Place
     Chicago, Illinois 60629

     Editor: Vytautas Kavolis   Circulation: 1,000
     Sponsor: Metmenys Co.   Frequency: semi-annually
     Language: Lithuanian   Subscription: 4 issues $10.00

Publishes avant-garde works in literature, philosophy, the arts, and the social sciences.

625. MOTERU DIRVA.   Women's Field.   1914–
     9428 South Harding Avenue
     Evergreen Park, Illinois 60642

     Editor: Mrs. Dale Murray   Circulation: 2,050
     Sponsor: American-Lithuanian Roman Catholic Frequency: bi-monthly
               Women's Alliance   Subscription: $2.50
     Language: Lithuanian and English

In addition to organizational information and chapter news, this bi-monthly publishes stories (both fictional and historical) and biographical data on women in literature, the arts, etc. (both past and present).

626. MŪSU SPARTAI.   Our Wings.   1950–
     5718 South Richmond Street
     Chicago, Illinois 60629

     Editor: Povilas Dilys   Circulation: n.i.
     Sponsor: Lithuanian Ev. Reformed Church Frequency: quarterly
     Language: Lithuanian   Subscription: n.i.

A Lithuanian evangelical religious quarterly.

627. MŪSŲ VYTIS.   Our Knight.   1948–
    168 Morningstar Court   (716) 632-7221
    Williamsville, New York 14221

    Editor: L. Grinius   Circulation: n.i.
    Sponsor: Collegiate Division of the Lithuanian   Frequency: quarterly
        Scout Association, Inc.   Subscription: $6.00
    Language: Lithuanian

Lithuanian Scouting journal aimed at collegiate youth and Scout leaders throughout the free world.

628. MŪSŲ ŽINIOS.   Our News.   1972–
    2345 West 56th Street   (312) 737-8400
    Chicago, Illinois 60636

    Editor: Algimantas Kezys   Circulation: 2,000
    Sponsor: Lithuanian Jesuit Fathers   Frequency: semi-monthly
    Language: Lithuanian   Subscription: n.i.

An informational bulletin covering the cultural activities in the Lithuanian Jesuit youth center. Occasionally features news on events occurring within the Lithuanian community. Illustrated.

629. NAUJIENOS.   The Lithuanian Daily.   1914–
    1739 South Halsted Street
    Chicago, Illinois 60608

    Editor: Martin Gudelis   Circulation: 26,000
    Sponsor: Lithuanian News Publishing Co.   Frequency: daily
    Language: Lithuanian   Subscription: $26.00

Covers national, international, and social news of interest to the Lithuanian-American community. Anti-communist.

630. NAUJOJI VILTIS.   The New Hope.   1970–
    7150 South Spaulding Avenue   (312) 778-7707
    Chicago, Illinois 60629

    Editor: Jonas Balys   Circulation: 1,000
    Sponsor: Fraternity Neo-Lithuania and National   Frequency: semi-annual
        Lithuanian Society of America, Inc. Subscription: $6.00
    Language: Lithuanian

Conservative in orientation, this journal is devoted primarily to politics and culture.

631. PASAULIO LIETUVIS.   The World Lithuanian.   1963–
    6804 South Maplewood Avenue   (312) 776-4028
    Chicago, Illinois 60629

    Editor: Stasys Barzdukas   Circulation: 3,400
    Sponsor: Lithuanian World Community, Inc.   Frequency: monthly
    Language: Lithuanian   Subscription: $3.00

Provides coverage of the activities within Lithuanian communities throughout the world, promoting the retention of the Lithuanian culture and traditions and participation in Lithuanian activities and organizations. Encourages action for the national independence of Lithuania.

632. PRO PATRIA.   For Fatherland.   1975–
    4259 South Maplewood Avenue   (312) 254-7450
    Chicago, Illinois 60632

    Editor: Jolanta Mockaitis   Circulation: 500
    Sponsor: Korp. Neo-Lithuania   Frequency: n.i.
    Language: Lithuanian   Subscription: free

Covers national affairs and the organization's activities in the United States, Canada, Australia, England, and West Germany.

633. SANDARA.   The League.   1914–
840 West 33rd Street   (312) 827-4789
Chicago, Illinois 60608

Editors: Michael Vaidyla and Joseph Kapacinskas   Circulation: 15,000
Sponsor: Lithuanian National League of America   Frequency: weekly
Language: Lithuanian   Subscription: $7.00

General news coverage, with an emphasis on the local Lithuanian community.

634. SĖJA.   The Sowing.   1953–
5921 South Fairfield Avenue   (312) 776-5674
Chicago, Illinois 60629

Editor: Liudvikas Šmulkštys   Circulation: 750
Sponsor: The Fund of Bell Publishings   Frequency: quarterly
Language: Lithuanian   Subscription: $5.00

This journal serves as a forum for the Democratic Political Party, originally established at the
end of the 19th century in Lithuania. Objective: Lithuanian independence.

635. SKAUTU AIDAS.   The Scouts Echo.   1923–
6842 South Campbell Avenue
Chicago, Illinois 60629

Editor: Sofija Jelioniene   Circulation: 1,061
Sponsor: Lithuanian Scouts Association   Frequency: monthly
Language: Lithuanian   Subscription: $5.00

This Scouting journal focuses on retaining the Lithuanian culture and language.

636. ŠV. FRANCIŠKAUS VARPELIS.   The Bell of St. Francis.   1942–
Beach Street   (207) 967-2011
Kennebunkport, Maine 04046

Editor: Rev. Dr. Victor Gidžiūnas   Circulation: 3,100
Sponsor: Franciscan Fathers   Frequency: 10 copies/year
Language: Lithuanian   Subscription: $3.00

This religious-patriotic monthly is read primarily by members of the Lithuanian St. Francis
Order in the United States and other countries.

637. TAUTOS PRAEITIS.   The Past of a Nation.
4439 South Talmon Avenue
Chicago, Illinois 60632

Editor: Jonas Dainauscas   Circulation: n.i.
Sponsor: Lithuanian Historical Society   Frequency: irregular
Language: Lithuanian   Subscription: $16.00

This scholarly historical publication includes various historical materials on Lithuania. Recently
changed its title to *Lietuvin Tantos Praetis* (Lithuanian Historical Review).

638. TECHNIKOS ŽODIS.   The Engineering Word.   1951–
5859 South Whipple Street   (312) 778-0699
Chicago, Illinois 60629

Editor: Victor Jautokas   Circulation: 725
Sponsor: American Lithuanian Engineers and   Frequency: quarterly
        Architects Association   Subscription: $6.00
Language: Lithuanian

Provides a forum for the exchange of ideas and information between Lithuanian engineers,
scientists, and architects throughout the world. Highlights activities of various chapters and
individual members.

639. TEVYNE.   Motherland.   1889–
    307 West 30th Street   (212) 524-5529
    New York, New York 10001

Editor: Genevieve Meiliunas   Circulation: 5,000
Sponsor: Lithuanian Alliance of America   Frequency: semi-monthly
Language: Lithuanian and English   Subscription: $4.00

Tevyne, the official organ of the Lithuanian Alliance of America (a fraternal benefit society), is published to inform its members of various traditional and cultural activities. It also covers current and general news of the society's affairs.

640. TIESA.   The Truth.   1930–
    104-107 102nd Street   (212) 641-6699
    Ozone Park, New York 11417

Editor: John Siurba   Circulation: 3,000
Sponsor: Association of Lithuanian Workers   Frequency: monthly
Language: Lithuanian and English   Subscription: free to members

Published for the Association's members, this monthly highlights news of organizational activities, etc. Communist oriented.

641. VARPAS.   Bell.   1889–
    1214 North 16th Avenue
    Melrose Park, Illinois 60160

Editor: Antanas Kucys   Circulation: 1,000
Sponsor: Lithuanian Alumni Association, Varpas   Frequency: annually
Language: Lithuanian   Subscription: $2.50

"Journal for propagation of freedom and independence of Lithuania, individual and national freedom, Lithuanian culture and liberal ideology" (editor's statement).

642. VIENYBE.   Unity.   1886–
    192 Highland Boulevard
    Brooklyn, New York 11207

Editor: Jonas Valaitis   Circulation: 2,530
Sponsor: n.i.   Frequency: semi-monthly
Language: Lithuanian   Subscription: $7.00

The oldest Lithuanian newspaper. This publication provides general news and Lithuanian news.

643. VILNIS.   The Surge.   1920–
    3116 South Halsted Street   (312) 842-7325
    Chicago, Illinois 60608

Editor: Stanislovas J. Jokubka   Circulation: 5,350
Sponsor: Workers Publishing Association, Inc.   Frequency: 3 times/week
Language: Lithuanian   Subscription: $12.00

This communist-oriented newspaper publishes items relating to labor, world, and national events.

644. VYTIS.   The Knight.   1915–
    c/o I. K. Sankus
    1467 Force Drive
    Mountainside, New Jersey 07092

Editor: Irene K. Sankus   Circulation: 1,600
Sponsor: Knights of Lithuania   Frequency: bi-monthly
Language: English and Lithuanian   Subscription: $4.00

This is the house organ of the Knights of Lithuania organization.

Lithuanian Publications in English

645. LITUANUS.   1954–
    6621 South Troy
    Chicago, Illinois 60629

Editor: A. Klimas   Circulation: 5,000
Sponsor: Lituanus Foundation, Inc.   Frequency: quarterly
Language: English   Subscription: $10.00

"Baltic States journal of arts and sciences, the only English language quarterly about Lithuania, Latvia, and Estonia, presenting a forum for free-world scholars to express their views on the history and people of the Baltic area" (editor's statement).

646. VILTIS.   Hope.   1942–
    P. O. Box 1225
    Denver, Colorado 80201

Editor: Vyts F. Beliajus   Circulation: 2,500
Sponsor: None   Frequency: bi-monthly
Language: English   Subscription: $5.00

Contains ethnic news and information on folklore, folk dances, customs, recipes, background material, ballads, club activities.

647. VOICE OF THE LITHUANIAN AMERICAN COUNCIL.   1940–
    2606 West 63rd Street   (312) 778-6900
    Chicago, Illinois 60629

Editor: Irene Blinstrubas   Circulation: n.i.
Sponsor: Lithuanian American Council, Inc.   Frequency: bi-weekly
Language: English   Subscription: n.i.

Official bulletin of the Lithuanian American Council, a nationwide anti-communist organization.

LUXEMBOURG PRESS
Luxembourg Publications in English

648. LUXEMBOURG NEWS OF AMERICA.   1966–
    496 North Northwest Highway   (312) 394-8252
    Park Ridge, Illinois 60068

Editor: Victor Jacoby   Circulation: 650
Sponsor: Luxembourgers of America   Frequency: monthly
Language: English   Subscription: $5.00

"Communication medium for Luxembourgers living in the United States; also their descendants and friends. News items of Luxembourg Societies. Also anything of general interest in the Grand Duchy of Luxembourg" (editor's statement).

NEGRO PRESS
See Black American Press

NORWEGIAN PRESS
See also Scandinavian Press

Norwegian and Norwegian-English Publications

649. MINNESOTA POSTEN.   Minnesota Post.   1956–
    1455 West Lake Street
    Minneapolis, Minnesota 55408

Editor: Jenny A. Johnsen   Circulation: 4,840
Sponsor: Friend Publishing Company   Frequency: weekly
Language: Norwegian   Subscription: $5.00

MINNESOTA POSTEN (cont'd)
Contains cultural news from Norway and news about Norwegian activities in the United States.
Articles inform readers about the industry, government, and social thinking of Norway. Pertinent articles from American publications are occasionally printed, and Norwegian organizational
activities of the Twin Cities area are publicized and promoted.

650. **NORDISK TIDENDE.**   The Norwegian News.   1891—
    8104 5th Avenue   (212) 238-1100
    Brooklyn, New York 11209

    Editor: Sigurd Daasvand   Circulation: 8,000
    Sponsor: Norse News Inc.   Frequency: weekly
    Language: Norwegian and English   Subscription: $12.00

This weekly provides local news about Norwegians, mainly in the Greater New York area, and
includes information concerning American relations with Norway. A special feature is church
news and interviews with visitors from Norway and Americans who have visited Norway.
Illustrated.

651. **NORDMANNS FORBUNDET.**   The Norseman.   1907—
    P. O. Box 1
    Coon Valley, Wisconsin 54623

    Editor: Johan Hambro   Circulation: 30,000
    Sponsor: The Norsemen Federation   Frequency: monthly
    Language: Norwegian   Subscription: $10.00

Features articles about Norway (political, cultural and social issues) and materials on Norwegians
in the United States.

652. **NORSK UNGDOM.**   Norwegian Youngpeople.   1913—
    1134 South 8th Street   (612) 332-7635
    Minneapolis, Minnesota 55404

    Editor: The Rev. Jacob Andreasen   Circulation: 2,097
    Sponsor: Lutheran Mission Societies, Inc.   Frequency: monthly
    Language: Norwegian and English   Subscription: $3.00

A religious monthly dedicated to the interpretation of the Gospel of Jesus Christ, this paper also
includes news from Norway and news about various Christian groups and religious life around
the world.

653. **NORTHWOOD EMISSAEREN.**   The Northwood Emissary.   1914—
    Northwood, North Dakota 58267

    Editor: Rev. John O. Johanson   Circulation: 1,510
    Sponsor: Northwood Deaconess Hospital and   Frequency: monthly
        Home   Subscription: $1.00
    Language: English and Norwegian

The purpose of this house organ is "to tell the story and to reflect the activities of the Northwood
Deaconess Hospital and Home" (editor's statement).

654. **VALDRES SAMBAND BUDSTIKKEN.**   1970—
    RFD No. 3   (612) 564-3408
    Granite Falls, Minnesota 56241

    Editors: Carl T. Narvestad and Amy A. Narvestad Circulation: 1,365
    Sponsor: Valdres Samband   Frequency: semi-annually
    Language: English and Norwegian   Subscription: free/membership

Its main objective is "to inform and educate Valdres Americans about all aspects of their Valdres
ancestral background. In addition to covering current activities of the Samband and of its members we research and publish historical data of the Valdres area" (editor's statement). Illustrated.

655. WESTERN VIKING.   1889–
2040 Northwest Market Street   (206) 784-4617
Seattle, Washington 98107

Editor: Henning C. Boe   Circulation: 6,000
Sponsor: None   Frequency: weekly
Language: Norwegian and English   Subscription: $11.00

"Provides news from Norway and from many Norwegian-American societies and lodges in the
cities and towns along the Pacific Coast, including Canada, as well as from the midwest states"
(editor's statement). It has weekly feature articles by well-known writers on the West Coast
and the Midwest. Its main objectives are to foster an interest in Norwegian culture and to
maintain contact with Norway. Illustrated.

Norwegian Publications in English

656. THE AUGSBURG NOW.   1929–
701-707 21st Avenue South
Minneapolis, Minnesota 55404

Editor: n.i.   Circulation: n.i.
Sponsor: Augsburg College and Theological   Frequency: monthly
          Seminary   Subscription: $3.00
Language: English

657. EBENEZER.   1934–
2545 Portland Avenue
Minneapolis, Minnesota 55404

Editor: Fernanda U. Malmin   Circulation: 25,000
Sponsor: Ebenezer Home Society   Frequency: quarterly
Language: English   Subscription: $1.00

This illustrated house organ contains news of interest to members of the Ebenezer Home Society.

658. FAITH AND FELLOWSHIP.   1920–
Box 655
Fergus Falls, Minnesota 56537

Editor: Rev. Robert Overgaard   Circulation: 2,800
Sponsor: Lutheran Brethren Publishing Frequency: bi-weekly
          Company   Subscription: $3.50
Language: English

Publishes articles on religious and literary subjects.

659. NEWS OF NORWAY.   1942–
825 Third Avenue   (212) 421-7333
New York, New York 10022

Editor: Director of Information Service   Circulation: 9,000
Sponsor: The Norwegian Information Service Frequency: semi-monthly
          in the United States   Subscription: free
Language: English

Provides a general presentation of modern Norway including trends and events in all areas of
Norwegian society. Special features include "Norwegian Diary," "Books and Booklets,"
"Feature Stories."

660. THE NORSEMAN.   1907–
P. O. Box 1
Coon Valley, Wisconsin 54623

Editor: Johan Hambro   Circulation: 30,000
Sponsor: The Norsemen Federation   Frequency: bi-monthly
Language: English   Subscription: $10.00

THE NORSEMAN (cont'd)
Contains articles and news on the political, economic, social, and cultural scene in Norway, and articles concerning persons of Norse descent around the world. Illustrated.

661. NORWEGIAN AMERICAN STUDIES. 1925–
St. Olaf College (507) 645-9311
Northfield, Minnesota 55057

Editor: Kenneth O. Bjork   Circulation: 1,155
Sponsor: Norwegian-American Historical   Frequency: irregular
    Association   Subscription: varies
Language: English

This is a series of publications by the Norwegian-American Historical Association (organized in 1925). The Association publishes the following series: 1, *Studies and Records* (vol. 1, 1926–); 2, *Travel and Description Series* (vol. 1, 1926–); 3, *Authors' Series. Studies and Records* contains scholarly articles and source material on Norwegian immigration.

662. THE NORWEGIAN SOCIETY OF WASHINGTON D. C. NEWSLETTER. 1972–
130 South Columbus Street (703) 892-6443
Arlington, Virginia 22204

Editor: Alfred B. Moe   Circulation: 150
Sponsor: The Norwegian Society of   Frequency: monthly
    Washington D. C.   Subscription: n.i.
Language: English

General information on local, national, and international news about Norwegians, traditional and special events, or American events of Norwegian interest. News about and profiles of members.

663. SANGER HILSEN. Singers' Greeting. 1894–
3316 Xenwood Avenue South (612) 925-4658
Minneapolis, Minnesota 55416

Editor: Erling Stone   Circulation: 1,005
Sponsor: Norwegian Singers Association of   Frequency: bi-monthly
    America   Subscription: n.i.
Language: English

664. THE SONS OF NORWAY VIKING. 1903–
1455 West Lake Street (612) 827-3611
Minneapolis, Minnesota 55408

Editor: Bent Vanberg   Circulation: 72,200
Sponsor: Sons of Norway   Frequency: monthly
Language: English   Subscription: $6.00

Primarily a membership magazine for the Sons of Norway, is also the main publication for all Norwegian-American-Canadian cultural and educational interests. Includes articles on Norway and Norwegians in North America.

PAKISTANI PRESS
See also **Asian Press**

Pakistani Publication in English

665. PAKISTAN AFFAIRS.
2315 Massachusetts Avenue, N. W. (202) 332-8330
Washington, D. C. 20008

Editor: Camille Wallace   Circulation: n.i.
Sponsor: Embassy of Pakistan   Frequency: bi-weekly
Language: English   Subscription: free

PAKISTAN AFFAIRS (cont'd)
An official newsletter of the Embassy designed to keep interested Americans informed of developments in Pakistan. Provides information on job opportunities for Pakistani students studying in the United States.

PALESTINIAN PRESS
See **Arabic Press**

POLISH PRESS
Polish and Polish-English Publications

666. AVE MARIA.   Hail Mary.   1924–
    600 Doat Street   (716) 892-4141
    Buffalo, New York 14211

    Editor: Sister Mary Donata Slominski   Circulation: 4,100
    Sponsor: Felician Sisters   Frequency: bi-monthly
    Language: Polish   Subscription: $2.00

"Objectives are: 1) to promote devotion to the Blessed Virgin Mary; 2) to give concise news of the Catholic world in general, and in Poland and the Felician community in particular, with special emphasis on the Church itself, the liturgy, and Our Lady–all in an easily readable form" (editor's statement).

667. BIULETYN.   The Bulletin.   1944–
    381 Park Avenue South   (212) 683-4342
    New York, New York 10016

    Editor: Michael Budny   Circulation: 1,200
    Sponsor: Pilsudski Institute of America for   Frequency: annual
          Research in the Modern History   Subscription: free to members
          of Poland
    Language: Polish and English

Published by the Jozef Pilsudski Institute of America (established 1943), which is a major Polish scholarly organization in the United States. Sent to all members of the Institute, the bulletin contains annual reports, statements, obituaries, and historical or educational articles.

668. BULLETIN–NMDA NAS.   1913–
    6130 North Sheridan Road   (312) 743-2600
    Chicago, Illinois 60660

    Editor: Henry E. Bielinski   Circulation: 2,100
    Sponsor: National Medical and Dental   Frequency: semi-annual
          Association of America and   Subscription: $3.00
          National Advocates Society
    Language: English and Polish

Contains reports of the annual joint convention of the National Medical and Dental Association of America and National Advocates Society; this convention brings together once a year the officers, families, etc. of Polish American physicians, dentists, and lawyers.

669. DZIENNIK POLSKI.   Polish Daily News.   1904–
    2310 Cass
    Detroit, Michigan 48201

    Editor: Stanley Krajewski   Circulation: 16,100
    Sponsor: Polish Daily News, Inc.   Frequency: daily
    Language: Polish   Subscription: $28.00

Includes international and national news while also covering the activities of Polish organizations and Poles in the United States. It also "helps candidates of Polish descent in their bids for elective or appointive office" (editor's statement). Illustrated.

670. DZIENNIK ZWIAZKOWY.   **Polish Daily Zgoda.**   1908–
    1201 North Milwaukee Avenue   (312) 278-8700
    Chicago, Illinois 60622

Editor: John F. Krawiec   Circulation: 20,000
Sponsor: Alliance Printers & Publishers, Inc.   Frequency: daily
Language: Polish   Subscription: $31.50

Provides international, national, and local news coverage, with feature articles on politics, culture, literature, economy, sports, and other topics, as well as valuable material on the activities of Polish organizations and people in the United States. Illustrated.

671. GLOS LUDOWY.   **The People's Voice.**   1909–
    5854 Chene Street
    Detroit, Michigan 48211

Editors: Conrad Komorowski and Stanley Nowak Circulation: 3,150
Sponsor: Conrad Komorowski and Stanley Nowak Frequency: weekly
Language: Polish and English   Subscription: $10.00

This weekly contains general news, as well as articles on political, cultural, social, and other activities.

672. GLOS NARODU.   **The Voice of the People.**   1900–
    410 Matchaponix Avenue
    Jamesburg, New Jersey 08831

Editor: Kaz. Kolodziejczyk   Circulation: 4,900
Sponsor: n.i.   Frequency: weekly
Language: Polish   Subscription: $5.00

General and local news of interest to the Polish community in the United States, with material on the activities of Polish religious and other organizations, as well as news about Poland. Illustrated.

673. GLOS POLEK.   **Polish Women's Voice.**   1910–
    1309 North Ashland Avenue   (312) 278-2524
    Chicago, Illinois 60622

Editors: Maria Lorys and A. Logodzinska   Circulation: 65,000
Sponsor: Polish Women's Alliance of America   Frequency: semi-monthly
Language: Polish and English   Subscription: membership

This is the official publication of the Polish Women's Alliance of America. While the publication is primarily devoted to P.W.A.A. activities, it also aims at preserving Polish customs, tradition, and language. Illustrated.

674. GWIAZDA.   **Polish Star.**   1902–
    3022 Richmond Street   (215) 739-7571
    Philadelphia, Pennsylvania 19134

Editor: G. Nowaczyk   Circulation: 8,500
Sponsor: Union of Polish Women in America   Frequency: weekly
Language: Polish and English   Subscription: $6.00

Features articles and other materials concerning the Polish community in the United States, with a special section on the activities of the Union of Polish Women in America.

675. GWIAZDA POLARNA.   **Northern Star.**   1908–
    3535 Jefferson Street
    Stevens Point, Wisconsin 54481

Editor: Frank Kmietowicz   Circulation: 22,000
Sponsor: Worzalla Publishing Co.   Frequency: weekly
Language: Polish and English   Subscription: $14.00

GWIAZDA POLARNA (cont'd)
This weekly contains national, international, and local news. Articles cover historical, political, social, cultural, and other topics, and a special section contains information on Polish activities in America. A small portion of material is published in English. Illustrated.

676. **JEDNOSC POLEK.** Unity of Polish Women. 1924–
   6905 Lansing Avenue (216) 641-9234
   Cleveland, Ohio 44105

   Editor: Joseph Ptak Circulation: 1,329
   Sponsor: Association of Polish Women of the Frequency: semi-monthly
         United States Subscription: $3.00
   Language: Polish

A fraternal magazine.

677. **KURYER.** Courier. 1923–
   6905 Lansing Avenue (216) 641-9234
   Cleveland, Ohio 44105

   Editor: Joseph Ptak Circulation: 21,005
   Sponsor: Union of Poles Frequency: semi-monthly
   Language: Polish and English Subscription: $4.00

A fraternal magazine.

678. **LEGIONNAIRE.** 1943–
   6009 Fleet Avenue
   Cleveland, Ohio 44105

   Editor: Julian S. Kubit Circulation: 2,500
   Sponsor: Polish Legion of American Veterans Frequency: bi-monthly
         of U.S.A. Subscription: n.i.
   Language: Polish and English

679. **MIESIĘCZNIK FRANCISZKAŃSKI.** Franciscan Monthly. 1907–
   Franciscan Publishers (414) 822-5833
   Pulaski, Wisconsin 54162

   Editor: Rev. Sebastian M. Kus Circulation: 10,300
   Sponsor: Province of the Franciscan Fathers Frequency: monthly
         at Pulaski Subscription: $3.00
   Language: Polish

Features popular articles on current religious, moral, and social issues. Since it is directed to readers of Polish descent, it frequently includes articles on Polish culture, customs, and history. Illustrated.

680. **MIGRANT ECHO.** 1972–
   6100 Dorothy Avenue
   Detroit, Michigan 48211

   Editor: Andrew N. Woznicki Circulation: 575
   Sponsor: Society of Christ for Polish Migrants Frequency: quarterly
   Language: English and Polish Subscription: $4.00

The magazine "is dedicated to the examination of socio-religious problems of migration movement, with emphasis on Polish ethnic groups all over the world" (editor's statement). It features articles on Polish culture and education as well as articles on the past and present of Polish-American communities in the United States.

681. NAROD POLSKI. The Polish Nation. 1897–
984 Milwaukee Avenue (312) 278-3215
Chicago, Illinois 60622

Editor: Joseph W. Zurawski Circulation: 45,200
Sponsor: Polish Roman Catholic Union of Frequency: semi-monthly
America Subscription: $2.00
Language: English and Polish

Reports on the activities of the members and societies of the Polish Roman Catholic Union of America. Fraternal news, membership news, cultural and educational news, and sports and youth news. Regular book review section. Illustrated.

682. NOWINY MINNESOCKIE. Minnesota News. 1915–
440 Thomas Avenue
St. Paul, Minnesota 55103

Editor: J. M. Koleski Circulation: 1,595
Sponsor: Polish Fraternal, Social, and Civic Frequency: weekly
Organizations Subscription: n.i.
Language: Polish

683. NOWY DZIENNIK. Polish Daily News. 1971–
15 Exchange Place
Jersey City, New Jersey 07302

Editor: Editorial Board Circulation: 6,500
Sponsor: Bicentennial Publishing Corporation Frequency: daily
Language: Polish Subscription: $26.00

Articles cover historical, political, cultural, social, and other topics of interest to the Polish community in the United States, with emphasis on the activities of Polish organizations and individual Poles.

684. OBYWATEL AMERYKANSKI. American Citizen.
410 Matchaponix Avenue
Jamesburg, New Jersey 08831

Editor: n.i. Circulation: 4,900
Sponsor: n.i. Frequency: weekly
Language: Polish and English Subscription: $5.00

Contains international, national, and local news, emphasizing the activities of Polish organizations and Poles in general in the United States. Illustrated.

685. PATRON. 1943–
607 Humboldt Street
Brooklyn, New York 11222

Editor: Rev. Carol J. Wawak Circulation: 1,200
Sponsor: St. Stanislaus Kostka Parish Frequency: weekly
Language: Polish and English Subscription: $3.00

This house organ features parish announcements, news of parish activities, and other material relevant to the members of the Stanislaus Kostka parish.

686. PITTSBURCZNIN. The Pittsburgher. 1920–
3515 Butler Street
Pittsburgh, Pennsylvania 15201

Editor: Dora M. Alski Circulation: 10,456
Sponsor: Pittsburgh Polish Daily Publishing Frequency: weekly
Company, Inc. Subscription: $5.00
Language: Polish

Containing general and local news, this weekly serves Polish Americans in western Pennsylvania by promoting Polish culture and language.

687. POLAK AMERYKANSKI. Polish American. 1919–
410 Matchaponix Avenue
Jamesburg, New Jersey 08831

Editor: Kaz. Kolodziejczyk
Sponsor: n.i.
Language: Polish

Circulation: 4,900
Frequency: weekly
Subscription: n.i.

688. POLKA. Polish Woman. 1935–
1004 Pittston Avenue
Scranton, Pennsylvania 18505

Editor: J. Mastalski
Sponsor: United Women's Societies of the
Most Blessed Sacrament
Language: Polish and English

Circulation: n.i.
Frequency: quarterly
Subscription: $1.00

This journal, devoted to the Polish-American woman, contains articles on the family and on the role of women in society, as well as items on the activities and events of the Society.

689. POLONIA. 1971–
1200 North Ashland Avenue (312) 276-8323
Chicago, Illinois 60622

Editor: Joseph T. Bialasiewicz
Sponsor: Independent Publishing Co.
Language: Polish

Circulation: 5,700
Frequency: weekly
Subscription: $15.00

Contains international, national, and local news of interest to Polish-Americans, with special emphasis on Polish activities in the United States and in Poland. Articles cover political, historical, religious, cultural, and other topics. Aimed at the "old generation of Polish American" (editor's statement). Illustrated.

690. POLONIAN. 1969–
165 Eleventh Street
San Francisco, California 94103

Editor: Dalegor Wladyslaw Suchecki
Sponsor: Polish Community Service Center
Language: English and Polish

Circulation: 5,500
Frequency: bi-monthly
Subscription: $5.00

Contains items on topics that have general ethnic group interest, especially to the Polish communities in northern California.

691. POSLANIEC MATKI BOSKIEJ SALETYNSKIEJ. Messenger of
Virgin Mary.
Twin Lakes, Wisconsin 53131

Editor: Saletyni Missionaries
Sponsor: La Salette Missionary Fathers
Language: Polish

Circulation: n.i.
Frequency: monthly
Subscription: n.i.

692. PRZEGLĄD POLSKI. Polish Review. 1972–
2539 North Kedzie Boulevard (312) 772-1788
Chicago, Illinois 60647

Editor: Rev. Michael P. Pawelek
Sponsor: New Polonia Confraternity of America
Language: Polish

Circulation: 5,000
Frequency: quarterly

This quarterly presents news of the New Polonia Confraternity in America and news from Poland. Its religious and cultural articles are designed to be of interest to the Polish community.

693. ROLA BOZA. God's Field.   1923–
529 East Locust Street
Scranton, Pennsylvania 18505

Editor: Rt. Rev. Anthony M. Rysz   Circulation: 6,200
Sponsor: Polish National Catholic Church   Frequency: semi-monthly
Language: Polish and English   Subscription: $5.00

This Polish-English semi-monthly is devoted primarily to religious issues, including the activities and events of various Polish parishes. It is the official organ of the Polish National Catholic Church.

694. RÓŻE MARYI. Roses of Mary.   1944–
Eden Hill, The Marian Fathers & Brothers   (617) 413-3691
Stockbridge, Massachusetts 01262

Editor: Brother Albin Milewski   Circulation: 7,000
Sponsor: Association of Marian Helpers   Frequency: monthly
Language: Polish   Subscription: $2.00

"The objective of the *Róże Maryi* is, primarily, the education of Polish-speaking people in the area of religion–new developments in the Catholic Church as well as historical information. Also included are articles of interest on the culture and patriotic events of Poland" (editor's statement).

695. SLOWO I LITURGIA.   1970–
Orchard Lake Schools   (313) 682-1885, ext. 23
P. O. Box 5042
Orchard Lake, Michigan 48033

Editor: Rev. Eugene Edyk   Circulation: 365
Sponsor: Polish-American Liturgical Center   Frequency: quarterly
Language: Polish   Subscription: $10.00

Designed as a sermon-preparing aid for priests who preach in the Roman Catholic Church in Polish but who are not fluent in the Polish language.

696. SODALIS.   1920–
Orchard Lake, Michigan 48033

Editor: Rt. Rev. Valerius J. Jasinski   Circulation: 1,658
Sponsor: SS. Cyril and Methodius Seminary   Frequency: monthly
Language: Polish   Subscription: $4.00

This faculty publication deals with religious, social, pedagogic, and historical topics of interest to American Catholics of Polish descent.

697. SOKOL POLSKI. Polish Falcon.   1896–
97 South 18th Street   (412) 431-0305
Pittsburgh, Pennsylvania 15203

Editor: Mieczysław J. Wasilewski   Circulation: 16,500
Sponsor: Polish Falcons of America   Frequency: semi-monthly
Language: Polish and English   Subscription: membership

The official publication of the Polish Falcons of America, this paper features news and articles on the Falcon (Sokol) organization and its members. Sometimes includes valuable historical material. Illustrated.

698. STRAŻ. The Guard.   1897–
1004 Pittston Avenue   (717) 347-1911
Scranton, Pennsylvania 18505

Editor: Theodore L. Zawistowski   Circulation: 10,000
Sponsor: Polish National Union of America   Frequency: weekly
Language: English and Polish   Subscription: $7.00

STRAŻ (cont'd)
Provides official and social reports and news about the Polish National Union, the Polish National Catholic Church, and affiliated organizations and parishes. Covers cultural activities, philately, and fraternal activities. Includes book reviews.

699. **TATRA EAGLE.**
264 Palsa Avenue
East Paterson, New Jersey 07407

Editor: Thaddeus V. Gromada
Sponsor: Polish Tatra Mountaineers Alliance, Inc.
Language: Polish and English

Circulation: 10,000
Frequency: quarterly
Subscription: $1.50

Devoted to the Tatra Highlander (góral) folk culture, this publication reports on the activities of the highlanders now living in the United States as well as on activities in the Podhale region of Poland. It attempts to preserve the best elements of this folklore and to study its impact on Polish culture in general.

700. **UNIA POLSKA. Polish Union.** 1920–
761 Fillmore Avenue   (716) 893-1365
Buffalo, New York 14212

Editor: Thaddeus L. Sielski
Sponsor: Polish Union of America
Language: Polish and English

Circulation: 6,600
Frequency: semi-monthly
Subscription: membership

This is the official organ of the Polish Union of America. It presents the various fraternal activities of the Union and of individual members.

701. **WETERAN. Veteran.** 1921–
17 Irving Place   (212) 475-5585
New York, New York 10003

Editor: Zbigniew A. Konikowski
Sponsor: Polish Army Veterans Association
of America, Inc.
Language: Polish

Circulation: 4,950
Frequency: monthly
Subscription: $4.00

The official organ of the Polish Army Veterans Association of America, this monthly covers historical, military, and current events, as well as news of various Polish veterans' organizations around the world.

702. **ZGODA. Unity.** 1881–
1201 North Milwaukee Avenue   (312) 276-0700
Chicago, Illinois 60622

Editor: Joseph Wiewiora
Sponsor: Polish National Alliance
Language: English and Polish

Circulation: 160,000
Frequency: semi-monthly
Subscription: membership

This official publication of the Polish National Alliance provides coverage of fraternal, cultural, and sports activities and general news. It includes features on prominent Americans of Polish descent, emphasizing "Polish-American participation in the mainstream of American life" (editor's statement).

703. **ZWIAZKOWIEC. The Alliancer.** 1896–
6966 Broadway Avenue   (216) 883-3131
Cleveland, Ohio 44105

Editor: Roman Tretczyk
Sponsor: Alliance of Poles in America
Language: Polish and English

Circulation: 4,800
Frequency: semi-monthly
Subscription: $7.00

A fraternal publication.

Polish Publications in English

704. AMERICAN POLONIA REPORTER.   1957–
21 East 17th Street
New York, New York 10003

Editor: Leopold Dende   Circulation: 3,250
Sponsor: Amerpol Publishing Corporation   Frequency: quarterly
Language: English   Subscription: n.i.

705. AM-POL EAGLE.   1960–
1335 East Delavan Avenue
Buffalo, New York 14215

Editor: Matthew W. Pelczynski   Circulation: 7,200
Sponsor: n.i.   Frequency: weekly
Language: English   Subscription: $6.50

Published primarily for Polish Americans who reside in western New York, it includes general news items of special interest to Polish Americans and provides coverage of the activities of Polish clubs, parishes, societies, and organizations.

706. GAZETA READINGSKA.   Reading Newspaper.   1909–
5th and Penn Streets   (215) 215-0919
Reading, Pennsylvania 19603

Editor: L. Fruchter   Circulation: 5,500
Sponsor: Graphic Publishing Corp.   Frequency: monthly
Language: English   Subscription: $2.00

Provides news and articles of interest to the Polish community.

707. THE KOSCIUSZKO FOUNDATION NEWSLETTER.   1925–
15 East 65th Street   (212) 734-2130
New York, New York 10021

Editor: Eugene Kusielewicz   Circulation: 4,100
Sponsor: The Kosciuszko Foundation   Frequency: monthly
Language: English   Subscription: $10.00

"Publishes the reports and activities of The Kosciuszko Foundation as a cultural and exchange institution. The Foundation's activities focus on expanding cultural and scholarship exchange between the United States and Poland, as well as to foster the development of Polish American ethnic studies in this country" (editor's statement). The newsletter publishes two major articles per issue devoting the remainder of the space to cultural news of Polish Americans.

708. THE NATIONAL P.L.A.V.   1958–
3024 North Laramie Avenue   (312) 283-9161
Chicago, Illinois 60641

Editor: Julian S. Kubit   Circulation: n.i.
Sponsor: Polish Legion of American Veterans   Frequency: quarterly
    of U.S.A.   Subscription: n.i.
Language: English

709. PERSPECTIVES.   1970–
700 7th Street, S. W.   (202) 554-4267
Washington, D. C. 20024

Editor: Marta Korwin-Rhodes   Circulation: 8,000
Sponsor: Board of Editors   Frequency: bi-monthly
Language: English   Subscription: $3.00

PERSPECTIVES (cont'd)

This is an "independent apolotical non-profit bi-monthly devoted mainly to the current social and cultural scene. It aims at the cultivation of the Polish-American heritage" (editor's statement). Contains valuable historical and other material on Polish life in America. Includes a book review section.

710. POLISH AMERICAN CONGRESS NEWSLETTER. 1959–
1200 North Ashland Avenue
Chicago, Illinois 60622

Editor: Valentine Janicki	Circulation: n.i.
Sponsor: Polish American Congress	Frequency: quarterly
Language: English	Subscription: free to members

This is the official organ of the Polish American Congress, a secular central organization of Americans of Polish descent. It presents items on the organization's various activities.

711. POLISH AMERICAN HISTORICAL ASSOCIATION BULLETIN. 1945–
984 Milwaukee Avenue (312) 278-3210
Chicago, Illinois 60622

Editor: Anthony Milnar	Circulation: 1,000
Sponsor: Polish Institute of Arts & Sciences	Frequency: quarterly
Language: English	Subscription: free to members

712. POLISH AMERICAN JOURNAL. 1911–
413 Cedar Avenue (717) 343-2012
Scranton, Pennsylvania 18505

Editor: Henry J. Dende	Circulation: 29,067
Sponsor: Dende Press, Inc.	Frequency: monthly
Language: English	Subscription: $3.00

This is "the official newspaper of the following fraternal benefit societies: Polish Union of U.S. of N.A., Polish Beneficial Association" (editor's statement). The Chicago Edition is sponsored by the Polish American Congress, Illinois State Division. It carries international, national, and local news of special interest to Americans of Polish descent, with sections devoted to letters to editors, achievements of individuals of Polish descent, news of various groups, church news, sports activities, women's corner, and educational and cultural notes.

713. POLISH AMERICAN STUDIES. 1944–
984 North Milwaukee Avenue (312) 384-3252
Chicago, Illinois 60622

Editor: Frank Renkiewicz	Circulation: 750
Sponsor: Polish American Historical Association	Frequency: semi-annually
Language: English	Subscription: $5.00

Carries articles, criticism, edited documents, bibliographies, and reviews that deal with all aspects of the history and culture of Poles in the United States. Articles place the Polish-American experience in historical and comparative perspective by examining its roots in Europe and its relationship to other ethnic groups.

714. POLISH AMERICAN WORLD. 1959–
3100 Grand Boulevard
Baldwin, New York 11510

Editor: Thomas Poster	Circulation: 5,000
Sponsor: Polish American World	Frequency: weekly
Language: English	Subscription: $4.00

This weekly provides coverage of events and activities occurring in Polish-American communities in the United States, plus commentaries on political matters that affect Americans of Polish descent. It also contains reports on events occurring in Poland.

715. THE POLISH REVIEW.   1956–
  59 East 66th Street   (212) 861-8668
  New York, New York 10021

  Editor: Ludwik Krzyzanowski   Circulation: 2,000
  Sponsor: The Polish Institute of Arts and   Frequency: quarterly
              Sciences in America, Inc.   Subscription: $10.00
  Language: English

Scholarly journal devoted to all aspects of Polish history and culture, including the Polish-American community. It publishes articles concerning political and social contemporary affairs, history, economics, creative and critical literature, theatre, and Polish-American ethnicity. Includes book reviews, bibliography.

716. POST EAGLE.   1962–
  800 Van Houten Avenue   (201) 473-5414
  Clifton, New Jersey 02013

  Editor: Chester Grabowski   Circulation: 11,000
  Sponsor: Post Publishing Co., Inc.   Frequency: weekly
  Language: English   Subscription: $6.00

Designed to keep Americans of Polish heritage informed on Polonian life, accomplishments, and functions. Covers all subjects pertaining to Polonian life in the United States and abroad, including such topics as defamation and equality, sports news, and support of Polonians in political life and business life.

717. THE QUARTERLY REVIEW.   1949–
  6300 Lakeview Drive   (703) 256-4333
  Falls Church, Virginia 22041

  Editor: Irene Prazmowska Coulter   Circulation: 3,500
  Sponsor: American Council of Polish   Frequency: quarterly
              Cultural Clubs   Subscription: $3.00
  Language: English

This is the official organ of the American Council of Polish Cultural Clubs, a confederation of 25 affiliates in 21 cities. Its purpose is to propagate "the knowledge and appreciation of the culture and civilization of Poland" (editor's statement). It contains articles on Polish culture in the United States and on the activities of Polish cultural clubs, plus editorials, letters to the editor, and book reviews.

718. VOICE OF THE WHITE EAGLE.   1957–
  Villa Anneslie   (301) 377-4352
  Anneslie Maryland 21212

  Editor: Leonard Suligowski   Circulation: 1,500
  Sponsor: Polish Nobility Association Frequency: quarterly
  Language: English   Subscription: n.i.

Contains materials on heraldry and genealogy, often including news of interest to Polish nobility or to students of Polish genealogy.

PORTUGUESE PRESS
Portuguese and Portuguese-English Publications

719. BOLETIM DA S.P.R.S.I.   Bulletin of the S.P.R.S.I.
  3031 Telegraph Avenue   (415) 658-4310
  Oakland, California 94609

  Editor: Etelvina S. Vaz   Circulation: 12,025
  Sponsor: Portuguese Society Queen Saint Isabel   Frequency: monthly
  Language: Portuguese and English   Subscription: free to members

BOLETIM DA S.P.R.S.I. (cont'd)
Fraternal publication devoted to SPRSI activities. Contains articles of interest to the membership, in Portuguese and English, plus both Portuguese and English recipes. Historical and religious stories furnished by Portuguese government prior to April 25, 1975.

720. **CORREIO OPERARIO NORTEAMERICANO.**   North American
     Labor News.   1963–
     815 16th Street, N. W.   (202) 637-5041
     Washington, D. C. 20006

     Editor: George Meany   Circulation: 6,000
     Sponsor: AFL-CIO   Frequency: semi-monthly
     Language: Portuguese   Subscription: free

This publication provides pertinent labor news from North America to organized labor in
Brazil.

721. **FRIENDS OF THE FOUNDATION.**   1970–
     P. O. Box 1768   (415) 452-4465
     Oakland, California 94604

     Editor: Barbara Angeja   Circulation: 200
     Sponsor: Luso-American Education Foundation   Frequency: quarterly
     Language: English and Portuguese   Subscription: n.i.

Promotes the goals and purposes of the Luso-American Education Foundation, whose aim is to
preserve the Portuguese language and culture.

722. **JORNAL PORTUGUÊS.**   **Portuguese Journal.**   1888–
     3240 East 14th Street   (415) 532-4141
     Oakland, California 94601

     Editor: Alberto S. Lemos   Circulation: 6,200
     Sponsor: Portuguese Journal   Frequency: weekly
     Language: Portuguese and English   Subscription: $9.00

Provides "its thousands of Portuguese and Brazilian readers access to local and political events
in their communities in the U.S.A. and informs them of latest happenings in their Mother-Land"
(editor's statement). Its main objective is to keep alive Portuguese language, tradition, and culture; at the same time, it provides the best link between the land of birth of the Portuguese
and Brazilian people and the United States. Illustrated.

723. **LUSO-AMERICANO.**   1928–
     88 Ferry Street
     Newark, New Jersey 07105

     Editor: Vasco Jardim, Jr.   Circulation: 7,000
     Sponsor: Luso-Americano Company, Inc.   Frequency: weekly
     Language: Portuguese and English   Subscription: $8.00

Provides general and local news, plus special features of interest to Portuguese-speaking communities in America.

724. **NOTICIARIO DO SINDICALISMO LIVRE.**   Free Trade Union News.   1945–
     815 16th Street, N. W.   (202) 637-5041
     Washington, D. C. 20006

     Editor: George Meany   Circulation: 15,000
     Sponsor: AFL-CIO   Frequency: monthly
     Language: Portuguese   Subscription: free to members

International labor news.

725. PORTUGUESE TIMES.   1972–
  61 West Rodney French Boulevard (617) 997-3118
  New Bedford, Massachusetts 02744

  Editor: António Alberto Costa   Circulation: 5,000
  Sponsor: Portuguese Times, Inc.   Frequency: weekly
  Language: Portuguese   Subscription: $10.00

International, national, and local news of interest to Portuguese communities. The major Portuguese publication in the United States, it includes materials on Portugal and Portuguese Americans. Illustrated.

726. UPEC LIFE. **Portuguese Union of the State of California Life.** 1885–
  1120 East 14th Street   (415) 483-7676
  San Leandro, California 94577

  Editor: Carlos Almeida   Circulation: 5,400
  Sponsor: Supreme Council of U.P.E.C. Frequency: quarterly
  Language: Portuguese and English Subscription: free with membership

Features activities of the Portuguese Union as well as articles on Portuguese culture. It is the oldest fraternal Portuguese magazine in California. Illustrated.

727. VOZ DE PORTUGAL. **Voice of Portugal.**   1960–
  368 A Street   (415) 537-9503
  Hayward, California 94541

  Editor: Lourenco Costa Aguiar Circulation: 3,970
  Sponsor: Voice of Portugal   Frequency: 3 times/month
  Language: Portuguese   Subscription: $6.00

General, local, and group news of interest to Portuguese-speaking people.

Portuguese Publications in English

728. PORTU-INFO.   1961–
  43 Dundee Road   (203) 322-2922
  Stamford, Connecticut 06903

  Editor: Henry H. Gaylord, III Circulation: 300
  Sponsor: The International Society for Frequency: quarterly
     Portuguese Philately Subscription: $4.00
  Language: English

Dissemination of philatelic news and articles pertaining to Portugal and her colonies.

PUERTO RICAN PRESS
See **Spanish Press**

ROMANIAN PRESS
Romanian and Romanian-English Publications

729. CREDINTA. **The Faith.**   1950–
  19959 Riopelle   (313) 366-1998
  Detroit, Michigan 48203

  Editor: V. Rev. Archimandrite B. V. Anania Circulation: 1,600
  Sponsor: The Romanian Orthodox Missionary Frequency: monthly
     Archdiocese in America Subscription: $5.00
  Language: Romanian and English

The main objective of this publication is to promote the Eastern Orthodox faith and to provide information on religious, cultural, and social events of the Romanian communities in the United States and Canada.

730. LUMINATORUL.   Illuminator.   1926–
    7009 Detroit Avenue   (216) 961-5013
    Cleveland, Ohio 44102

    Editor: Luca Sezonov   Circulation: n.i.
    Sponsor: Romanian Baptist Association of   Frequency: monthly
        the United States   Subscription: $7.50
    Language: Romanian and English

This religious weekly is primarily concerned with religious issues and the Romanian Baptist
Church in the United States. A small section is published in English.

731. ROMANIA.   1956–
    500 Fifth Avenue   (212) 524-6951
    New York, New York 10036

    Editor: Editorial Committee   Circulation: 2,000
    Sponsor: Romanian National Tourist Office   Frequency: bi-monthly
    Language: Romanian   Subscription: n.i.

732. SOLIA.   The Herald.   1936–
    11341 Woodward Avenue   (313) 883-7845
    Detroit, Michigan 48202

    Editor: The Rt. Rev. Bishop Valerian (D. Trifa)   Circulation: 4,579
    Sponsor: The Romanian Orthodox Episcopate   Frequency: monthly
        of America   Subscription: $6.00
    Language: Romanian and English

This is the official organ of the Romanian Orthodox Episcopate of America. It features articles
on the Orthodox faith, on church activities, and on religious education.

733. UNIREA.   The Union.   1949–
    4309 Olcott Avenue   (219) 398-3760
    Chicago, Illinois 46312

    Editor: Rev. George C. Muresan   Circulation: 1,850
    Sponsor: Association of Romanian Catholics   Frequency: monthly
        of America, Inc.   Subscription: $2.50
    Language: English and Romanian

Contains general instructional and informational material of an ecclesiastical nature. Principally
concerned with the specific interest of Romanian Catholics. Book reviews are occasionally
included.

734. ZIARUL ROMÂNESC "AMERICA."   America-Romanian News.   1906–
    15 Lawrence Street   (313) 866-1718
    Detroit, Michigan 48202

    Editor: Ilie Olteanu   Circulation: 2,520
    Sponsor: Union and League of Romanian   Frequency: semi-monthly
        Societies of America   Subscription: $8.00
    Language: Romanian and English

The main objective is to promote the interest of the Union and League and to keep active the
national consciousness among Romanians in America and Canada. It provides news items on
Romanian organizations and group activities in the United States and Canada. Illustrated.

Romanian Publications in English

735. ROMANIAN BULLETIN.   1968–
    866 Second Avenue   (201) 935-1067
    New York, New York 10017

ROMANIAN BULLETIN (cont'd)

Editor: n.i.
Sponsor: Romanian Library
Language: English

Circulation: n.i.
Frequency: monthly
Subscription: free

Communist-oriented, this publication provides information on current events in Romania. Includes book reviews.

RUSSIAN PRESS
Russian and Russian-English Publications

736. **EZHEGODNIK PRAVOSLAVNOI TSERKVI V AMERIKE.** Annual of the Orthodox Church in America. 1975–
P. O. Box 675   (516) 922-0550
Syosset, New York 11791

Editor: Archbishop Sylvester
Sponsor: Orthodox Church in America
Language: Russian

Circulation: 1,000
Frequency: annual
Subscription: $6.00

Features religious news and guidance for Russian-speaking clergy and laity of the Orthodox Church in America. It reports events, activities, appointments, and transfers of clergy from Orthodox churches all over the world. It also includes doctrinal instruction, biographies of religious figures, and messages from members of the clergy.

737. **KORPUSNIK.**
349 West 86th Street
New York, New York 10024

Editor: Dimitry Vertepov
Sponsor: St. Alexander Nevsky Foundation, Inc.
Language: Russian

Circulation: 650
Frequency: monthly
Subscription: free

738. **NOVAYA ZARYA.** New Dawn. 1928–
2078 Sutter Street
San Francisco, California 94115

Editor: G. T. Soohoff
Sponsor: n.i.
Language: Russian

Circulation: 2,818
Frequency: daily
Subscription: $8.50

This independent Russian daily provides general news coverage.

739. **NOVOYE RUSSKOYE SLOVO.** New Russian Word. 1910–
243 West 56th Street   (212) 265-5500
New York, New York 10019

Editor: Andrei Sedych
Sponsor: Novoye Russkoye Slovo Publishing
         Corp.
Language: Russian

Circulation: 26,000
Frequency: daily (except Monday)
Subscription: $45.00

The oldest and largest Russian language daily outside Russia. It provides readers with national and international news as well as news of Russian-oriented activities in the United States. Articles cover politics, culture, history, and other topics of interest to the Russian community. Special features include articles on Russian literature and publication of underground material received from the Soviet Union through the publication's own sources of communication. Anti-communist in outlook.

740. NOVYJ ZHURNAL.   New Review.   1942–
2700 Broadway   (212) 666-1692
New York, New York 10025

Editor: Roman B. Goul   Circulation: 1,400
Sponsor: New Review Inc.   Frequency: quarterly
Language: Russian   Subscription: $20.00

This literary and scholarly quarterly features critical review articles and original works of literature. Designed for scholars and specialists on the USSR and Russian affairs.

741. PO STOPAM KHRISTA.   Following the Steps of Christ.   1950–
1908 Essex Street
Berkley, California 94703

Editor: V. Rev. N. Vieglais   Circulation: 900
Sponsor: Orthodox Press   Frequency: quarterly
Language: Russian   Subscription: $2.00

This quarterly provides religious news and guidance for followers of the Orthodox faith. It includes international news of Orthodox churches, hymns and publications of interest, and commentaries by members of the clergy. Since 1957 each issue contains a supplement with church music.

742. PRAVOSLAVNAYA RUS.   Orthodox Russia.   1928–
Holy Trinity Monastery
Jordanville, New York 13361

Editor: Fr. Constantine   Circulation: 1,600
Sponsor: Holy Trinity Monastery   Frequency: semi-monthly
Language: Russian   Subscription: $8.00

Features articles and news on Eastern Orthodoxy "from the view of the Russian Orthodox Church outside Russia" (editor's statement).

743. PRAVOSLAVNAYA ZHIZN'.   Orthodox Life.   1950–
Holy Trinity Monastery
Jordanville, New York 13361

Editor: Fr. Constantine   Circulation: 1,650
Sponsor: Holy Trinity Monastery   Frequency: monthly
Language: Russian   Subscription: $3.00

"Lives of Saints and features of the Eastern Orthodox Christianity of the Russian Orthodox Church outside Russia" (editor's statement).

744. RODINA.   Fatherland.   1950–
Chadwick Street 20
Glen Cove, New York 11542

Editor: Boris Solonevitch   Circulation: 200
Sponsor: n.i.   Frequency: bi-monthly
Language: Russian   Subscription: free

This "Russian independent anti-communist magazine" is non-commercial and is intended for Russian emigrees and all "serious readers of anti-communist thought" (editor's statement). It stresses political theory and opinion, often on a particular theme. Articles discuss both historical and current topics.

745. RODNIYE DALI.   Native Vistas.   1954–
1117 North Berendo Street   (213) 662-7866
Los Angeles, California 90029

Editor: Alexander Doll (Dolgopolov)   Circulation: 320
Sponsor: Rodniye Dali Company   Frequency: monthly
Language: Russian   Subscription: $7.00

RODNIYE DALI (cont'd)

This independent, anti-communist, social and literary publication has a monthly column on current political events; it also includes fiction, travels, memoirs, historical articles, articles of general interest (medicine, technology), reviews of new Russian books, a monthly children's page, news of the activities of various local Russian organizations, and other topics relevant to the Russian community.

746. **ROSSIYA.   Russia.**   1933–
        216 West 18th Street
        New York, New York 10011

        Editor: George Alexandrovsky   Circulation: 1,650
        Sponsor: Newspaper Rossiya Company   Frequency: semi-weekly
        Language: Russian   Subscription: $18.00

General news coverage.

747. **RUSSKAYA ZHIZN'.   Russian Life.**   1920–
        2458 Sutter Street
        San Francisco, California 94115

        Editor: Ariadna Delianich   Circulation: 2,500
        Sponsor: Russian Life, Inc.   Frequency: 5 times/week
        Language: Russian   Subscription: $25.00

This publication serves the American-Russian community and Russian nationals abroad, with the aim of preserving the Russian language, culture, and literature. Its viewpoint is "conservative, American" (editor's statement). It gives worldwide news of politics, literature, history, science, and social events, plus news of emigre organizations, Orthodox churches, and accomplishments of members of the Russian emigre community.

748. **RUSSKOYE DELO.   The Russian Cause.**   1958–
        349 West 86th Street
        New York, New York 10024

        Editor: Alexander V. Rummel   Circulation: 656
        Sponsor: Russian Immigrants Representative   Frequency: monthly
                Association in America, Inc.   Subscription: $4.00
        Language: Russian

"Critical analysis of the theory, practice and propaganda of communism. Survey of the current political events from the anti-communist point of view and immigrants' life chronicle" (editor's statement).

749. **RUSSKY GOLOS.   Russian Voice.**   1917–
        130 East 16th Street
        New York, New York 10003

        Editor: Victor A. Yakhontoff   Circulation: 2,584
        Sponsor: n.i.   Frequency: weekly
        Language: Russian   Subscription: $9.00

Provides general international, national, and local news coverage, plus coverage of Russian life in the United States.

750. **SOGLASIYE.   Agreement.**   1950–
        1019 South Longwood Avenue
        Los Angeles, California 90019

        Editor: Dimitri Frank   Circulation: 990
        Sponsor: Soglasiye Publishing Co.   Frequency: monthly
        Language: Russian   Subscription: $5.00

This anti-communist political magazine serves "special needs of the newcoming emigrants and special needs of Russian cultural activities in the U.S.A." (editor's statement).

751. STRANNIK. **Pilgrim.** 1945–
P. O. Box 206
Garfield, New Jersey 07026

Editor: A. V. Chubkowsky
Sponsor: Christian Evangelical Pentecostal Faith
Language: Russian
Circulation: 2,000
Frequency: quarterly
Subscription: n.i.

752. NOVOSTI TOLSTOVSKOGO FONDA. **Tolstoy Foundation News.** 1934–
250 West 57th Street, Room 1004-1030 (212) 247-2922
New York, New York 10019

Editor: Tatiana Schaufuss
Sponsor: Tolstoy Foundation, Inc.
Language: English and Russian
Circulation: 8,000
Frequency: semi-annual
Subscription: n.i.

News about current programs and progress reports on Tolstoy Foundation activities. Illustrated.

753. TSERKOVNAYA ZHIZN'. **Church Life.** 1934–
75 East 93rd Street
New York, New York 10028

Editor: Synod of Bishops of the Russian
      Orthodox Church
Sponsor: Synod of Bishops of the Russian
      Orthodox Church
Language: Russian
Circulation: 350
Frequency: irregular
Subscription: $3.00

Contains "information of Church events and commentary of ecclesiastical issues; publication of documents" (editor's statement).

754. VESTNIK OBSHCHESTVA RUSSKIKH VETERANOV VELIKOI VOINY.
Messenger of the Russian Veterans of World War I. 1926–
2041 Lyon Street
San Francisco, California 94115

Editor: Collegia
Sponsor: Society of Russian Veterans of
      World War I
Language: Russian
Circulation: 200
Frequency: irregular
Subscription: $.35/copy

The main objective of this publication is "to save memoirs of military character by members of the Society and other men of different Russian armies" (editor's statement).

755. ZAPISKI RUSSKOY AKADEMICHESKOY GRUPY C.W.A. **Transactions**
of the Association of Russian-American Scholars. 1948–
85-20 114th Street (212) 846-6410
Richmond Hill, New York 11418

Editor: Constantine Belousow
Sponsor: Association of Russian-American
      Scholars
Language: Russian and English
Circulation: 500
Frequency: annual
Subscription: $10.00

Contains articles by distinguished Russian and American specialists in various fields of scholarship.

756. ZNAMYA ROSSII. **The Banner of Russia.** 1946–
3544 Broadway
New York, New York 10031

Editor: Nicholas N. Chuhnov
Sponsor: n.i.
Language: Russian
Circulation: 1,200
Frequency: monthly
Subscription: $4.00

ZNAMYA ROSSII (cont'd)
This publication is "an organ of Russian independent monarchical thought dedicated to anti-communist political views" (editor's statement). It has articles on socio-political topics, both historical and current, relating to Russia and Russian emigres. Includes international news, a chronicle of Russian life, information on funds for emigres, and occasional political poems.

Russian Publications in English

757. ONE CHURCH.   1947–
c/o Rt. Rev. Feodor Kovalchuk
727 Miller Avenue
Youngstown, Pennsylvania 44502

Editor: Rt. Rev. Photius Donahue   Circulation: 2,500
Sponsor: Russian Orthodox Church   Frequency: bi-monthly
Language: English   Subscription: $5.00

Contains religious news and guidance for followers of the Orthodox faith. News articles include information on church life and political developments around the world. Editorials, sermons, commentaries on current events, and answers to doctrinal questions provide spiritual guidance. Book and record reviews are also included. Occasionally a Russian section is featured.

758. THE ORTHODOX HERALD.   1952–
116 Eastridge Drive
San Antonio, Texas 78227

Editor: V. Rev. W. Basil Stroyen   Circulation: 5,020
Sponsor: The Orthodox Herald, Inc.   Frequency: monthly
Language: English   Subscription: $1.25

Features news of the Orthodox world and spiritual guidance for followers of the Orthodox faith. It includes international news of recent events, religious discussions and quizzes, answers to doctrinal questions, and Bible reading schedules. Religious poetry, recipes for Russian dishes, and light articles are also included.

759. ORTHODOX LIFE.   1950–
Holy Trinity Monastery
Jordanville, New York 13361

Editor: V. Rev. Archimandrite Constantine Circulation: 1,250
Sponsor: Holy Trinity Monastery   Frequency: bi-monthly
Language: English   Subscription: $3.00

"Dedicated to the preservation of traditional Orthodox Christianity of the Russian Church" (editor's statement).

760. THE RUSSIAN REVIEW.   1941–
Stanford, California 94305   (415) 497-2067

Editor: Terence Emmons   Circulation: 1,850
Sponsor: Hoover Institution on War,   Frequency: quarterly
         Revolution and Peace   Subscription: $12.00
Language: English

Features scholarly materials in the fields of Russian history, politics and society, literature, and the arts. Provides a forum for work on Russian-American and Soviet-American relations. Publishing reviews by leading specialists of important new books from the United States, the Soviet Union, and other countries.

761. ST. VLADIMIR'S THEOLOGICAL QUARTERLY.   1952–
575 Scarsdale Road
Crestwood, New York 10707

Editor: John Meyendorf   Circulation: 1,300
Sponsor: St. Vladimir's Orthodox Theological Frequency: n.i.
Language: English   Subscription: $4.00

SCANDINAVIAN PRESS
See also Danish, Finnish, Norwegian and Swedish Presses

Scandinavian Publications in English

762. THE AMERICAN-SCANDINAVIAN REVIEW.　　　　　　1911–
　　　127 East 73rd Street　　　　　　　　(212) 879-9779
　　　New York, New York 10021

　　　Editor: Erik J. Friis　　　　　　　　Circulation: 6,100
　　　Sponsor: The American-Scandinavian Foundation　Frequency: quarterly
　　　Language: English　　　　　　　　Subscription: $7.50

Features articles on Sweden, Norway, Denmark, Finland, and Iceland, plus Scandinavian fiction
in English translation. Illustrated.

763. SCAN.　　　　　　　　　　　　　　　1940–
　　　127 East 73rd Street　　　　　　　　(212) 879-9779
　　　New York, New York 10021

　　　Editor: Gene G. Gage　　　　　　　　Circulation: 6,300
　　　Sponsor: American-Scandinavian Foundation　Frequency: monthly
　　　Language: English　　　　　　　　Subscription: free

Contains information on the activities of the American-Scandinavian Foundation.

764. SCANDINAVIAN-AMERICAN BULLETIN.　　　　1965–
　　　5817 Eighth Avenue
　　　Brooklyn, New York 11220

　　　Editor: Erik J. Friis　　　　　　　　Circulation: n.i.
　　　Sponsor: n.i.　　　　　　　　　　Frequency: monthly
　　　Language: English　　　　　　　　Subscription: n.i.

765. SCANDINAVIAN STUDIES.　　　　　　　1911–
　　　Department of Germanic Languages　　　(413) 545-0314
　　　University of Massachusetts
　　　Amherst, Massachusetts 01002

　　　Editor: Harald Naess　　　　　　　　Circulation: 915
　　　Sponsor: Society for the Advancement of　Frequency: quarterly
　　　　　　　Scandinavian Study　　　　　Subscription: $15.00
　　　Language: English

"Publishes articles of scholarly distinction on: 1) philological and linguistic problems of the
Scandinavian languages, medieval and modern; 2) the literatures of Denmark, the Faroes,
Finland (Finno-Swedish and Finnish), Iceland, Norway, and Sweden; and 3) the history,
culture, and society of the North. Each issue of the journal includes reviews of important
Scandinavica, news of periodical literature, and announcements of relevant local, national,
and international meetings. A comprehensive bibliography and an index are published
annually" (editor's statement).

SCOTTISH PRESS
Scottish Publications in English

766. HEATHER NOTES.　　　　　　　　　1961–
　　　408 Brady Lane　　　　　　　　　(512) 327-0875
　　　Austin, Texas 78746

　　　Editor: Harry Gordon　　　　　　　　Circulation: 750
　　　Sponsor: Scottish Society of Texas and　Frequency: semi-annual
　　　　　　　Scots of Austin　　　　　　Subscription: free
　　　Language: English

HEATHER NOTES (cont'd)

Promotes Scottish customs, dress, traditions, and "good fellowship and social contacts between Scots and Scot-Americans" (editor's statement). Contains news on Scottish activities in the Southwest, especially in Texas.

767. THE HIGHLANDER. 1962–

P. O. Box 397　　　　　　　　　　　(312) 381-5617
Barrington, Illinois 60010

Editor: Angus J. Ray　　　　　　　　Circulation: 4,700
Sponsor: Angus J. Ray　　　　　　　Frequency: quarterly
Language: English　　　　　　　　　Subscription: $3.75

News of Scottish-oriented activities in the United States and Canada.

768. THE RAMPANT LION. 1964–

2137 MacLarie Lane　　　　　　　　(215) 446-1242
Broomall, Pennsylvania 19008

Editor: Blair C. Stonier　　　　　　　Circulation: 550
Sponsor: Scottish Historic & Research Society　　Frequency: monthly
　　　　of the Delaware Valley, Inc.　　Subscription: $5.00
Language: English

Features articles on all phases of Scottish culture, travel, history, and other topics. Book review section included. Illustrated.

769. THE SCOTIA NEWS. 1964–

P. O. Box 3194, Grand Central Station
New York, New York 10017

Editor: L. Rutledge Franks　　　　　Circulation: n.i.
Sponsor: Scotia Publications　　　　　Frequency: monthly
Language: English　　　　　　　　　Subscription: $3.00

Promotes Scottish heritage and culture in the United States.

SERBIAN PRESS
Serbian and Serbian-English Publications

770. AMERIKANSKI SRBOBRAN.　American Serb Defender. 1929–

3414 Fifth Avenue　　　　　　　　　(412) 621-6600
Pittsburgh, Pennsylvania 15213

Editor: Robert Rade Stone　　　　　　Circulation: 9,600
Sponsor: Serb Nation Federation　　　Frequency: 3 issues/week
Language: Serbian and English　　　　Subscription: $16.00

The oldest and largest Serbian newspaper in America, and the official organ of the Serb National Federation. Its purpose is to keep alive the "traditions and ideals of Serbian people and to promote 100% Americanism" (editor's statement). Contains articles on people and events in the Serbian community in the United States and Canada and publicizes the national sports program. Illustrated.

771. RADNICKA BORBA.　Workers' Struggle. 1907–

14302 Schoolcraft
Detroit, Michigan 48227

Editor: Peter Slepcevich　　　　　　Circulation: n.i.
Sponsor: South Slavonian Federation of the　Frequency: semi-monthly
　　　　Socialist Labor Party　　　　Subscription: $2.00
Language: Serbian

Political party newspaper of the Yugoslav Federation of the Socialist Labor Party (Socialist Labor Party of America). Its articles are largely devoted to political theory, political news, and news of meetings and events. A column is regularly devoted to letters from readers.

772. **SERBIA.** Voice of Serbian Freedom Fighters. 1960–
    9663 Maple Avenue
    Gary, Indiana 46403

Editor: Momchilo Djujich
Sponsor: Serbian Chetniks
Language: Serbian

Circulation: 3,500
Frequency: bi-monthly
Subscription: n.i.

Anti-communist political magazine.

773. **SLOBODA.** Liberty. 1950–
    3909 West North Avenue   (312) 772-7878
    Chicago, Illinois 60647

Editor: Dragisha Kasikovich
Sponsor: Serbian National Defense Council
Language: Serbian

Circulation: 3,500
Frequency: weekly
Subscription: $15.00

Features political, cultural, and other articles of interest to Serbian community. Its aim is to preserve Serbian language and culture in the United States.

774. **SRPSKA BORBA.** The Serbian Struggle. 1946–
    448 Barry Avenue   (312) 549-6111
    Chicago, Illinois 60657

Editor: Slobodan M. Draskovich
Sponsor: Serbian Literary Association
Language: Serbian and English

Circulation: 16,160
Frequency: n.i.
Subscription: $12.00

The purpose of this publication is "to preserve, strengthen, and develop the spirit of freedom, individual and national, among all Serbs scattered in thirty-six countries of the free world, as well as in communist-occupied Yugoslavia" (editor's statement). Every issue has a review of world events. Articles cover historical, political, social, literary, theatrical, and other topics, and social and political aspects of the United States are also explained.

775. **YUGOSLOVENSKI AMERICKI GLASNIK.** Yugoslav-American Herald. 1909–
    235 Starbird Drive
    Monterey Park, California 91754

Editor: Mike Perko
Sponsor: Yugoslav-American Publishers, Inc.
Language: English and Serbo-Croatian

Circulation: 1,700
Frequency: monthly
Subscription: $5.00

Provides political, social, religious, and cultural news to all peoples of Yugoslav origin, attempting to give equal coverage to each. It includes information on activities and meetings, laws and rights in the United States, and churches and sports. It also advertises books and records available in Yugoslav languages.

Serbian Publications in English

776. **SERBIAN DEMOCRATIC FORUM.** 1972–
    2400 West Wilson Street, Apartment 303   (312) 271-6323
    Chicago, Illinois 60625

Editor: George M. Radoyevich
Sponsor: Serbian National Committee
Language: English

Circulation: 5,000
Frequency: irregular
Subscription: $5.00/copy

Political anti-communist organ featuring articles on the present political situation in Yugoslavia as well as historical materials pertaining to Serbia. Aims at a free and democratic Serbia.

SLOVAK PRESS
Slovak and Slovak-English Publications

777. AVE MARIA.   1916–
  2900 East Boulevard
  Cleveland, Ohio 44104

  Editor: Rev. Andrew Pier   Circulation: n.i.
  Sponsor: Slovak Benedictine Fathers   Frequency: monthly
  Language: Slovak   Subscription: n.i.

778. BRATSTVO.   Brotherhood.   1899–
  9 East North Street   (717) 823-2847
  Wilkes-Barre, Pennsylvania 18702

  Editor: Stephen J. Tkach   Circulation: 3,028
  Sponsor: Pennsylvania Slovak Catholic Union   Frequency: monthly
  Language: Slovak and English   Subscription: $2.00

This fraternal publication provides general news coverage of interest to the Slovak community. Includes reports of the Union's activities.

779. DOBRY PASTIER.   Good Shepherd.   1927–
  205 Madison Street
  Passaic, New Jersey 07055

  Editor: Rev. Joseph Altany   Circulation: 4,000
  Sponsor: Slovak Catholic Federation of America   Frequency: monthly
  Language: Slovak and English   Subscription: $2.00

780. FLORIDSKY SLOVAK.   Floridian Slovak.   1952–
  463 Jerpo Road
  Maitland, Florida 32751

  Editor: Charles Belohlavek   Circulation: n.i.
  Sponsor: n.i.   Frequency: quarterly
  Language: Slovak and English   Subscription: n.i.

This house organ includes news of special interest to retired Slovaks, especially articles on Slovak culture.

781. FRATERNALLY YOURS.   1914–
  24950 Chagrin Boulevard   (216) 464-8015
  Beachwood, Ohio 44122

  Editor: Anne M. Fusillo   Circulation: 33,050
  Sponsor: First Catholic Slovak Ladies   Frequency: monthly
             Association   Subscription: $1.50
  Language: Slovak and English

The name of this official organ of a fraternal insurance society has been changed from *Zenska Jednota* to *Fraternally Yours*. Articles cover the activities of the Association, Slovak culture, and Slovak leaders. Illustrated.

782. JEDNOTA.   The Union.   1891–
  P. O. Box 150   (216) 341-3355
  Middletown, Pennsylvania 17057

  Editor: Joseph C. Krajsa   Circulation: 37,866
  Sponsor: First Catholic Slovak Union   Frequency: weekly
  Language: Slovak and English   Subscription: $6.00

This is the official organ of the First Catholic Slovak Union of the United States and Canada. Its objectives are "to promote and preserve the Catholic faith of the Slovak people, their language, and identity. To provide news of the fraternity" (editor's statement). The largest Slovak newspaper in the United States. Illustrated.

783. **KATOLICKY SOKOL.** Catholic Falcon. 1915–
205 Madison Street (201) 777-2605
Passaic, New Jersey 07055

Editor: John C. Sciranka Circulation: 19,200
Sponsor: Slovak Catholic Sokol Frequency: weekly
Language: Slovak and English Subscription: $3.50

A fraternal publication.

784. **LISTY SVATEHO FRANTISKA.** Leaflets of St. Francis. 1924–
232 South Home Avenue
Pittsburgh, Pennsylvania 15202

Editor: Rev. Rudolf Dilong Circulation: 3,000
Sponsor: Slovak Franciscan Fathers Frequency: monthly
Language: Slovak Subscription: $3.00

Contents are primarily religious and spiritual, although some educational materials are also published.

785. **LUDOVE NOVINY.** People's News. 1905–
1510 West 18th Street
Chicago, Illinois 60608

Editor: Paul Hodos Circulation: 1,200
Sponsor: n.i. Frequency: weekly
Language: Slovak Subscription: $6.00

Provides general news coverage of special interest to Slovaks.

786. **MOST.** Bridge. 1954–
2900 East Boulevard
Cleveland, Ohio 44104

Editor: Nicholas Sprinc Circulation: 1,000
Sponsor: The Slovak Institute Frequency: quarterly
Language: Slovak Subscription: $5.00

This cultural and literary quarterly features articles on Slovak literature, fine arts, history, social sciences, and philosophy by Slovak authors outside Slovakia.

787. **NÁRODNÉ NOVINY.** National News. 1910–
516 Court Place (412) 281-5728
Pittsburgh, Pennsylvania 15219

Editor: Edward Kovac Circulation: 10,000
Sponsor: National Slovak Society Frequency: semi-monthly
Language: Slovak and English Subscription: $4.00

Emphasizes the events and activities of the fraternal organization.

788. **PRIATEL DIETOK.** The Children's Friend. 1911–
205 Madison Street
Passaic, New Jersey 07055

Editor: John C. Sciranka Circulation: 8,336
Sponsor: Junior Slovak Catholic Sokol Frequency: monthly
Language: Slovak Subscription: $1.00

A children's magazine.

789. SION. Zion. 1929–
157 McNeilly Road
Pittsburgh, Pennsylvania 15226

Editors: Rev. John Kovacik and Rev. Jan Adam   Circulation: 1,771
Sponsor: Slovak Zion Synod   Frequency: monthly
Language: Slovak and English   Subscription: $2.00

Official organ of the Slovak Lutheran Church in America.

790. SLOBODNÁ TRIBÚNA. Free Tribune. 1972–
P. O. Box 291   (212) 744-1367
New York, New York 10008

Editor: Jerry Jaroslav Krúpa   Circulation: 500
Sponsor: Slovak-American Cultural Center   Frequency: irregular
Language: Slovak   Subscription: $1.00/copy

Features cultural, educational, scientific articles of interest to the Slovak community in the
United States. Also includes information on Slovakia.

791. SLOVAK V AMERKE. Slovak in America. 1889–
P. O. Box 150
Middletown, Pennsylvania 17057

Editor: Draga Pauco   Circulation: 1,980
Sponsor: Joseph Pauco, Publisher   Frequency: weekly
Language: Slovak   Subscription: $6.00

The oldest Slovak newspaper in America, it provides coverage of national, international, and
local news of special concern to its Slovak readers. It "champions the right of Slovak people
to the re-establishment of their own national state" (editor's statement).

792. SLOVENSKY SOKOL. Sokol Times. 1905–
276 Prospect Street   (201) 676-0280
East Orange, New Jersey 07019

Editor: Karol Bednar   Circulation: 11,000
Sponsor: Slovak Gymnastic Union Sokol   Frequency: weekly
    of U.S.A.   Subscription: $6.00
Language: English and Slovak

Official publication of a fraternal and physical education organization, with articles on the
history and program of the Sokol movement, gymnastics, and sports.

793. SVEDOK. The Witness. 1906–
342 Boulevard of the Allies
Pittsburgh, Pennsylvania 15222

Editor: Rev. John J. Pelikan, Sr.   Circulation: 1,925
Sponsor: Synod of Evangelical Lutheran Churches Frequency: monthly
Language: Slovak   Subscription: $1.50

A magazine for Lutheran Slovaks.

794. SVORNOST. Harmony. 1912–
342 Boulevard of the Allies
Pittsburgh, Pennsylvania 15222

Editor: Rev. Thomas Harnyak   Circulation: 981
Sponsor: Catholic Slovak Brotherhood   Frequency: bi-monthly
Language: Slovak   Subscription: $1.00

A fraternal religious magazine.

795. ZIVENA. 1908
1235 Woodland Avenue, N.S.
Pittsburgh, Pennsylvania 15212

Editor: John Cieker   Circulation: 1,975
Sponsor: Zivena Beneficial Society   Frequency: monthly
Language: Slovak and English   Subscription: n.i.

A fraternal publication.

796. ZORNIČKA.   Morning Star. 1941
315 Oak Hill Drive
Middletown, Pennsylvania 17057

Editor: Edward Kovac, Jr.   Circulation: 5,000
Sponsor: Ladies Pennsylvania Slovak   Frequency: monthly
          Catholic Union   Subscription: $1.00
Language: Slovak and English

This fraternal monthly publishes general news and news of the Union. Illustrated.

Slovak Publications in English

797. CALVIN. 1907
342 Boulevard of the Allies
Pittsburgh, Pennsylvania 15222

Editor: Rev. George Virchick   Circulation: 1,000
Sponsor: Presbyterian Beneficial Union   Frequency: monthly
Language: English   Subscription: $1.25

Prior to June 1960 this publication had the title *Slovak Presbyterian*. Fraternal in nature, it publishes articles and reports on the activities of the Union.

798. SLOVAKIA. 1951
313 Ridge Avenue   (717) 944-9933
Middletown, Pennsylvania 17057

Editor: Joseph Paučo   Circulation: 2,600
Sponsor: Slovak League of America   Frequency: annual
Language: English   Subscription: $4.00

Features scholarly articles on history, culture, and economic and social affairs of the Slovaks in the United States and elsewhere. Book review section included.

799. SOKOL TIMES. 1905
P. O. Box 468   (201) 676-0280
East Orange, New Jersey 08862

Editor: Karol Bednar   Circulation: 11,000
Sponsor: Slovak Gymnastic Union Sokol   Frequency: semi-monthly
          in U.S.A.   Subscription: n.i.
Language: English

800. THE UNITED LUTHERAN. 1903
223 East Main Street   (412) 238-9505
Ligonier, Pennsylvania 15658

Editor: Daniel M. Zornan   Circulation: 8,000
Sponsor: United Lutheran Society   Frequency: monthly
Language: English   Subscription: n.i.

Fraternal publication.

SLOVENE PRESS
Slovene and Slovene-English Publications

801. AMERIKANSKI SLOVENEC–GLASILO K.S.K. JEDNOTE. American
Slovenian–Official Organ of the American Slovenian Catholic Union.   1891–
    6117 St. Clair Avenue   (216) 524-6263
    Cleveland, Ohio 44103

    Editor: Ernest Racic   Circulation: 15,500
    Sponsor: American Slovenian Catholic Union   Frequency: weekly
    Language: Slovenian and English   Subscription: $5.00

Provides general and local news of special interest to Slovenian readers, as well as fraternal news.

802. AMERISKA DOMOVINA. American Home.   1898–
    6117 St. Clair Avenue
    Cleveland, Ohio 44103

    Editors: James Debevec and Vinko Lipovee   Circulation: 9,000
    Sponsor: American Home Publishing Company   Frequency: daily
    Language: Slovenian and English   Subscription: $23.00

This publication, the oldest Slovenian daily, provides general national and local news of interest to readers, including coverage of national Slovenian organizations. The Friday edition has an English page.

803. AVE MARIA. Hail Mary.   1906–
    1400 Main Street   (312) 257-2494
    Lemont, Illinois 60439

    Editor: Father Fortunat Zorman   Circulation: 2,760
    Sponsor: The Slovenian Franciscan Fathers   Frequency: monthly
    Language: Slovenian   Subscription: $2.50

This Catholic monthly publishes materials about the Catholic faith and life, with a special news section entitled "The Church in the World." Its aim is to preserve the Slovenian language. Illustrated.

804. FRATERNAL VOICE.   1938–
    5809 West 38th Avenue   (303) 421-3320
    Denver, Colorado 80212

    Editors: Anthony Jersin and Mary Volk   Circulation: 3,982
    Sponsor: The Western Slavonic Association   Frequency: monthly
    Language: English and Slovenian   Subscription: $1.20

"The purpose of our fraternal publication is to help promote the growth of our Association and to unite our whole membership and develop fraternity, brotherhood and cooperation to the highest degree" (editor's statement). Illustrated.

805. NAS GLAS. Our Voice.   1910–
    6401 St. Clair Avenue   (216) 361-0886
    Cleveland, Ohio 44103

    Editor: Margot A. Klima   Circulation: 7,800
    Sponsor: American Mutual Life Association   Frequency: semi-monthly
    Language: English and Slovenian   Subscription: $2.00

Contains general news of interest to Association members–mainly social events sponsored by the organization. Some insurance news and features, ethnic news, senior citizen news.

806. NOVA DOBA.   New Era.   1925–
      6233 St. Clair Avenue
      Cleveland, Ohio 44103

Editor: Julia Pirc   Circulation: 8,578
Sponsor: American Fraternal Union   Frequency: semi-monthly
Language: Slovenian   Subscription: $1.50

This fraternal publication provides general news coverage.

807. NOVI SVET.   New World Herald.   1938–
      2032 West Cermak Road
      Chicago, Illinois 60608

Editor: Ludwig A. Leskovar   Circulation: 1,700
Sponsor: Novi Svet Publishing Company   Frequency: quarterly
Language: Slovenian and English   Subscription: $2.00

This quarterly features articles on educational topics and family life.

808. PROSVETA.   Enlightenment.   1906–
      2657 South Lawndale Avenue   (312) 762-4904
      Chicago, Illinois 60623

Editor: Louis Beniger   Circulation: 8,832
Sponsor: Slovene National Benefit Society   Frequency: daily
Language: Slovenian and English   Subscription: $15.00

This daily covers general national and international news of interest to the Slovenian community, as well as fraternal news.

809. ZARJA.   The Dawn.   1928–
      1937 West Cermark Road   (312) 247-2014
      Chicago, Illinois 60608

Editor: Corinne Leskovar   Circulation: 8,105
Sponsor: Slovenian Women's Union of America Frequency: monthly
Language: English and Slovenian   Subscription: $5.00

The objective of this official publication of the Slovenian Women's Union of America is to uphold "the ideals of sisterhood and perpetuate the traditions of the Slovenian nationality" (editor's statement). It features news and views of its membership and promotes the organization's causes and programs.

Slovene Publications in English

810. FRATERNAL VOICE.   1938–
      5809 West 38th Street   (303) 421-3320
      Denver, Colorado 80212

Editors: Anthony Jersin and Mary Volk   Circulation: 3,980
Sponsor: Anthony Jersin and Mary Volk   Frequency: monthly
Language: English   Subscription: free to members

Fraternal publication.

811. THE VOICE OF YOUTH.   1922–
      2657 South Lawndale Avenue   (312) 762-4904
      Chicago, Illinois 60623

Editor: Louis Beniger   Circulation: 11,350
Sponsor: Slovene National Benefit Society   Frequency: monthly
Language: English   Subscription: $3.00

A youth magazine.

SPANISH PRESS

Editor's Note: This section includes ethnic Spanish publications of Cuban Americans, Mexican Americans, Argentinian Americans, and Puerto Rican Americans, which are published in the United States.

Spanish and Spanish-English Publications

812. AMERICA SPANISH NEWS. 1953–
2448 Mission Street
San Francisco, California 94110

Editor: Felipe Marquez
Sponsor: n.i.
Language: Spanish and English

Circulation: 25,000
Frequency: semi-monthly
Subscription: n.i.

Provides general national, international, and local news coverage.

**813. AZTLÁN–INTERNATIONAL JOURNAL OF CHICANO STUDIES
RESEARCH.** 1969–
405 Hilgard Avenue (213) 825-2642
Los Angeles, California 90024

Editors: Reynaldo F. Macías, Teresa McKenna,
and Juan Gómez-Quiñones
Sponsor: Chicano Studies Center
Language: Spanish and English

Circulation: 2,000
Frequency: tri-annual
Subscription: $7.00

This interdisciplinary scholarly journal serves as a forum for research and essays related to Chicano studies. "Its focus is critical analysis, research, theory and methodology in the study of the Chicano as they relate to the group and to the United States and to Mexico" (editor's statement). Articles are on a variety of subjects, such as sociology, politics, history, law, economics, health, nutrition, bilingualism, art, theatre, education, etc.

814. BANCOS Y ECONOMÍA. **Banks and Economics.** 1973–
P. O. Box 013913 (305) 643-4220
Miami, Florida 33101

Editor: Luis Fernandez Walpole
Sponsor: Luis Fernandez Walpole
Language: Spanish

Circulation: 2,000
Frequency: monthly
Subscription: $2.40

Primarily publishes articles relating to socioeconomic affairs and to conditions of the Cuban exiles.

815. BERNALILLO TIMES. 1931–
P. O. Box B
Bernalillo, New Mexico 87004

Editor: Cruz Segura
Sponsor: Independent Publishing Company
Language: Spanish and English

Circulation: 720
Frequency: weekly
Subscription: $2.50

**816. BOLETIN INFORMATIVO DE LA ASOCIACIÓN ARGENTINA DE
DETROIT.** **Informative Bulletin of Argentine Association of Detroit.** 1970–
P. O. Box 81
Clawson, Michigan 48017

Editor: Juan C. Carioni
Sponsor: Argentine Association
Language: Spanish

Circulation: 200
Frequency: bi-monthly
Subscription: $2.00

Contains information on Argentinian community living in the Detroit area. Covers social and cultural events of interest to the Argentinian community.

817. BUEN HOGAR. Good Home. 1966–
5535 N. W. 7th Avenue
Miami, Florida 33127

Editor: Frank Calderon Circulation: 375,000
Sponsor: Continental Publishing Company, Inc. Frequency: monthly
Language: Spanish Subscription: $6.00

This family magazine provides articles on food, fashion, beauty, home furnishings, health and medicine, children and babies, horoscopes, family problems, along with novels and feature stories. Edited for the 18- to 35-year-old married women in the rising middle-income category. Covers all Spanish-speaking countries of Latin America, plus the United States.

818. EL CAMAGÜEYANO, INC. The Camagueyano, Inc. 1966–
P. O. Box 5164 (305) 573-8155
Miami, Florida 33101

Editor: María A. Crespí Circulation: 2,500
Sponsor: María A. Crespí Frequency: monthly
Language: Spanish Subscription: $12.00

This anti-communist magazine, which serves Cuban exiles from the Province of Camaguey, features historical and political articles. Illustrated.

819. CARACOL. Snail. 1974–
1151 Culebra (512) 734-5004
San Antonio, Texas 78201

Editors: Cecilio García-Camarillo and Circulation: 1,000
  Mia García-Camarillo Frequency: monthly
Sponsor: Texas Institute for Educational Subscription: $3.50
  Development
Language: English and Spanish

This bilingual journal was established to fill a "gap that exists in relation to the news media for Chicanos . . .to raise the consciousness of [the Chicanos] in the United States" (editor's statement). The point of view is strictly Chicano. Covers sociopolitical-economic affairs, literature, art, human interest stories, children's drawings, etc.

820. EL CENTINELA Y HERALDO DE LA SALUD. The Sentinel and
Herald of Health. 1895–
1350 Villa Street (415) 961-2323
Mountain View, California 94042

Editor: Tulio N. Peverini Circulation: 170,000
Sponsor: Pacific Press Publishing Association Frequency: monthly
Language: Spanish Subscription: $7.00

Along with international and national news coverage, this monthly publishes articles on religious liberty, temperance, health, and other topics.

821. CHICANO TIMES. 1970–
1903 Saunders (512) 224-2507
San Antonio, Texas 78207

Editor: José Luis Rodriguez Circulation: 21,406
Sponsor: n.i. Frequency: semi-monthly
Language: Spanish and English Subscription: $7.00

The newspaper's objective is "to represent the interests of the Mexican American community of Central and South Texas" (editor's statement). The paper advocates action against governmental programs that are seen as discriminatory against the Mexican-American population.

822. EL COMUNERO MESTIZO.   The Halfbreed Commoner.   1975–
2229 MacDonald Avenue   (415) 232-6050
Richmond, California 94801

Editor: Wilma Bonet   Circulation: 1,000
Sponsor: United Council of Spanish Speaking   Frequency: monthly
      Organizations, Inc.   Subscription: no rates set.
Language: Spanish and English

Primarily a community newsletter, *El Comunero Mestizo*, provides information on the activities of the confederation's member organizations, as well as other general information, such as consumer news and employment matters. Encourages community members to submit articles for publications.

823. EL CONTINENTAL.   Continental.   1925–
909 East San Antonio Street
El Paso, Texas 79901

Editor: Raul Cuellar   Circulation: 8,000
Sponsor: El Continental Publishing Company   Frequency: daily
Language: Spanish   Subscription: $16.00

The objectives of this daily are to provide "general information to the public with news from all over the world. This is a modern newspaper that works like any other regular daily in the U.S.A." (editor's statement).

824. CORPUS CHRISTI AMERICANO.
1012 Leopard Street
Corpus Christi, Texas 78401

Editor: P. R. Ochoa   Circulation: n.i.
Sponsor: Ochoa Newspapers   Frequency: weekly
Language: Spanish   Subscription: $10.00

This general newspaper contains articles, editorials, and announcements of interest to the Chicano community.

825. COSTILLA COUNTY FREE PRESS.   1948–
P. O. Box 116
San Luis, California 81152

Editor: Alfonso J. LaCombe   Circulation: n.i.
Sponsor: n.i.   Frequency: weekly
Language: English and Spanish   Subscription: $2.00

An independent weekly that publishes general and local news.

826. DE COLORES: JOURNAL OF EMERGING RAZA PHILOSOPHIES.   1973–
2633 Granite N. W.   (505) 242-8075
Albuquerque, New Mexico 87104

Editor: Jose Armas   Circulation: 1,000
Sponsor: Pajarito Publications   Frequency: quarterly
Language: English and Spanish   Subscription: $8.00

This quarterly publishes limited editions of the best in Chicano expression and thought. Its purpose is "to shape and create an aesthetic in the area of Chicano literature" (editor's statement).

827. EL DIARIO–LA PRENSA.   The Daily Press.   1913–
181 Hudson Street
New York, New York 10013

Editor: Sergio Santelices   Circulation: 109,000
Sponsor: El Diario Publishing Co.   Frequency: daily
Language: Spanish   Subscription: $50.48

EL DIARIO–LA PRENSA (cont'd)
This daily newspaper is published for the Spanish-speaking population of New York and surrounding areas. International, national, and local news coverage.

828. **DIARIO LAS AMERICAS.**   **The Americas Daily.**   1953–
      2900 N. W. 39th Street   (305) 633-3341
      Miami, Florida 33142

      Editor: Horacio Aguirre   Circulation: 54,397
      Sponsor: The Americas Publishing Co.   Frequency: daily
      Language: Spanish   Subscription: $24.00 (Miami);
                                      $48.00 (rest of U.S.)

Complete coverage of world, national, state, and local news, emphasizing Latin American
affairs.

829. **LA ESPAÑA LIBRE.**   **Free Spain.**   1936–
      231 West 18th Street
      New York, New York 10011

      Editor: Marcos C. Marí   Circulation: 2,500
      Sponsor: Confederated Spanish Societies of   Frequency: bi-monthly
              U.S.A.   Subscription: $5.00
      Language: Spanish and English

General news coverage of interest to the Spanish-speaking population.

830. **THE FORUMEER.**   1964–
      127 Graham Avenue   (408) 289-9439
      San Jose, California 95110

      Editor: E. David Sierra   Circulation: 7,500
      Sponsor: American GI Forum   Frequency: monthly
      Language: English and Spanish   Subscription: $10.00

To inform the Chicano GI of the activities within the organization, and to keep the general
public aware of Chicano activities in the United States.

831. **LA GACETA.**   **The Gazette.**   1922–
      2015 15th Street
      Tampa, Florida 33605

      Editor: Roland Manteiga   Circulation: 9,825
      Sponsor: La Gaceta Publishing Company   Frequency: weekly
      Language: Spanish, English and Italian   Subscription: $5.00

Devoted to general news coverage.

832. **GRAFICA.**   **Graphic.**   1947–
      705 North Windsor Boulevard   (213) 462-2481
      Hollywood, California 90038

      Editor: Armando del Moral   Circulation: n.i.
      Sponsor: Orbe Publications, Inc.   Frequency: bi-monthly
      Language: Spanish   Subscription: $5.50

This general interest magazine touches briefly on all topics–art, music, movies, sports, politics,
etc.

833. **EL HERALDO DE BROWNSVILLE.**   **Brownsville Herald.**   1892–
      13th and Adams Streets
      Brownsville, Texas 78520

      Editor: D. R. Segal   Circulation: 12,800
      Sponsor: Freedom Newspapers, Inc.   Frequency: daily
      Language: Spanish and English   Subscription: $26.00

834. EL HISPANO. The Spanish.   1966–
    900 Park Avenue, S. W.   (505) 243-6161
    Albuquerque, New Mexico 87102

    Editor: A. B. Collado   Circulation: 8,600
    Sponsor: El Hispano, Inc.   Frequency: weekly
    Language: Spanish   Subscription: $5.00

This weekly newspaper carries many ads and legal notices, as well as local news of special interest to the Spanish-speaking population. Includes local sports news and syndicated columns on women and entertainment.

835. EL INDEPENDIENTE. The Independent.   1885–
    114 Grand Avenue N. W.
    Albuquerque, New Mexico 87101

    Editor: Mary Beth Acuff   Circulation: 1,000
    Sponsor: Independent Publishing Company   Frequency: weekly
    Language: English and Spanish   Subscription: $3.00

"Legal newspaper containing political commentary and problems of the legal profession. . . . Our papers serve lawyers and political activists of all ethnic groups" (editor's statement).

836. LA JUSTICIA. Justice.   1933–
    1710 Broadway
    New York, New York 10019

    Editor: Anthony Lespier   Circulation: 83,000
    Sponsor: International Ladies' Garment   Frequency: monthly
            Workers' Union   Subscription: $2.00
    Language: Spanish

This monthly is "primarily an organ of union information. All aspects of union news. Also editorial comment on national and local issues. Political education, rights and responsibilities and involvement in community affairs" (editor's statement).

837. LA LUZ. The Light.   1971–
    360 South Monroe   (303) 388-5807
    Denver, Colorado 80209

    Editor: Daniel Valdes y Tapia   Circulation: 77,000
    Sponsor: La Luz Publications, Inc.   Frequency: monthly
    Language: English and Spanish   Subscription: $12.00

Hispano-oriented general interest pictorial magazine for people who want to know more about the life, literature, and culture of Hispano Americans (Mexican-Americans, Chicano, Puerto Ricans, Boricuas, Cuban-Americans, and other Latin Americans in the United States)" (editor's statement). Articles deal with such topics as education, history, politics, music, etc.

838. LA LUZ. The Light.   1931–
    8259 Niles Center Road
    Skokie, Illinois 60076

    Editor: Jorge J. Rodriguez-Florido   Circulation: 16,000
    Sponsor: National Textbook Company   Frequency: monthly
    Language: Spanish   Subscription: $4.00

A magazine for high school students of Spanish. Includes news articles of interest to teenagers, historical articles, short stories, cartoons, movie and book reviews, sports stories, and articles on the customs and culture of Spanish-speaking countries.

839. EL MUNDO DE NUEVA YORK. New York World. 1970–
115 East 69th Street
New York, New York 10021

Editor: Stanley Ross
Sponsor: El Mundo Enterprises
Language: Spanish

Circulation: n.i.
Frequency: monthly
Subscription: n.i.

This general magazine, aimed primarily at the Spanish-speaking population of New York City, contains local news of the more sensational type, state and national news, feature articles, and news from Spanish-speaking countries. Feature articles include some true-confession type material with quite sensational illustrations.

840. MUNDO HISPANO. Spanish World. 1970–
2448 Mission Street
San Francisco, California 94110

Editors: Felipe Marquez and Thomas Berkley
Sponsor: Alameda Publishing Company
Language: Spanish

Circulation: 10,000
Frequency: weekly
Subscription: $7.50

This weekly newspaper contains local, state, national, and international news, both general and of special appeal to Spanish-speaking population. Contains all regular newspaper features such as editorials, women's news, etc.

841. NOTICIERO DEL MOVIMIENTO SINDICAL LIBRE. Free Trade
Union News. 1945–
815 16th Street, N. W. (202) 637-5041
Washington, D. C. 20006

Editor: George Meany
Sponsor: AFL-CIO
Language: Spanish

Circulation: 15,000
Frequency: monthly
Subscription: free

Although this publication is sponsored by the AFL-CIO, its objectives are to reach the Spanish-speaking population. Provides coverage of international labor news.

842. NOTICIERO OBRERO NORTEAMERICANO. North American
Labor News. 1944–
815 16th Street, N. W. (202) 637-5041
Washington, D. C. 20006

Editor: George Meany
Sponsor: AFL-CIO
Language: Spanish

Circulation: 10,500
Frequency: semi-monthly
Subscription: free

Primarily intended for Spanish-speaking ethnics, this AFL-CIO publication covers American labor news.

843. LA OPINION. The Opinion. 1926–
1436 South Main Street (213) 748-1191
Los Angeles, California 90015

Editor: Ignacio E. Lozano, Jr.
Sponsor: Lozano Enterprises, Inc.
Language: Spanish

Circulation: 22,543
Frequency: daily
Subscription: $30.00

"*La Opinion* is a daily newspaper of general interest and content, published in the Spanish language. It covers local, national, and international news, with emphasis on news of particular interest to the Spanish-speaking community of Southern California" (editor's statement).

844. LA PALABRA DIARIA.   Daily Word.   1955–
Unity Village, Missouri 64065   (816) 524-3550

Editor: Martha Smock   Circulation: 35,000
Sponsor: Unity School of Christianity   Frequency: monthly
Language: Spanish   Subscription: $2.00

Includes short stories, poems, and meditations.

845. PALADIN & DON QUIXOTE.   1963–
21 East Santa Clara Street
San Jose, California 95113

Editor: P. C. Ramirez   Circulation: 5,000
Sponsor: MIM Diaz-Infante   Frequency: semi-monthly
Language: Spanish   Subscription: n.i.

This publication includes general and local news of interest to the Spanish-speaking community in California.

846. PIMIENTA.   Pepper.   1958–
1515 Northwest 7th Street   (305) 642-3633
Miami, Florida 33125

Editor: Efraim Caballero   Circulation: 101,200
Sponsor: Pimienta Publishing Corp.   Frequency: monthly
Language: Spanish   Subscription: $8.00

This male-oriented magazine is very similar to *Playboy* in format and content.

847. EL PORVENIR.   The Outlook.   1934–
200 East Third Street
Mission, Texas 78572

Editor: Rogelio Cantu   Circulation: 4,500
Sponsor: Border Printing Service   Frequency: bi-weekly
Language: Spanish   Subscription: n.i.

848. THE POST–EL INFORMADOR.   1967–
Box 489, 2973 Sacramento Street
Berkeley, California 94701

Editor: Thomas L. Berkley   Circulation: 40,000
Sponsor: n.i.   Frequency: monthly
Language: Spanish and English   Subscription: $7.80

This monthly provides general news and items of group interest.

849. LA RAZA.   1967–
P. O. Box 31004   (213) 261-0128
Los Angeles, California 90031

Editor: Raul Ruiz   Circulation: 1,500
Sponsor: El Barrio Communications Project   Frequency: monthly
Language: Spanish and English   Subscription: $12.00

Publishes articles on the cultural and historical contributions of the Chicano to the American society, with an analysis of the socioeconomic conditions of the Mexican-American. Contributors are Chicano workers, students, and professors.

850. REVISTA CHICANO-RIQUEÑA.   Chicano-Puerto Rican Review.   1973–
3400 Broadway   (219) 887-0111
Gary, Indiana 46408

Editors: Nicolás Kanellos and Luis Dávila   Circulation: 1,000
Sponsor: Indiana University Northwest   Frequency: quarterly
Language: Spanish and English   Subscription: $5.00

REVISTA CHICANO-RIQUEÑA (cont'd)
Devoted to Chicano and Puerto Rican literature, art, literary criticism, and book reviews.

851. **RIO GRANDE SUN.**   1956–
Box 790
Española, New Mexico 87532

Editor: Robert Trapp   Circulation: 2,979
Sponsor: Sun Company, Inc.   Frequency: weekly
Language: English and Spanish   Subscription: $4.00

This independent newspaper provides general and local coverage.

852. **EL SOL. The Sun.**   1968–
18566 Northridge Drive, P. O. Box 81   (408) 449-7708
Salinas, California 93901

Editor: Oscar S. Parodi   Circulation: 7,200
Sponsor: El Sol de Salinas, Inc.   Frequency: weekly
Language: Spanish   Subscription: $5.00

General newspaper covering international, national, and local news of interest to the Spanish-speaking community.

853. **TAMPA INDEPENDENT.   El Tampa Independiente.**
P. O. Box 1838
Tampa, Florida 33601

Editor: Robert L. Jerome, Jr.   Circulation: 1,496
Sponsor: Tampa Independent Publishers Frequency: weekly
Language: Spanish   Subscription: n.i.

854. **TEJIDOS.**   1973–
P. O. Box 7383
Austin, Texas 78712

Editors: René Cisneros and Elizabeth A. Leone   Circulation: 300
Sponsor: Tejidos, Inc.   Frequency: quarterly
Language: Spanish and English   Subscription: $6.00

"Bilingual journal for the expression of Chicano thought and creativity" (editor's statement). Published by Tejidos, a non-profit corporation devoted to the publication of Chicano art, the journal welcomes "all serious literary works, in any style or format–traditional, modern, or barrio" (editor's statement).

855. **TEMAS. Topics.**   1950–
1560 Broadway
New York, New York 10036

Editor: José de la Vega   Circulation: 78,200
Sponsor: Club Familiar, Inc.   Frequency: monthly
Language: Spanish   Subscription: $4.00

This publication is "a family magazine containing general information, special features, interviews, beauty and health topics" (editor's statement). Also covers entertainment news, women's features, etc.

856. **EL TIEMPO. The Times.**   1963–
116 West 14th Street
New York, New York 10011

Editor: Stanley Ross   Circulation: 45,000
Sponsor: n.i.   Frequency: daily
Language: Spanish   Subscription: $30.00

General coverage of local, national, and international news.

857. EL TIEMPO DE LAREDO. The Laredo Times. 1881—
111 Esperanza Drive (512) 723-2901
Laredo, Texas 78040

Editor: William H. Baker Circulation: 18,502
Sponsor: Laredo Newspapers, Inc. Frequency: daily
Language: English and Spanish Subscription: $28.00

"Standard daily newspaper. Spanish pages utilize local news copy, the A. P., and Copley News Service. No special interests or axes to grind" (editor's statement).

858. LA TRIBUNA DE NEW JERSEY. The New Jersey Tribune. 1962—
70 Kossuth Street (201) 589-3742
Newark, New Jersey 07101

Editor: Carlos G. Bidot Circulation: 60,000
Sponsor: La Tribuna de New Jersey Frequency: semi-monthly
Language: Spanish Subscription: $6.00

Contains information of interest to the Spanish-speaking population. Editorials are published on a variety of subjects—political, educational, economic, social, and others.

859. LA TROMPETA. The Trumpet. 1912—
905 Bluntzer Street
Corpus Christi, Texas 78405

Editor: Rev. Maurice M. Caldwell Circulation: 200
Sponsor: Christian Triumph Company Frequency: monthly
Language: Spanish Subscription: free

860. LA VERDAD. The Truth. 1937—
910 Francisca Street (512) 882-7853
Corpus Christi, Texas 78405

Editor: Santos de la Paz Circulation: 7,000
Sponsor: La Verdad Publishing Co. Frequency: weekly
Language: Spanish and English Subscription: $3.50

This publication contains heavily editorialized articles on labor, welfare, economics, education, etc. Covers events in Corpus Christi and surrounding areas.

861. THE VOICE. La Voz. 1959—
6201 Biscayne Boulevard
Miami, Florida 33138

Editor: George H. Monahan Circulation: 63,212
Sponsor: n.i. Frequency: weekly
Language: English and Spanish Subscription: $5.00

"*The Voice* is the official publication of the Catholic Archdiocese of Miami. Its news function is that of bringing developments within the Church to the people of South Florida. Also. . . emphasis on social action problems. . .articles concerning the plight of the poor, of migrants, of the Cuban refugees, the Spanish-speaking members of the younger generation who are estranged from society, etc." (editor's statement).

Spanish Publications in English

862. DEFENSOR-CHIEFTAIN. Socorro County News. 1904—
P. O. Box Q, 204 Manzanares N. E.
Socorro, New Mexico 87801

Editor: Robert Klipsch Circulation: 1,843
Sponsor: n.i. Frequency: semi-weekly
Language: English Subscription: $6.50

Primarily carries news of a local orientation, but also provides brief coverage of major national and international affairs.

863. EL GALLO NEWS. The Rooster.   1967
    1567 Downing   (303) 832-1146
    Denver, Colorado 80218

Editor: Rodolfo Gonzales   Circulation: 1,100
Sponsor: Crusade for Justice   Frequency: irregular
Language: English   Subscription: $3.50

Aimed at the Chicano community, this publication is militant in its approach. Deals with political and social affairs and provides coverage of Chicano activities.

864. THE JOURNAL OF MEXICAN AMERICAN HISTORY.   1970
    P. O. Box 13861 (UCSB)   (805) 968-5915
    Santa Barbara, California 93107

Editor: Joseph Peter Navarro   Circulation: n.i.
Sponsor: Joseph Peter Navarro   Frequency: monthly
Language: English   Subscription: $15.00

This journal "was formally incorporated in 1970 to do something about the scholarly neglect of the history of Mexicans in the United States" (editor's statement). The journal, which consists of articles, reviews, and selective bibliography, deals exclusively with Mexican-American history in the United States.

865. MANO A MANO.   1971
    3520 Montrose, Suite 216   (713) 524-0595
    Houston, Texas 77006

Editor: Editorial Board   Circulation: 400
Sponsor: Chicano Training Center, Inc.   Frequency: bi-monthly
Language: English   Subscription: $4.00

This is "a Chicano social service/mental health periodical" (editor's statement).

866. RIO GRANDE HERALD.   1923
    102 North Corpus, P. O. Box 452
    Rio Grande City, Texas 78582

Editor: Cris Quintxnilla   Circulation: 910
Sponsor: Starr County Publishing Company   Frequency: weekly
Language: English   Subscription: $6.50

General and local news coverage.

867. SANTA ROSA NEWS.   1924
    P. O. Drawer P
    Santa Rosa, New Mexico 88435

Editor: Darrel Freeman   Circulation: 1,800
Sponsor: n.i.   Frequency: weekly
Language: English   Subscription: $4.00

This weekly features general and local news of interest to the Santa Rosa community.

868. THE TAOS NEWS.   1959
    P. O. Box U   (505) 758-2241
    Taos, New Mexico 87571

Editor: Richard Everett   Circulation: 4,500
Sponsor: Taos Publishing Corp.   Frequency: weekly
Language: English   Subscription: $7.80

The objective of this weekly is to serve as a "primary local news source for county of 18,000 population, of which 65 per cent is of Spanish descent" (editor's statement). Occasional news and editorials in Spanish. Publishes legal notices in English and Spanish.

869. THE TIMES.   1935–
P. O. Box 856, 683 West Main Street
Raymondville, Texas 78580

Editor: A. R. Rodriguez   Circulation: 820
Sponsor: n.i.   Frequency: weekly
Language: English   Subscription: $3.00

General and local news for Americans of Spanish descent.

SWEDISH PRESS
See also Scandinavian Press

Swedish and Swedish-English Publications

870. THE LEADING STAR. Ledstjarnan.   1920–
1410 Fifth Avenue
Seattle, Washington 98101

Editor: Carl L. Helgren   Circulation: 3,600
Sponsor: Order of Runeberg   Frequency: monthly
Language: English and Swedish   Subscription: $1.50

This is the official organ of the international order of Runeberg, a fraternal order of Swedish-Finnish origin.

871. MUSIKTIDNING. Music Tidings.   1905–
6132 North Winchester Avenue   (312) 238-9500
Chicago, Illinois 60626

Editor: Gunnar A. Bloom   Circulation: 1,100
Sponsor: American Union of Swedish Singers   Frequency: monthly
Language: English and Swedish   Subscription: $3.00

Promotes teaching and cultivation of chorus singing, principally in Swedish.

872. NORDEN. The North.   1896–
8104 5th Avenue   (212) 238-4433
Brooklyn, New York 11209

Editor: Erik R. Hermans   Circulation: 1,385
Sponsor: Norden News, Inc.   Frequency: weekly
Language: Swedish and English   Subscription: $12.00

Contains news from Finland and Scandinavian countries and from different immigrant colonies in the United States and Canada, plus general news. "The main objective is to give the fewer and fewer immigrants a newspaper that is written in their mother tongue. This paper is the only news medium for Swedish-speaking people from Finland" (editor's statement).

873. NORDSTJERNAN-SVEA. The North Star-Svea.   1872–
4 West 22nd Street
New York, New York 10010

Editor: Gerhard T. Rooth   Circulation: 7,500
Sponsor: n.i.   Frequency: weekly
Language: English and Swedish   Subscription: $8.00

This weekly, the oldest Swedish newspaper in the United States, provides general national and local news coverage.

874. SVENSKA AMERIKANAREN TRIBUNEN. Swedish American Tribune. 1876–
5301 North Clark Street   (312) 878-1018
Chicago, Illinois 60640

Editors: Arthur B. Hendricks and Einar O. Enard Circulation: 16,500
Sponsor: Swedish American Newspaper Co.   Frequency: weekly
Language: Swedish   Subscription: $9.00

SVENSKA AMERIKANAREN TRIBUNEN (cont'd)
Provides extensive coverage of Swedish life in the United States, as well as general news coverage. Independent in religion and politics.

875. **SVENSKA POSTEN.**   Swedish Post.   1885–
      2228 First Avenue
      Seattle, Washington 98121

      Editor: Harry Fabbe   Circulation: 2,800
      Sponsor: Consolidated Press Printing Company   Frequency: weekly
      Language: Swedish   Subscription: $6.00

This weekly publishes international, national, and local news, with particular attention to events in Sweden and Swedish life in the United States.

876. **VESTKUSTEN.**   West Coast.   1885–
      435 Duboce Avenue
      San Francisco, California 94117

      Editor: Karin Person   Circulation: 1,994
      Sponsor: n.i.   Frequency: weekly
      Language: Swedish   Subscription: $6.00

877. **THE WESTERN NEWS.**   1888–
      1210 California   (303) 825-2305
      Denver, Colorado 80204

      Editor: Glenn D. Peterson   Circulation: 1,050
      Sponsor: Enoch Peterson   Frequency: semi-monthly
      Language: English and Swedish   Subscription: $4.00

Provides information on Swedish, Norwegian, Danish, and Finnish people and their clubs, lodges, and churches. Illustrated. Prior to 1941 was published in Swedish.

Swedish Publications in English

878. **BETHPHAGE MESSENGER.**   1913–
      Bethphage Mission   (308) 743-2401
      Axtell, Nebraska 68924

      Editor: Robert A. Turnquist   Circulation: 19,500
      Sponsor: Bethphage Mission, Inc.   Frequency: monthly
      Language: English   Subscription: free

Religious newsletter (Lutheran). Illustrated.

879. **CALIFORNIA VECKOBLAD.**   California Weekly.   1910–
      P. O. Box 3156 Terminal Annex
      Los Angeles, California 90054

      Editor: Mary Hendricks   Circulation: 2,200
      Sponsor: n.i.   Frequency: weekly
      Language: English   Subscription: $5.00

This independent weekly provides general and local news.

880. **EVANGELICAL BEACON.**   1931–
      1515 East 66th Street
      Minneapolis, Minnesota 55423

      Editor: George M. Keck   Circulation: 23,000
      Sponsor: Evangelical Free Church of America   Frequency: bi-weekly
      Language: English   Subscription: $5.00

This is the newsletter of the Evangelical Free Church, which was organized in Iowa in the 1880s as the Swedish Evangelical Free Mission. Contains news about church activities, religious articles, poetry, and other creative writing. Illustrated.

881. HERALD OF FAITH.   1934–
  P. O. Box 118
  Prairie View, Illinois 60069

Editor: Joseph Mattsson-Boze   Circulation: 6,950
Sponsor: Full Gospel Faith and Fellowship–   Frequency: monthly
          Herald of Faith, Inc.   Subscription: n.i.
Language: English

882. NEWS FROM SWEDEN.   1948–
  825 Third Avenue   (212) 751-5900
  New York, New York 10022

Editor: Eli L. Weisman   Circulation: 2,200
Sponsor: Swedish Information Service   Frequency: monthly
Language: English   Subscription: free

Features brief news on Swedish cultural, political, and economic life.

883. PACIFIC SOUTHWEST COVENANTER.
  P. O. Box 1007
  Turlock, California 95380

Editor: Virgil Hanson   Circulation: 5,689
Sponsor: Pacific Southwest Conference of the   Frequency: monthly
          Evangelical Covenant Church   Subscription: $5.00
Language: English

Carries religious articles and news concerning the Pacific Southwest Conference of the Evangelical Covenant Church. Illustrated.

884. SVITHIOD JOURNALEN.   The Svithiod Journal.   1898–
  5520 West Lawrence Avenue   (312) 736-1191
  Chicago, Illinois 60630

Editor: Harold Wennersten   Circulation: 6,025
Sponsor: Independent Order of Svithiod   Frequency: monthly
Language: English   Subscription: $1.00

A fraternal publication published in Sweden until 1940. Reports the social and charitable
activities of Svithiod lodges and other news of interest to the fraternity.

885. SWEDISH INSTITUTE YEARBOOK.
  639 38th Street
  Rock Island, Illinois 61201

Editor: n.i.   Circulation: 500
Sponsor: Augustana College   Frequency: irregular
Language: English   Subscription: n.i.

Consists of essays by Swedish authors on Swedish Americans and Sweden. Objective is "to
preserve elements of the Swedish heritage in America" (editor's statement).

886. THE SWEDISH PIONEER HISTORICAL QUARTERLY.   1950–
  5125 North Spaulding Avenue   (312) 583-5722
  Chicago, Illinois 60625

Editor: H. Arnold Barton   Circulation: 1,521
Sponsor: The Swedish Pioneer Historical   Frequency: quarterly
          Society, Inc.   Subscription: $7.00
Language: English

The purpose of the quarterly is "to record the achievements of the Swedish pioneers" (editor's
statement). Covers the history of Swedish community in the United States, with an emphasis
on the history of Swedish immigrants in the nineteenth century. Includes scholarly articles
and primary sources (diaries, letters, etc.) book reviews, genealogical notes, and news items
of interest to members of the Society.

887. SWEDISH STANDARD. Svenska Standaret. 1910–
1233 Central Street (312) 328-8500
Evanston, Illinois 60201

Editor: Donald E. Anderson Circulation: 27,000
Sponsor: Baptist General Conference Frequency: semi-monthly
Language: English Subscription: $6.00

Promotes the ministry of churches and boards of the Baptist Central Conference. Illustrated.

888. THE VASASTJÄRNAN. The Vasa Star. 1968–
3720 Daryl Drive (717) 898-8526
Landisville, Pennsylvania 17538

Editor: Ruth Peterson Circulation: 23,343
Sponsor: The Vasa Order of America Frequency: monthly
Language: English Subscription: $2.00

Reports news of organizational activities and promotes mutual cooperation between Sweden and the United States. Its aim is to preserve the Swedish cultural heritage in America.

889. VIKINGEN. Vikings. 1901–
157 East Ohio Street
Chicago, Illinois 60611

Editor: William A. Johnson Circulation: 9,100
Sponsor: Grand Lodge of Independent Order Frequency: monthly
  of Vikings Subscription: n.i.
Language: English

A fraternal monthly.

SWISS PRESS

Swiss Publications in German, French, Italian, and English

890. SWISS AMERICAN REVIEW. 1868–
608 Fifth Avenue (212) 247-0459
New York, New York 10020

Editor: Editorial Board Circulation: 2,500
Sponsor: Swiss Publishing Company Frequency: weekly
Language: English, German, French and Italian Subscription: $12.00

This weekly provides coverage of Switzerland (politics, culture, finance, local news, sports) and news of the Swiss in the United States (Swiss clubs, Swiss companies, and other). Also includes general and United States news. About half the paper is published in German.

891. SWISS JOURNAL. 1918–
548 Columbus Avenue
San Francisco, California 94133

Editor: Mario Muschi Circulation: 3,000
Sponsor: Swiss Journal Company Frequency: weekly
Language: English, German and Italian Subscription: $8.00

General news on Switzerland, the Swiss people, and Swiss organizations in the United States.

Swiss Publications in English

892. THE SWISS AMERICAN. 1869–
33 Public Square, Room 1008 (216) 771-2414
Cleveland, Ohio 44113

Editor: Anton Haemmerle Circulation: 3,600
Sponsor: The North American Swiss Alliance Frequency: monthly
Language: English Subscription: membership

THE SWISS AMERICAN (cont'd)
This monthly promotes fraternalism and good fellowship among the Swiss, Swiss-Americans and their descendants. Includes information on the social activities of various Swiss societies, financial reports, etc.

893. **SWISS AMERICAN HISTORICAL SOCIETY NEWSLETTER.** 1927—
Old Dominion University
Norfolk, Virginia 23508

Editor: Heinz K. Meier Circulation: 205
Sponsor: Swiss American Historical Society Frequency: 3 times/year
Language: English Subscription: $7.00 (membership)

Features scholarly articles on various aspects of the Swiss in America and Swiss-American relations. Also includes book reviews and society news.

SYRIAN PRESS
See **Arabic Press**

TURKISH PRESS
Turkish and Turkish-English Publications

894. **FLORIDADAN "TÜRK SESI."** "Turkish Voice" from Florida. 1974—
2217 Northeast 2nd Street (305) 943-6626
Pompano Beach, Florida 33062

Editor: Kaya Kocaman, President, Board of Circulation: 200
   Directors Frequency: monthly
Sponsor: Florida Turkish-American Association Subscription: n.i.
   for Cultural Exchange, Inc.
Language: Turkish and English

News from Turkey and about the Turkish community in the United States.

895. **NEWS FROM TURKEY.** 1965—
1472 Broadway (212) 524-3447
New York, New York 10472

Editor: M. Peker Circulation: n.i.
Sponsor: Turkish-American Association for Frequency: semi-annual
   Cultural Exchange Subscription: n.i.
Language: Turkish

896. **TÜRK EVI.** **Turkish Home.** 1970—
60 East 42nd Street (212) 682-8787
New York, New York 10017

Editor: Aykut Gorkey Circulation: 1,500
Sponsor: The McNaught Publishing Co. Frequency: monthly
Language: Turkish and English Subscription: $15.00

Features articles on social and cultural activities of Turkish-American societies and on American-Turkish relationships. Illustrated.

897. **TURKISH REVIEW.** 1970—
P. O. Box 7546
Pittsburgh, Pennsylvania 15213

Editor: n.i. Circulation: n.i.
Sponsor: Turkish Society of Pittsburgh Frequency: quarterly
Language: Turkish Subscription: n.i.

898. TURKIYE. Turkey. 1970–
7676 New Hampshire Avenue, Suite 120
Langley Park, Maryland 20783

Editor: Akif Leblebicioglu Circulation: 4,697
Sponsor: Turkiye Magazine and Publishing Frequency: quarterly
    Corporation Subscription: $15.00
Language: Turkish and English

This quarterly includes a broad range of general news articles on Turkey and Turkish activities in the United States.

Turkish Publications in English

899. TURKISH DIGEST. 1965–
2523 Massachusetts Avenue, N. W.
Washington, D. C. 20008

Editor: n.i. Circulation: 3,000
Sponsor: Turkish Embassy Office of the Press Frequency: monthly
Language: English Subscription: n.i.

UKRAINIAN PRESS
Ukrainian and Ukrainian-English Publications

900. AMERYKA. America. 1912–
817 North Franklin Street (412) 627-4519
Philadelphia, Pennsylvania 19123

Editor: Lew Shankowsky Circulation: 6,500
Sponsor: The Providence Association of Frequency: daily
    Ukrainian Catholics in America Subscription: $15.00
Language: Ukrainian and English

This is the only Ukrainian Catholic daily. It publishes news on international, national, and local events of special interest to Ukrainians, emphasizing developments within the Ukrainian Catholic Church. Cultural, educational, political, and other activities and events by Ukrainian organizations and individuals within Ukrainian communities in the United States, Canada, and Europe are also covered. Includes editorials, commentaries, letters to the editor, and by-lined articles on a variety of topics. There is a special English language edition.

901. ANNALY SVITOVOI FEDERATSII LEMKIV. Annals of the World
Lemkos' Federation.
P. O. Box 202
Camillus, New York 13031

Editor: John Hvosda Circulation: n.i.
Sponsor: World Lemkos' Federation Frequency: irregular
Language: Ukrainian Subscription: $7.00

Features articles covering all aspects of Lemko life (history, religion, art, economy, etc.), and also includes Lemko poetry and prose. It reflects the objectives of the World Lemkos' Federation, whose main task is "to do all possible it can to help Ukrainian Lemkos in Poland, to preserve interest in the Lemko affairs and their culture among the people of good will throughout the world" (preface to the first issue). Contains English summary of minor articles.

902. BIBLOS. 1955–
238 East 6th Street (212) 475-1190
New York, New York 10003

Editor: Nicholas Sydor-Czartorysky Circulation: 1,000
Sponsor: Nicholas Sydor-Czartorysky Frequency: quarterly
Language: Ukrainian Subscription: $4.00

BIBLOS (cont'd)
"This bibliographical magazine includes news items on Ukrainian publications outside Ukraine; bibliographical listings and brief book reviews" (editor's statement).

903. **BIULETEN'. Bulletin.**   1962–
P. O. Box 3295 Country Fair Station   (217) 356-4195
Champaign, Illinois 61820

Editor: Dmytro Shtohryn   Circulation: 300
Sponsor: Ukrainian Librarians' Association   Frequency: irregular
     of America   Subscription: free to members
Language: Ukrainian

This is the official organ of the Ukrainian Librarians' Association of America. Includes news on activities of the Association, bibliographical notes, and brief articles.

904. **EKONOMICHNO-HROMADS'KYI VISNYK. The Herald of the Economic
and Social Events.**   1975–
923 North Western Avenue   (312) 342-1447
Chicago, Illinois 60622

Editor: Mychailo Bida and others   Circulation: 2,000
Sponsor: The Association of the Ukrainian   Frequency: irregular
     American Merchants, Manufacturers Subscription: $5.00
     and Professionals in Chicago
Language: Ukrainian

Features articles on Ukrainian industrial and economic establishments in the United States, especially in Chicago, with news also on Ukrainian organizations. Illustrated.

905. **EKRAN. ILLUSTROVANYI, DVO-MISIACHNYK UKRAINSKOHO
ZYTTIA. Screen. Illustrated Bimonthly of Ukrainian Life.**   1960–
2222 West Erie Street
Chicago, Illinois 60612

Editor: A. Antonovych   Circulation: 3,000
Sponsor: Ukrainian School Societies of Chicago Frequency: irregular
Language: Ukrainian   Subscription: $4.00

This is an illustrated Ukrainian magazine for youth and adults. Illustrations represent historical, religious, cultural, and political events in the Ukrainian community in the United States and other countries.

906. **FENIKS–ZHURNAL MOLODYKH. Phoenix–Journal of Social and
Political Thought.**   1951–
P. O. Box 141
Riverton, New Jersey 08077

Editor: Nicholas G. Bohatiuk   Circulation: 1,000
Sponsor: The Michnowsky Ukrainian Students   Frequency: irregular
     Association   Subscription: $2.00
Language: Ukrainian and English

Includes articles on aspects of Ukrainian culture, history, politics, humanities, and social thought. Also contains occasional book reviews and news about the activities of the Michnowsky Ukrainian Students Association.

907. **HOTUJS'. Be Ready.**   1958–
144 Second Avenue   (212) 982-4530
New York, New York 10003

Editor: Lesja Chraplyva   Circulation: 1,000
Sponsor: Plast, Inc.   Frequency: monthly
Language: Ukrainian   Subscription: $3.00

Magazine for Ukrainian children who are members of the Plast youth organization.

908. HROMADSKYJ HOLOS.　Voice of the Commonwealth.　1941–
Box 218, Cooper Station
New York, New York 10003

Editor: Vladimir Levitsky
Sponsor: Ukrainian Publishing Association
Language: Ukrainian

Circulation: 1,600
Frequency: bi-monthly
Subscription: $2.50

This communist-oriented publication features articles on Ukrainian political and social events.

909. HUTSULIYA.　1967–
2453 West Chicago Avenue　(312) 276-3918
Chicago, Illinois 60622

Editor: N. Domashevsky
Sponsor: Hutsul Association, Inc.
Language: Ukrainian

Circulation: 1,150
Frequency: quarterly
Subscription: $7.00

Dedicated to the study of the Ukrainian ethnic Hutsul group, their land, history, art, and culture (editor's statement). Includes news on the activities of the Hutsul Association in the United States and Hutsul life in the Ukraine.

910. INFORMATYWNYJ LYSTOK OBJEDNANNIA UKRAJINSKYCH WETERYNARNYCH LIKARIW.　Information Bulletin Journal of the
Ukrainian Veterinary Medical Association.　1950–
2457 West Rice Street　(312) 384-4237
Chicago, Illinois 60622

Editor: Roman Baranowskyj
Sponsor: Ukrainian Veterinary Medical
　　　Association in U.S.A.
Language: Ukrainian

Circulation: 250
Frequency: quarterly
Subscription: free/membership

Contains veterinary medical articles, abstracts, and news from domestic and foreign veterinary medical literature, reports, and others.

911. KRYLATI.　The Winged Ones.　1963–
315 East Tenth Street
New York, New York 10009

Editor: Editorial Committee
Sponsor: Central Committee of Ukrainian
　　　American Youth Association
Language: Ukrainian

Circulation: 6,000
Frequency: monthly
Subscription: $5.00

This youth magazine features articles on Ukrainian history and culture and on current events in the Ukrainian community and the Ukrainian American Youth Association.

912. LEMKIVS'KI VISTI.　Lemko News.　1950–
P. O. Box 202
Camillus, New York 13031

Editor: John Hvosda
Sponsor: Organization for the Defense of
　　　Lemkivshchyna
Language: Ukrainian

Circulation: 2,200
Frequency: monthly
Subscription: $4.00

This Ukrainian newspaper is "devoted to the affairs of the Ukrainian ethnographic territory of Lemkivshchyna, as well as to the inhabitants thereof" (editor's statement). Serves Ukrainian Lemkos in the United States, Canada, and Europe.

913. HOLOS LEMKIVSHCHYNY.   The Lemko Voice.   1963–
149 Park Avenue   (914) 476-6503
Yonkers, New York 10703

Editor: Stephan Zeneckyj   Circulation: 4,000
Sponsor: The Kardaty Publishers   Frequency: monthly
Language: Ukrainian   Subscription: $4.00

This independent Ukrainian monthly is dedicated to Lemko affairs in the Ukraine, Poland, America, and other parts of the world. General and local news coverage is also provided. Anti-communist orientation.

**914. LIKARSKYI VISNYK. ZHURNAL UKRAINSKOHO LIKARSKOHO
TOVARYSTVA PIVNICHNOI AMERYKY.**   Journal of the Ukrainian
Medical Association of North America, Inc.   1954–
Two East 79th Street   (212) 288-8660
New York, New York 10021

Editor: Paul J. Dzul   Circulation: 1,200
Sponsor: Ukrainian Medical Association of   Frequency: quarterly
           North America, Inc.   Subscription: $12.00
Language: Ukrainian

Publishes scientific medical papers in Ukrainian. Includes Ukrainian medical terminology. Presents news about the activities of the Association.

915. LITOPYS BOYKIVSHCHYNY.   Journal Boykivshchyna.   1969–
2222 Brandywine Street   (215) 567-3186
Philadelphia, Pennsylvania 19130

Editor: Alexander Bereznyckyj   Circulation: 575
Sponsor: Association "Boykivshchyna"   Frequency: quarterly
Language: Ukrainian   Subscription: $4.00

Dedicated to the study of the Ukrainian Boikian ethnic group and the Boikian land (Boykivshchyna). Features historical and ethnological articles, and other relevant materials.

916. LYS MYKYTA.   The Fox.   1951–
4933 Larkins   (313) 842-7476
Detroit, Michigan 48210

Editor: Edward Kozak   Circulation: 2,800
Sponsor: "The Fox" Ukrainian Publishing Co.   Frequency: monthly
Language: Ukrainian   Subscription: $5.50

Satirical periodical with numerous illustrations and short stories.

917. MISIONAR.   The Missionary.   1917–
1825 West Lindley Avenue   (412) 329-7217
Philadelphia, Pennsylvania 19141

Editor: Sister M. Modesta   Circulation: 1,600
Sponsor: Sisters of St. Basil the Great   Frequency: monthly
Language: Ukrainian   Subscription: $4.00

Catholic religious magazine.

918. MISIYA UKRAINY.   Mission of Ukraine.   1957–
P. O. Box 38, Greenpoint Station   (212) 383-5019
Brooklyn, New York 11222

Editor: Valentyn Koval   Circulation: 2,500
Sponsor: Association for the Liberation of   Frequency: irregular
           Ukraine, Inc.   Subscription: $2.00
Language: Ukrainian and English

Features articles on political, cultural, and social topics related to Ukraine and to the activities of the Association. Anti-communist orientation.

919. MOLODA UKRAINA. 1951–
ODUM, 221 Edridge Way (301) 744-0168
Catonsville, Maryland 21228

Editor: Mykola Hawrysh Circulation: 1,300
Sponsor: Central Committee of the Ukrainian Frequency: monthly
   Democratic Youth Association Subscription: $6.00
Language: Ukrainian

Its objective is "to inform the Ukrainian public about the work of ODUM; to allow for the Ukrainian authors to publish their works preferably about the problems of young people. The subject areas covered range from poetry–both traditional and contemporary–to historical, political, and editorial essays" (editor's statement).

920. MYRIANYN. The Layman. 1968–
1219 North Avers Avenue
Chicago, Illinois 60651

Editor: Jurij Teodorovych Circulation: 1,000
Sponsor: n.i. Frequency: monthly
Language: Ukrainian Subscription: $6.00

Catholic lay magazine.

921. NARODNA VOLYA. Peoples Will. 1911–
440 Wyoming Avenue (717) 342-0937
Scranton, Pennsylvania 18503

Editor: Vasyl M. Verhan Circulation: 5,600
Sponsor: Ukrainian Workingmen's Association Frequency: weekly
Language: Ukrainian and English Subscription: $7.20

This fraternal publication features articles on past and present Ukrainian affairs (history, politics, literature, social issues), plus information on Ukrainian life in the United States and other parts of the world and on the activities of the Ukrainian Workingmen's Association. Each issue has an English supplement.

922. NASH SVIT. Our World. 1948–
98 Second Avenue (212) 777-1336
New York, New York 10003

Editor: Vyacheslav Davedenko Circulation: 3,310
Sponsor: Association of American Ukrainians Frequency: bi-monthly
   "Selfreliance" Subscription: $2.50
Language: Ukrainian

Journal of "Selfreliance," a cooperative fraternity. Features articles on Ukrainian economic life in the United States as well as the Association's activities.

923. NASHA BATKIVSHCHYNA. Our Fatherland. 1962–
133 East Fourth Street
New York, New York 10003

Editor: Sydir Krawec Circulation: 1,700
Sponsor: Batkivshchyna (Fatherland), Inc. Frequency: semi-monthly
Language: Ukrainian Subscription: $7.00

General national and local news of interest to the Ukrainian community of the Orthodox faith. Features articles on Ukrainian history, political life, culture, and religious life.

924. NASHE ZYTTIA. Our Life. 1944–
108 Second Avenue (212) 674-5508
New York, New York 10003

Editor: Ulana Liubovych Circulation: 4,330
Sponsor: Ukrainian National Women's League Frequency: monthly
   of America, Inc. Subscription: $9.00
Language: Ukrainian and English

NASHE ZYTTIA (cont'd)
Features organizational articles and articles on Ukrainian literature, folk art, and other topics. Each issue includes a separate children's section and a "practical section" (articles on hygiene, recipes, etc.). One section in the magazine is in English.

925. NAZARETH. 1971–
2208 West Chicago Avenue
Chicago, Illinois 60622

Editor: Editorial Board   Circulation: n.i.
Sponsor: Ecumenical Center of St. Atanazii   Frequency: monthly
     Velykyi   Subscription: $1.00/copy
Language: Ukrainian

Ukrainian Catholic missionary magazine.

926. NOTATKY Z MYSTECTVA.   **Ukrainian Art Digest.**   1963–
1022 North Lawrence Street   (215) 922-2647
Philadelphia, Pennsylvania 19123

Editor: Petro Mehyk   Circulation: 1,000
Sponsor: Ukrainian Artists' Association   Frequency: irregular
Language: Ukrainian   Subscription: $5.00

The purpose of this publication is to acquaint the reader with many aspects of art. "The emphasis is on Ukrainian art and its artists. Activities and works of students of the Ukrainian Art Studio are also included" (editor's statement). Color and black and white plates of paintings.

927. NOTATNYK.   **Diary.**   1961–
Box 2325, Grand Central Station
New York, New York 10017

Editor: L. Lyman   Circulation: n.i.
Sponsor: Notatnyk   Frequency: monthly
Language: Ukrainian   Subscription: $2.00

Features brief articles on Ukrainian affairs in the Ukraine and in other countries.

928. NOVA ZORYA.   **New Star.**   1965–
2208 West Chicago Avenue   (312) 772-1919
Chicago, Illinois 60622

Editor: Rev. Jaroslav Swyschuk   Circulation: 6,000
Sponsor: St. Nicholas Diocese Press   Frequency: weekly
Language: Ukrainian and English   Subscription: $6.00

This Ukrainian Catholic weekly includes articles on Catholic and other churches, education, religion, and Ukrainian culture. One section is published in English.

929. NOVI NAPRYAMY.   **New Directions.**   1968–
140-142 Second Avenue
New York, New York 10003

Editor: Alexander Motyl   Circulation: 2,000
Sponsor: n.i.   Frequency: quarterly
Language: Ukrainian   Subscription: $3.50

This independent Ukrainian youth magazine serves as an open forum for the discussion of political, cultural, and other matters of interest to the North American Ukrainian community.

930. OVYD.   **Horizon.**   1949–
2226 West Chicago Avenue   (312) 384-3868
Chicago, Illinois 60622

Editor: Mykola Denysiuk   Circulation: 1,200
Sponsor: Mykola Denysiuk Publishing Company   Frequency: quarterly
Language: Ukrainian   Subscription: $4.00

OVYD (cont'd)
Contains literary works (poetry and short stories), articles on Ukrainian literature and culture, art, politics, and social issues. Illustrated.

931. **OZNAKY NASHOHO CHASU.**   **Signs of our Time.**   1930–
    1350 Villa Street
    Mountain View, California 94040

Editor: Nicholas Ilchuk	Circulation: 3,500
Sponsor: Pacific Press Publishing Association	Frequency: monthly
Language: Ukrainian	Subscription: $4.00

This religious magazine is dedicated to the interpretation of the Bible.

932. **PISLANETS' PRAVDY.**   **Messenger of Truth.**   1927–
    247 East Roland Road, Parkside
    Chester, Pennsylvania 19015

Editor: Leon Zabko-Potapovich	Circulation: 1,000
Sponsor: Ukrainian Baptist Convention in	Frequency: bi-monthly
the U.S.A.	Subscription: $3.00
Language: Ukrainian	

This is the official organ of the Ukrainian Baptist Churches outside the Ukraine. It includes articles on religion, education, and other topics relevant to Ukrainian Baptists.

933. **PRAVNYCHYI VISNYK.**   **Law Journal.**   1955–
    536 East 14th Street   (212) 677-5963
    New York, New York 10003

Editor: Editorial Board	Circulation: 500
Sponsor: The Ukrainian Lawyers' Organization	Frequency: irregular
in the U. S.	Subscription: n.i.
Language: Ukrainian	

Contains scholarly articles on Ukrainian law and history, book reviews, and bibliographies. Resumes in English.

934. **PRAVOSLAVNYI UKRAINETS'.**   **Orthodox Ukrainian.**   1952–
    2710 West Iowa Street
    Chicago, Illinois 60622

Editor: Alexander Bykowetz	Circulation: 700
Sponsor: Ukrainian Autocephalous Church	Frequency: quarterly
in the U. S. A.	Subscription: n.i.
Language: Ukrainian	

Official organ of the Ukrainian Autocephalous Church in the U. S. A.

935. **PRYZMA.**   **Prism.**   1974–
    P. O. Box 40121   (301) 439-1573
    Washington, D. C. 20016

Editor: Eugene M. Iwanciw	Circulation: 4,000
Sponsor: Federation of Ukrainian Student	Frequency: monthly
Organizations of America, Inc.	Subscription: $4.00
(SUSTA)	
Language: Ukrainian and English	

Provides news on Ukrainian student life in the United States and throughout the world.

936. **SAMOSTIJNA UKRAINA.**   **Independent Ukraine.**   1948–
    2315 West Chicago Avenue   (312) 276-0066
    Chicago, Illinois 60622

Editor: Denys Kwitkowskyj	Circulation: 1,015
Sponsor: Organization for the Rebirth of Ukraine	Frequency: bi-monthly
Language: Ukrainian	Subscription: $10.00

SAMOSTIJNA UKRAINA (cont'd)

This periodical is "devoted to Ukrainian affairs in Ukraine and abroad. Includes articles on Ukrainian history, political life, culture, and social issues, as well as information on the activities and ideology of the Ukrainian Nationalist Organizations" (editor's statement).

937. **SHLAKH.   The Way.**   1940–
    805 North Franklin Street
    Philadelphia, Pennsylvania 19123

Editor: Lew Mydlowskyj   Circulation: 12,356
Sponsor: Apostolate, Inc.   Frequency: weekly
Language: Ukrainian and English   Subscription: $5.00

The main objective of this Ukrainian Catholic weekly is to "support the religious and national education of Ukrainians in the U. S. A." (editor's statement).

938. **SUMIVETZ.**   1953–
    315 East Tenth Street
    New York, New York 10009

Editor: D. Motruk   Circulation: n.i.
Sponsor: Ukrainian American Youth   Frequency: irregular
            Association   Subscription: n.i.
Language: Ukrainian

A Ukrainian youth magazine.

939. **SVOBODA. UKRAINSKYI SHCHODENNYK.**   **Liberty. Ukrainian Daily.** 1893–
    81-83 Grand Street   (201) 434-0237
    Jersey City, New Jersey 07303

Editor: Anthony Dragan   Circulation: 20,500
Sponsor: Ukrainian National Association, Inc.   Frequency: daily
Language: Ukrainian   Subscription: $30.00

The oldest Ukrainian daily in the United States, this publication provides international, national, and local news coverage, and features articles on Ukrainian political, cultural, religious, and social life in America and in the world. It "considers the Ukrainian people's current status as that of a subjugated and oppressed nation, upholds Ukraine's rights and aspirations for freedom and independence" (editor's statement). The paper maintains a non-partisan political view.

940. **TEREM. PROBLEMY UKRAINSKOI KULTURY, NEPERIODYCHNYI
    ILIUSTROVANYI ZHURNAL.**   **Terem. Problems of Ukrainian Culture.**   1962–
    13588 Sunset Street
    Detroit, Michigan 48212

Editor: Yurij Tys-Krochmaluk   Circulation: 1,400
Sponsor: Institute of Ukrainian Culture   Frequency: irregular
Language: Ukrainian   Subscription: $3.50/copy

This is the official publication of the Institute of Ukrainian Culture. Its purpose is "to gather information on the status and growth of Ukrainian culture in countries of the free world" (editor's statement). Each issue is devoted to an individual who has contributed to "the constantly expanding sphere of Ukrainian culture in the Western Hemisphere." Covers literature, art, and social sciences.

941. **TOVARYSTVO ABSOL'VENTIV UHA-UTHI. BIULETEN'.   Bulletin for
    the Alumni of the Ukrainian Technological Academy–Ukrainian Technical
    University (Ukrainska Hospodarska Akademia and Ukrainskyi Technichno
    Hospodarskyi Instytut).**   1956–
    136-19 Cherry Avenue
    Flushing, New York 11355

TOVARYSTVO ABSOL'VENTIV UHA-UTHI. BIULETEN' (cont'd)
Editor: Alex Kozlowsky
Sponsor: Association of the Alumni of the
    Ukrainian Technological Academy –
    Ukrainian Technical University
Language: Ukrainian

Circulation: 400
Frequency: irregular
Subscription: $2.00

An alumni publication.

942. TOVARYSTVO UKRAINSKYCH INZHINERIV AMERYKY BIULETEN.
Bulletin of the Ukrainian Engineers Society of America.   1969–
    2 East 79th Street   (212) 535-7676
    New York, New York 10021

Editor: Eugene Ivashkiv
Sponsor: Ukrainian Engineers Society of
    America
Language: Ukrainian

Circulation: 500
Frequency: quarterly
Subscription: $2.00

Features technological articles, news of the activities of UES members, and organization news.

943. TRYZUB.   Trident.   1960–
    202 First Avenue
    New York, New York 10009

Editor: Z. Ivanyshyn   Circulation: 750
Sponsor: Ukrainsko Nacionalno-Derzhavnyi Soiuz   Frequency: bi-monthly
Language: Ukrainian   Subscription: $3.00

This political magazine of democratic orientation includes articles on Ukrainian history and political life.

944. TSERKOVNY VISNYK.   Church Herald.   1968–
    2245 West Superior Street   (312) 829-5209
    Chicago, Illinois 60612

Editor: Very Rev. Marian Butrynsky
Sponsor: Saints Volodymyr & Olha Ukrainian
    Catholic Parish
Language: Ukrainian

Circulation: 1,800
Frequency: semi-monthly
Subscription: $5.00

"Promotes the cause of Ukrainian Catholic Church autonomy (Patriarchate), defends the traditions and the rite in that Church" (editor's statement). Covers church events in Ukraine, and the United States, and parish events.

945. TSERKVA I ZHYTTIA.   Church and Life.   1957–
    1055 North Wolcott Avenue
    Chicago, Illinois 60622

Editor: A. I. Jaremenko
Sponsor: Ukrainian Orthodox Brotherhood of
    Metropolitan Vasil Lypkivsky
Language: Ukrainian

Circulation: 1,000
Frequency: bi-monthly
Subscription: $2.00

This Orthodox religious magazine supports the Ukrainian Orthodox Autocephalous Church. Includes articles on church history, biographies of prominent Orthodox leaders, and other relevant religious materials.

946. UKRAINSKA KNYHA.   Ukrainian Book.   1971–
    4800 North 12th Street   (215) 457-0527
    Philadelphia, Pennsylvania 19141

Editor: Bohdan Romanenchuk   Circulation: 1,150
Sponsor: Kyiv Publishing   Frequency: quarterly
Language: Ukrainian   Subscription: $5.00

UKRAINSKA KNYHA (cont'd)
This Ukrainian bibliographical quarterly features articles on historical bibliography, reviews, and retrospective bibliographies dealing with special topics (literature, history, and others).

947. UKRAINSKE ISTORYCHNE TOVARYSTVO. BIULETEN'. Ukrainian Historical Association Bulletin.   1967–
573 Northeast 102nd Street
Miami Shores, Florida 33138

Editor: Roman O. Klimkevich   Circulation: 250
Sponsor: Ukrainian Historical Association   Frequency: irregular
Language: Ukrainian   Subscription: membership

Official publication of the Ukrainian Historical Association. Includes materials on the activities of the Association and its members, as well as some articles on the present status of Ukrainian scholarship in the United States and in other countries.

948. UKRAINSKE NARODNE SLOVO.   Ukrainian National Word.   1915–
P. O. Box 1948   (412) 261-2807
Pittsburgh, Pennsylvania 15230

Editor: Wolodymyr Masur   Circulation: 5,000
Sponsor: Ukrainian National Aid Association   Frequency: semi-monthly
            of America   Subscription: n.i.
Language: Ukrainian and English

This fraternal organ includes information on activities of various Ukrainian organizations in the United States. One section is published in English.

949. UKRAINSKE PRAVOSLAVNE SLOVO.   Ukrainian Orthodox Word.   1950–
P. O. Box 495
South Bound Brook, New Jersey 08880

Editor: Rev. M. Zemlachenko   Circulation: 2,000
Sponsor: Ukrainian Orthodox Church of the   Frequency: monthly
            U. S. A.   Subscription: $5.00
Language: Ukrainian

This is the official organ of the Ukrainian Orthodox Church in the United States. It features articles on the Orthodox Church and religious education. There is a separate news section on the Ukrainian Orthodox Church and its activities.

950. UKRAINSKE ZHYTTIA.   Ukrainian Life.   1955–
2534 West Chicago Avenue
Chicago, Illinois 60622

Editor: G. Stepowy   Circulation: 1,500
Sponsor: Ukrainian Life, Inc.   Frequency: semi-monthly
Language: Ukrainian   Subscription: $5.00

This independent weekly publishes articles on political, cultural, and social events in the Ukraine and in other parts of the world. Promotes "democratic ideas and philosophy" (editor's statement).

951. UKRAINSKI VISTI.   Ukrainian News.   1920–
85 East Fourth Street   (212) 473-1762
New York, New York 10003

Editor: Leon Tolopko   Circulation: 1,670
Sponsor: Ukrainian Daily News, Inc.   Frequency: weekly
Language: Ukrainian   Subscription: $5.00

General and local news. Communist orientation.

952. UKRAINSKYI FILATELIST. The Ukrainian Philatelist. 1951–
4176 Spring Crest Drive
Cleveland, Ohio 44144

Editor: Stepan Kikta
Sponsor: Society of Ukrainian Philatelists, Inc.
Language: Ukrainian

Circulation: 500
Frequency: irregular
Subscription: $5.00

Includes articles on Ukrainian stamps, descriptions of individual stamp collections, medals, and other related topics. The objective is "to bring together Ukrainian philatelists all over the world and to keep the level of interest in this field growing" (editor's statement).

953. UKRAINSKYI HOSPODARNYK. The Ukrainian Economist. 1954–
47 Ellery Avenue
Irvington, New Jersey 07111

Editor: Mykola Yelychkivsky
Sponsor: n.i.
Language: Ukrainian and English

Circulation: 500
Frequency: irregular
Subscription: $2.00

This journal of Ukrainian economists in the United States features articles on the economic development of the Ukrainian SSR, history of the Ukrainian economy, etc.

954. UKRAINSKYI ISTORYK. Ukrainian Historian. 1963–
P. O. Box 312
Kent, Ohio 44240

Editor: Lubomyr R. Wynar
Sponsor: Ukrainian Historical Association
Language: Ukrainian and English

Circulation: 1,000
Frequency: quarterly
Subscription: $15.00

The official journal of the Ukrainian Historical Association, this quarterly is devoted to the study of East European and Ukrainian history, emphasizing political, social, and cultural history. A special section includes articles on auxiliary historical sciences and archival materials. Reviews and bibliographical notes are included in each issue. The major scholarly journal of Ukrainian history outside the Soviet Ukraine.

955. UKRAINSKYI PRAVOSLAVNYI VISNYK. Ukrainian Orthodox Herald. 1933–
90-34 139th Street
Jamaica, New York 11435

Editor: Very Rev. Ivan Tkaczuk
Sponsor: Ukrainian Orthodox Church of
U. S. A. and Canada
Language: Ukrainian and English

Circulation: 1,000
Frequency: quarterly
Subscription: $2.00

Official organ of the Ukrainian Orthodox Church in America in the jurisdiction of the Ecumenical Patriarch. Includes articles on theological and educational matters.

**956. UKRAINSKYI ZHURNALIST. BIULETEN SPILKY UKRAINSKYCH
ZHURNALISTIV AMERYKY.** The Ukrainian Journalist. 1967–
14 Peck Avenue
Newark, New Jersey 07107

Editors: Roman Kryshtalskyj, Jaroslaw Shawiak,
and M. Dolnyckyj
Sponsor: Ukrainian Journalist's Association
of America
Language: Ukrainian

Circulation: 135
Frequency: irregular
Subscription: n.i.

Articles on journalism and events of interest to Association members.

957. UKRAJINSKE KOZATSTVO.   Ukrainian Cossackdom.   1968–
2100 West Chicago Avenue   (312) 276-5171
Chicago, Illinois 60622

Editor: Antin Kushchynskyj   Circulation: 1,000
Sponsor: Ukrainian Free Cossackdom Veterans   Frequency: quarterly
       Brotherhood   Subscription: $6.00
Language: Ukrainian

Magazine of Ukrainian veterans dedicated to the dissemination of the ideas of Ukrainian Cossacks. Contains articles on military Ukrainian history, Cossack traditions, and the activities of the "Ukrainian Free Cossacks Brotherhood."

958. VESELKA.   The Rainbow.   1954–
81-83 Grand Street   (201) 434-0237
Jersey City, New Jersey 07303

Editor: Wolodymyr Barahura   Circulation: 3,000
Sponsor: Ukrainian National Association   Frequency: monthly
Language: Ukrainian   Subscription: $4.00

This illustrated children's monthly magazine includes materials for pre-school and school age children (e.g., stories, fairy tales, puzzles, etc.). "The content of the magazine is designed to cultivate and preserve the Ukrainian spiritual heritage" (editor's statement).

959. VILNA UKRAINA.   Free Ukraine.   1953–
P. O. Box 4, Peter Stuyvesant Station
New York, New York 10009

Editor: Editorial Board   Circulation: 700
Sponsor: Ukrainian Free Society of America   Frequency: irregular
Language: Ukrainian   Subscription: $5.00

This quarterly political magazine features articles on Ukrainian history, politics, and social issues. Also has a book review section. Supports Ukrainian socialist ideology.

960. VIRA I NAUKA.   Faith and Science.   1962–
101 Cambridge Road   (215) 874-4976
Brookhaven, Pennsylvania 19015

Editor: Rev. John Berkuta   Circulation: 700
Sponsor: privately sponsored   Frequency: bi-monthly
Language: Ukrainian   Subscription: $4.00

The objective of this religious magazine is to provide "religious teaching along with scientific and educational news" (editor's statement).

961. VISNYK.   The Herald.   1947–
P. O. Box 304, Cooper Station   (212) 982-1170
New York, New York 10003

Editor: Board of Editors   Circulation: 2,000
Sponsor: Organization for Defense of Four   Frequency: monthly
       Freedoms for Ukraine, Inc.   Subscription: $6.00
Language: Ukrainian

This political monthly contains articles on Ukrainian political life, history, culture, and social issues. Supports the ideology of the Ukrainian Nationalist Organization.

962. VISTI UKRAINSKYKH INZHINERIV.   Ukrainian Engineering News.   1949–
Two East 79th Street   (212) 535-7676
New York, New York 10021

Editor: S. G. Prociuk   Circulation: 1,000
Sponsor: Ukrainian Engineers' Society of America   Frequency: quarterly
Language: Ukrainian   Subscription: $5.00

VISTI UKRAINSKYKH INZHINERIV (cont'd)
Includes original research papers in the field of technical sciences and articles on technological and economic developments in the Ukraine. Includes a book review section and current news on advanced technology. Section on English-Ukrainian technical dictionary.

963. **VISTI UVAN.** News of Academy. 1970–
206 West 100th Street (212) 222-1866
New York, New York 10025

Editor: Alexander Dombrovsky Circulation: 1,000
Sponsor: The Ukrainian Academy of Arts and Frequency: irregular
Sciences in the U. S. Subscription: free to members
Language: Ukrainian

Features articles on the activity of the Ukrainian Academy, biographical articles, bibliographies, and other news items.

964. **YEVANHELSKY RANOK.** Evangelical Morning. 1905–
5610 Trowbridge Drive (404) 394-7795
Dunwoody, Georgia 30338

Editor: Rev. Wladimir Borowsky Circulation: 700
Sponsor: Ukrainian Evangelical Alliance of Frequency: quarterly
North America Subscription: $3.00
Language: Ukrainian

Official organ of the Ukrainian Evangelical Alliance. Carries articles on religious and educational topics.

965. **ZA PATRIARCHAT.** For the Patriarchate. 1967–
P. O. Box 11012
Philadelphia, Pennsylvania 19141

Editor: Stephan Procyh Circulation: 1,000
Sponsor: Society for Promotion of the Frequency: quarterly
Patriarchal System in the Subscription: $2.00
Ukrainian Catholic Church
Language: Ukrainian

Features historical and current materials on the status of the Ukrainian Catholic Church. Supports the establishment of Ukrainian Catholic Patriarchate.

966. **ZHYTTIA I SHKOLA.** Life and School. 1954–
418 West Nittany Avenue
State College, Pennsylvania 16801

Editor: Wasyl Luciw Circulation: 1,000
Sponsor: n.i. Frequency: bi-monthly
Language: Ukrainian Subscription: $4.00

This publication consists mainly of reprinted older articles from various Ukrainian periodicals on Ukrainian culture, history, bibliography and other subjects. It also carries original articles on the same subjects.

Ukrainian Publications in English

967. **AMERYKA.** America.
817 North Franklin Street (215) 627-4519
Philadelphia, Pennsylvania 19123

Editor: Lew Shankovsky Circulation: 6,500
Sponsor: Providence Association of Ukrainian Frequency: weekly
Catholics Subscription: $4.00
Language: English

Weekly English supplement of Ukrainian daily, *Ameryka* (see number 900).

968. ANNALS OF THE UKRAINIAN ACADEMY OF ARTS AND SCIENCES. 1951–
206 West 100th Street (212) 222-1866
New York, New York 10025

Editor: Editorial Committee Circulation: 1,000
Sponsor: Ukrainian Academy of Arts and Frequency: irregular
    Sciences in the U. S. Subscription: $8.00
Language: English

A scholarly publication featuring articles on Ukrainian history, culture, literature, and other subjects in the humanities, social sciences, and sciences. Includes reviews, an obituary section, and a chronicle of UVAN activities.

969. FORUM–A UKRAINIAN REVIEW. 1967–
440 Wyoming Avenue (717) 347-5649
Scranton, Pennsylvania 18501

Editor: Andrew Gregorovich Circulation: 2,357
Sponsor: Ukrainian Workingmen's Association Frequency: quarterly
Language: English Subscription: $4.00

Publishes primarily popular articles on Ukraine and Ukrainians in Europe and North America for young adult and university student readers. Covers art, history, literature, biographies of outstanding people, sports, and book reviews. Well illustrated; printed in two or three colors.

970. HARVARD UKRAINIAN STUDIES NEWSLETTER. 1970–
1581-83 Massachusetts Avenue (617) 495-4053
Cambridge, Massachusetts 02138

Editor: Uliana Pasicznyk Circulation: 800
Sponsor: Harvard Ukrainian Research Frequency: bi-monthly
    Institute Subscription: n.i.
Language: English

Reports on the activities of Harvard Ukrainian Research Institute, the Ukrainian Studies Program, and their faculty, students, and associates. Regularly includes news about Institute publications, seminars, and library acquisitions.

971. MINUTES OF THE SEMINAR IN UKRAINIAN STUDIES HELD AT
HARVARD UNIVERSITY. 1970-71–
1581-83 Massachusetts Avenue (617) 495-4053
Cambridge, Massachusetts 02138

Editor: Uliana Pasicznyk Circulation: 250
Sponsor: Harvard Ukrainian Research Frequency: annual
    Institute Subscription: $8.00/3 years
Language: English

"Contains resumes of presentations and discussions and a selected bibliography for each Seminar session of the preceding academic year. Seminar topics are in the field of history, literature, linguistics, economics, art, archaeology, etc., and are presented by both guest lecturers and associates of Harvard's Ukrainian Studies Program. Each issue contains an index of Seminar speakers and topics" (editor's statement).

972. RECENZIJA. A Review of Soviet Ukrainian Literature. 1970–
1581-83 Massachusetts Avenue (617) 495-4053
Cambridge, Massachusetts 02138

Editor: Editors rotate (graduate students) Circulation: 700
Sponsor: Harvard Ukrainian Research Institute Frequency: semi-annual
Language: English Subscription: $4.00

Features reviews of "Soviet Ukrainian scholarly publications covering Ukrainian language periodicals and monographs in the social sciences and humanities" (editor's statement).

973. UKRAINIAN ORTHODOX WORD, ENGLISH EDITION. 1966–
P. O. Box 495
South Bound Brook, New Jersey 08880

Editor: Rev. M. Zemlachenko
Sponsor: Ukrainian Orthodox Church in U. S. A.
Language: English

Circulation: 2,000
Frequency: monthly
Subscription: $5.50

This is the English edition of *Ukrainske Pravoslavne Slovo* (see number 949). Includes a permanent section on the activities of the Ukrainian Orthodox League.

974. THE UKRAINIAN QUARTERLY. 1944–
302 West 13th Street (212) 924-5617
New York, New York 10014

Editor: Walter Dushnyck
Sponsor: Ukrainian Congress Committee of
America
Language: English

Circulation: 3,200
Frequency: quarterly
Subscription: $9.00

A journal of East European and Asian affairs. "Although in its editorial treatment of Eastern Europe *The Ukrainian Quarterly* places special emphasis on Ukraine, its overall editorial perspective embraces the other captive nations in the USSR" (editor's statement). Features articles on history, politics, ethnography, sociology, literature, art, and culture. A special feature is the chronicle of current events (Ukrainian life in the United States and other countries).

975. UKRAINIAN TIMES. 1975–
4315 Melrose Avenue
Los Angeles, California 90029

Editor: Orysia Bulczak
Sponsor: Ukrainian Culture Center
Language: English

Circulation: n.i.
Frequency: irregular
Subscription: $.25/copy

976. THE UKRAINIAN WEEKLY. 1933–
81-83 Grand Street (201) 434-0237
Jersey City, New Jersey 07303

Editor: Zenon Snylyk
Sponsor: Ukrainian National Association
Language: English

Circulation: 20,500
Frequency: weekly
Subscription: $4.50

This is the English language supplement of the *Svoboda* daily. "The weekly is designed primarily as a vehicle of information and an opinion forum for the American-born generation of Ukrainians" (editor's statement). Includes informative articles on Ukrainian affairs, creative literary pieces, social topics, sports news, and other relevant material.

WELSH PRESS
Welsh Publications in English

977. Y DRYCH. 1851–
P. O. Box 313
Milwaukee, Wisconsin 53201

Editor: Horace Breese Powell Circulation: 2,000
Sponsor: Drych Publishing Co. Frequency: monthly
Language: English Subscription: $3.00

This is the semi-official organ of the Welsh National Gymanta Ganu Association, an organization
of Welsh churches in America. Contains religious, social, and other news about Welsh in the United
States. Illustrated.

YIDDISH PRESS
See **Jewish Press**

YUGOSLAVIAN PRESS
See **Croatian, Serbian and Slovene Presses**

APPENDIX

ETHNIC PUBLICATIONS–STATISTICAL ANALYSIS

These tables present alphabetically arranged statistical analyses of individual ethnic presses. The entry for each press includes information on the frequency of publication in relation to language and circulation data. Publications that lack circulation figures are noted in the language column by means of a plus sign (i.e., "+1," "+3"). The titles of such publications are listed under each press.

MULTI-ETHNIC

BI-LINGUAL

	Number of Publications	Circulation
Semi-annual	1	1,100
(Subtotal)	(1)	(1,100)

ENGLISH

Weekly	1	1,000
Monthly	2	12,999
Bi-monthly	2	16,728
Quarterly	5 +1	11,515
Semi-annual	1	350
Other	2 +2	6,230
(Subtotal)	(16)	(33,822)
TOTAL	17	49,922

Circulation not given for these publications:
ETHNIC NEWSLETTER
ETHNICITY
THE NATIONAL ETHNIC STUDIES ASSEMBLY NEWSLETTER

ALBANIAN

NATIVE LANGUAGE

	Number of Publications	Circulation
Monthly	1	1,200
Quarterly	1 +1	2,000
(Subtotal)	(3)	(3,200)

BI-LINGUAL

Weekly	2	2,850
Quarterly	1	600
Other	1	500
(Subtotal)	(4)	(3,950)
TOTAL	7	7,150

Circulation not given for one publication:
ZËRI I BALLIT

ARABIC

NATIVE LANGUAGE

	Number of Publications	Circulation
Semi-weekly	1	2,750
Weekly	3	7,310
(Subtotal)	(4)	(10,060)

BI-LINGUAL

Weekly	2	1,600
Monthly	4 +1	18,300
(Subtotal)	(7)	(19,900)

ENGLISH

Weekly	2 +2	14,200
Semi-monthly	2	21,900
Monthly	3 +2	15,215
Bi-monthly	3	39,500
Quarterly	2	12,000
Other	1	400
(Subtotal)	(17)	(103,215)

TOTAL	28	133,175

Circulation not given for these publications:
FREE PALESTINE
ISLAMIC ITEMS
THE PALESTINIAN VOICE
PALESTINIAN DIGEST
THE VOICE

ARMENIAN

NATIVE LANGUAGE

	Number of Publications	Circulation
Daily	2	5,540
Semi-weekly	1	1,500
Monthly	2	6,500
Quarterly	1	500
(Subtotal)	(6)	(14,040)

BI-LINGUAL

Semi-weekly	2	4,126
Weekly	2	2,050
Monthly	8	26,810
Bi-monthly	1	800
Quarterly	2	3,150
Semi-annual	1	2,500
(Subtotal)	(16)	(39,436)

ARMENIAN (cont'd)

ENGLISH

	Number of Publications	Circulation
Weekly	5	15,440
Monthly	2	33,500
Quarterly	3	6,950
Semi-annual	1	2,500
Other	1	1,000
(Subtotal)	(12)	(59,390)
TOTAL	34	112,866

ASIAN

ENGLISH

	Number of Publications	Circulation
Weekly	+1	
Monthly	1	2,230
Bi-monthly	1	5,000
Quarterly	1	35,000
Other	+2	
(Subtotal)	(6)	(42,230)
TOTAL	6	42,230

Circulation not given for these publications:
AMERASIA JOURNAL
ASIAN STUDENT
THIRD WORLD NEWS

ASSYRIAN

BI-LINGUAL

	Number of Publications	Circulation
Monthly	1	1,700
(Subtotal)	(1)	(1,700)
TOTAL	1	1,700

BASQUE

BI-LINGUAL

	Number of Publications	Circulation
Monthly	1	1,296
(Subtotal)	(1)	(1,296)

BASQUE (cont'd)

	ENGLISH	
	Number of Publications	Circulation
Semi-annual	1	5,000
(Subtotal)	(1)	(5,000)
TOTAL	2	6,296

BELGIAN

	NATIVE LANGUAGE	
	Number of Publications	Circulation
Weekly	1	2,855
(Subtotal)	(1)	(2,855)
	ENGLISH	
Monthly	1	9,000
(Subtotal)	(1)	(9,000)
TOTAL	2	11,855

BULGARIAN

	NATIVE LANGUAGE	
	Number of Publications	Circulation
Bi-monthly	1	5,000
(Subtotal)	(1)	(5,000)
	BI-LINGUAL	
Weekly	1	2,501
Semi-monthly	1	818
Other	+1	
(Subtotal)	(3)	(3,319)
TOTAL	4	8,319

Circulation not given for one publication:
    AMERICAN BULGARIAN REVIEW

BYELORUSSIAN

	NATIVE LANGUAGE	
	Number of Publications	Circulation
Weekly	1	500
Monthly	1	2,100
Bi-monthly	1	400

BYELORUSSIAN (cont'd)

NATIVE LANGUAGE (cont'd)

	Number of Publications	Circulation
Quarterly	1	500
Semi-annual	2	2,200
Other	3 +1	1,300
(Subtotal)	(10)	(7,000)

BI-LINGUAL

Semi-annual	1	1,000
Other	1	2,000
(Subtotal)	(2)	(3,000)

ENGLISH

Bi-monthly	+1	
Quarterly	1	500
(Subtotal)	2	(500)

TOTAL	14	10,500

Circulation not given for these publications:
KAMUNIKATY
FACTS ON BYELORUSSIA

CARPATHO-RUTHENIAN

NATIVE LANGUAGE

	Number of Publications	Circulation
Weekly	1	18,000
Semi-monthly	1	2,488
Monthly	1	1,000
Bi-monthly	1	1,000
(Subtotal)	(4)	(22,488)

BI-LINGUAL

Semi-monthly	+1	
Monthly	1	4,500
Bi-monthly	1	2,000
(Subtotal)	(3)	(6,500)

ENGLISH

Weekly	2	26,900
Monthly	3	40,200
Bi-monthly	1	1,500
(Subtotal)	(6)	(68,600)

TOTAL	13	97,588

Circulation not given for one publication:
CERKOVNYJ VISTNIK

CHINESE

NATIVE LANGUAGE

	Number of Publications	Circulation
Daily	9 +1	66,887
Weekly	3	14,693
Semi-monthly	1 +1	9,000
Semi-annual	1	2,000
Other	1	7,040
(Subtotal)	(17)	(99,620)

BI-LINGUAL

Weekly	1	4,985
Monthly	1	2,000
Semi-annual	1	1,500
(Subtotal)	(3)	(8,485)

ENGLISH

Daily	3	26,245
Semi-weekly	1	3,100
Weekly	3	18,450
Monthly	1 +1	221
Bi-monthly	1	195
Quarterly	1	800
(Subtotal)	(11)	(49,011)
TOTAL	31	157,116

Circulation not given for these publications:
HWA PAO–MOTT STREET JOURNAL
MEI JO JIH PAO–THE CHINESE JOURNAL
BULLETIN OF THE CHINESE HISTORICAL SOCIETY OF AMERICA

COSSACK

BI-LINGUAL

	Number of Publications	Circulation
Other	1	250
(Subtotal)	(1)	(250)
TOTAL	1	250

CROATIAN

NATIVE LANGUAGE

	Number of Publications	Circulation
Weekly	2	5,410
Monthly	1	2,000
Bi-monthly	1	2,000
(Subtotal)	(4)	(9,410)

CROATIAN (cont'd)

	BI-LINGUAL	Circulation
Weekly	1	40,200
Semi-monthly	1	6,250
Bi-monthly	1	15,500
Quarterly	2	1,100
Other	1	500
(Subtotal)	(6)	(63,550)

	ENGLISH	
Other	2	4,200
(Subtotal)	(2)	(4,200)
TOTAL	12	77,160

CZECH

	NATIVE LANGUAGE Number of Publications	Circulation
Daily	1	8,291
Weekly	8	17,109
Semi-monthly	1	7,344
Monthly	2	3,830
Quarterly	1 +1	6,000
Other	1	3,400
(Subtotal)	(15)	(45,974)

	BI-LINGUAL	
Weekly	3	27,347
Monthly	8 +1	74,371
Bimonthly	+1	
Quarterly	2	6,750
(Subtotal)	(15)	(108,468)

	ENGLISH	
Monthly	3	9,860
(Subtotal)	(3)	(9,860)
TOTAL	33	164,302

Circulation not given for these publications:
SOKOL TYRS NEWSLETTER
TEXASKY ROLNIK
ZPRAVODAJ

DANISH

	NATIVE LANGUAGE Number of Publications	Circulation
Weekly	1	3,500
(Subtotal)	(1)	(3,500)

DANISH (cont'd)

	BI-LINGUAL	
	Number of Publications	Circulation
Semi-monthly	2	8,000
(Subtotal)	(2)	(8,000)

	ENGLISH	
Monthly	3	24,000
Bi-monthly	1	250
Quarterly	2	13,500
(Subtotal)	(6)	(37,750)
TOTAL	9	49,250

DUTCH

	NATIVE LANGUAGE	
	Number of Publications	Circulation
Semi-monthly	1	2,850
(Subtotal)	(1)	(2,850)

	BI-LINGUAL	
Weekly	1	8,200
Quarterly	1	18,600
(Subtotal)	(2)	(26,800)

	ENGLISH		
Weekly	1		45,200
Monthly	1	+1	3,500
Quarterly	1	+1	1,500
(Subtotal)	(5)		(50,200)
TOTAL	8		79,850

Circulation not given for these publications:
ATLANTIC OBSERVER
CALVINALIA

ESTONIAN

	NATIVE LANGUAGE	
	Number of Publications	Circulation
Weekly	1	4,000
Monthly	1	800
Bi-monthly	1	1,035
(Subtotal)	(3)	(5,835)
TOTAL	3	5,835

FILIPINO

ENGLISH

	Number of Publications	Circulation
Semi-monthly	1	25,000
Monthly	5 +1	25,450
Semi-annual	+1	
(Subtotal)	(8)	(50,450)
TOTAL	8	50,450

Circulation not given for these publications:
  CABLE MASONICO
  NINGAS-COGON

FINNISH

NATIVE LANGUAGE

	Number of Publications	Circulation
Semi-weekly	2	7,970
Weekly	3	6,224
Monthly	1	750
Quarterly	1	6,000
(Subtotal)	(7)	(20,944)

BI-LINGUAL

Semi-weekly	1	1,725
(Subtotal)	(1)	(1,725)

ENGLISH

Other	1	400
(Subtotal)	(1)	(400)
TOTAL	9	23,069

FRENCH

NATIVE LANGUAGE

	Number of Publications	Circulation
Weekly	2	36,900
Semi-monthly	1	3,900
Monthly	1	15,000
(Subtotal)	(4)	(55,800)

BI-LINGUAL

Weekly	1	14,000
Quarterly	2	50,500
(Subtotal)	(3)	(64,500)

FRENCH (cont'd)

ENGLISH

	Number of Publications	Circulation
Bi-monthly	2	3,500
Other	+1	
(Subtotal)	(3)	(3,500)
TOTAL	10	123,800

Circulation not given for one publication:
AMERICAN SOCIETY LEGION OF HONOR MAGAZINE

GEORGIAN

NATIVE LANGUAGE

	Number of Publications	Circulation
Bi-monthly	1	1,000
(Subtotal)	(1)	(1,000)
TOTAL	1	1,000

GERMAN

NATIVE LANGUAGE

	Number of Publications	Circulation
Daily	3	48,850
Weekly	20 +1	72,308
Semi-monthly	1	2,000
Monthly	11 +2	106,810
Bi-monthly	1	28,880
Quarterly	1	1,200
(Subtotal)	(40)	(260,048)

BI-LINGUAL

Weekly	3	37,430
Monthly	3	17,525
(Subtotal)	(6)	(54,955)

ENGLISH

Weekly	2	49,700
Semi-monthly	+1	
Monthly	3 +2	36,000
Bi-monthly	1	600
Quarterly	2	11,600
Semi-annual	1	250
Other	2	24,331
(Subtotal)	(14)	(122,481)
TOTAL	60	437,484

GERMAN (cont'd)

Circulation not given for these publications:
KATHOLISCHER JUGENFREUND
NINTH MANHATTAN MASONIC NEWS
THE STEUBEN NEWS
THE SWISS AMERICAN
VOICE OF AMERICANS OF GERMAN DESCENT
WASHINGTON JOURNAL

GREEK

NATIVE LANGUAGE

	Number of Publications	Circulation
Weekly	1	4,030
Semi-monthly	1	8,200
Monthly	2	10,000
Quarterly	1	2,500
(Subtotal)	(5)	(24,730)

BI-LINGUAL

Daily	1	18,942
Weekly	5	44,183
Semi-monthly	2	95,739
Monthly	2	17,250
Bi-monthly	1	3,000
Other	+1	
(Subtotal)	(12)	(179,114)

ENGLISH

Weekly	1	32,717
Semi-monthly	1	2,000
Monthly	1	2,000
Bi-monthly	2	30,100
Quarterly	1	1,200
Semi-annual	1	375
(Subtotal)	(7)	(68,392)

TOTAL	24	272,236

Circulation not given for one publication:
TRIBUNE OF G.A.P.A.

HUNGARIAN

NATIVE LANGUAGE

	Number of Publications	Circulation
Daily	1	10,830
Weekly	11	70,785
Semi-monthly	3	11,248
Monthly	3 +1	5,658
Quarterly	2	3,000
Other	1	1,000
(Subtotal)	(22)	(102,521)

HUNGARIAN (cont'd)

BI-LINGUAL

	Number of Publications	Circulation
Weekly	2	14,105
Monthly	3	23,786
Quarterly	3	38,500
(Subtotal)	(8)	(76,391)

ENGLISH

Quarterly	1	32,000
Other	+1	
(Subtotal)	(2)	(32,000)
TOTAL	32	210,912

Circulation not given for these publications:
NEMZETVEDELMI TAJEKOZTATO
HUNGARIAN STUDIES NEWSLETTER

INDIAN

ENGLISH

	Number of Publications	Circulation
Weekly	1	11,000
Other	1 +1	5,000
(Subtotal)	(3)	(16,000)
TOTAL	3	16,000

Circulation not given for one publication:
INDIA NEWS

IRANIAN

BI-LINGUAL

	Number of Publications
Other	+1
(Subtotal)	(+1)
TOTAL	1

Circulation not given for one publication:
THE IRAN TIMES

IRISH

ENGLISH

	Number of Publications	Circulation
Weekly	2 +1	57,450
Quarterly	1	5,200
Semi-annual	+1	
Other	1	5,300
(Subtotal)	(6)	(67,950)
TOTAL	6	67,950

Circulation not given for these publications:
THE BULLETIN OF THE AMERICAN IRISH HISTORICAL SOCIETY
IRISH WORLD

ITALIAN

NATIVE LANGUAGE

	Number of Publications	Circulation
Daily	1	69,735
Weekly	8	57,956
Semi-monthly	2	4,531
Monthly	3	65,602
Bi-monthly	2	5,300
Quarterly	1	1,820
(Subtotal)	(17)	(204,944)

BI-LINGUAL

Weekly	5	72,645
Semi-monthly	3	13,500
Monthly	7	86,503
Bi-monthly	1	1,600
Quarterly	2	2,100
(Subtotal)	(18)	(176,348)

ENGLISH

Weekly	4	37,234
Semi-monthly	+1	
Monthly	1 +1	12,000
Bi-monthly	1	10,000
Quarterly	2	7,350
Semi-annual	1	700
Other	2	33,600
(Subtotal)	(13)	(100,884)
TOTAL	48	482,176

Circulation not given for these publications:
COLUMBUS PRESS
THE NATIONAL ITALIAN AMERICAN NEWS

JAPANESE

BI-LINGUAL

	Number of Publications	Circulation
Daily	6	59,407
Semi-weekly	1	3,020
Weekly	2	2,066
Monthly	1	1,100
Other	1	910
(Subtotal)	(11)	(66,503)

ENGLISH

Weekly	1	22,250
Monthly	2	3,770
Other	1	425
(Subtotal)	(4)	(26,445)
TOTAL	15	92,948

JEWISH
(Hebrew and Hebrew English)

NATIVE LANGUAGE

	Number of Publications	Circulation
Weekly	2	9,600
Monthly	1	1,950
Bi-monthly	1	6,000
Other	1	850
(Subtotal)	(5)	(18,400)

Hebrew English BI-LINGUAL

Monthly	1	30,000
Quarterly	1	8,100
(Subtotal)	(2)	(38,100)
TOTAL	7	56,500

(Yiddish and Yiddish English)

NATIVE LANGUAGE

	Number of Publications	Circulation
Daily	2	13,091
Weekly	2	11,000
Semi-monthly	1	7,250
Monthly	6	30,600
Bi-monthly	1	1,200
Quarterly	3	5,000
Other	2	6,500
(Subtotal)	(17)	(74,641)

JEWISH (cont'd)

Yiddish English   BI-LINGUAL

	Number of Publications	Circulation
Monthly	1	26,000
Bi-monthly	1	1,500
Quarterly	2	11,500
Semi-annual	1	4,000
Other	1	25,000
(Subtotal)	(6)	(68,000)
TOTAL	23	142,641

(Jewish in German)

NATIVE LANGUAGE

	Number of Publications	Circulation
Weekly	1	31,000
(Subtotal)	(1)	(31,000)
TOTAL	1	31,000

(Jewish in English)

ENGLISH

	Number of Publications	Circulation
Weekly	42	756,368
Semi-monthly	8	53,500
Monthly	29	1,096,506
Bi-monthly	4	174,500
Quarterly	17 +2	510,820
Other	8	194,400
(Subtotal)	(110)	(2,786,094)
TOTAL	110	2,786,094

Circulation not given for these publications:
THE SOUTHWEST JEWISH CHRONICLE
WESTERN STATES JEWISH HISTORICAL QUARTERLY

KOREAN

NATIVE LANGUAGE

	Number of Publications	Circulation
Daily	1 +1	2,500
Weekly	+1	
Semi-monthly	+1	
Bi-monthly	1	2,800
(Subtotal)	(5)	(5,300)

BI-LINGUAL

	Number of Publications	Circulation
Weekly	1	120
Semi-monthly	1	494
(Subtotal)	(2)	(614)

KOREAN (cont'd)

ENGLISH

	Number of Publications	Circulation
Semi-monthly	1	1,200
(Subtotal)	(1)	(1,200)
TOTAL	8	7,114

Circulation not given for these publications:
GONG GAE PYUN JI
HAE OE MAN MIN BO
HANKOOK-SHINMON

LATVIAN

NATIVE LANGUAGE

	Number of Publications	Circulation
Semi-weekly	1	12,380
Semi-monthly	1	500
Monthly	4	4,210
Bi-monthly	1	570
Quarterly	1	230
Semi-annual	2	750
Other	3	6,900
(Subtotal)	(13)	(25,540)
TOTAL	13	25,540

LITHUANIAN

NATIVE LANGUAGE

	Number of Publications	Circulation
Daily	2	39,000
Semi-weekly	1 +1	17,000
Weekly	4	21,315
Semi-monthly	4	11,515
Monthly	8	14,573
Quarterly	2 +2	1,475
Semi-annual	2	2,000
Other	6 +1	11,150
(Subtotal)	(33)	(118,028)

BI-LINGUAL

Semi-monthly	1	5,000
Monthly	2	6,000
Bi-monthly	4	17,100
(Subtotal)	(7)	(28,100)

LITHUANIAN (cont'd)

ENGLISH

	Number of Publications	Circulation
Semi-monthly	+1	
Bi-monthly	1	2,500
Quarterly	1	5,000
(Subtotal)	(3)	(7,500)
TOTAL	43	153,628

Circulation not given for these publications:
LAISVE
MUSU SPARTA
MUSU VYTIS
TAUTOS PRAETIS
LITHUANIAN MUSEUM REVIEW

LUXEMBOURG

ENGLISH

	Number of Publications	Circulation
Monthly	1	650
(Subtotal)	(1)	(650)
TOTAL	1	650

NORWEGIAN

NATIVE LANGUAGE

	Number of Publications	Circulation
Weekly	1	4,840
Monthly	1	30,000
(Subtotal)	(2)	(34,840)

BI-LINGUAL

Weekly	2	14,000
Monthly	2	3,607
Semi-annual	1	1,365
(Subtotal)	(5)	(18,972)

ENGLISH

Semi-monthly	2	11,800
Monthly	2 +1	72,350
Bi-monthly	2	31,005
Quarterly	1	25,000
Other	1	1,155
(Subtotal)	(9)	(141,310)
TOTAL	16	195,122

Circulation not given for one publication:
THE AUGSBURG NOW

PAKISTANI

ENGLISH

	Number of Publications
Semi-monthly	+1
(Subtotal)	(+1)
TOTAL	+1

Circulation not given for one publication:
        PAKISTANI

POLISH

NATIVE LANGUAGE

	Number of Publications	Circulation
Daily	3	42,600
Weekly	5	27,551
Semi-monthly	1	1,329
Monthly	4 +1	23,908
Bi-monthly	1	4,100
Quarterly	2	5,365
(Subtotal)	(17)	(104,853)

BI-LINGUAL

Weekly	6	49,750
Semi-monthly	8	325,305
Bi-monthly	2	8,000
Quarterly	2 +1	10,575
Semi-annual	1	2,100
Other	1	1,200
(Subtotal)	(21)	(396,930)

ENGLISH

Weekly	3	23,200
Monthly	3	38,667
Bi-monthly	1	8,000
Quarterly	5 +2	11,250
Semi-annual	1	750
(Subtotal)	(15)	(81,867)
TOTAL	53	583,650

Circulation not given for these publications:
        POLKA–Polish Woman
        THE NATIONAL P.L.A.V.
        POLISH AMERICAN CONGRESS NEWSLETTER
        POSLANIEC MATKI BOSKIEJ SALETYNSKIEJ

PORTUGUESE

NATIVE LANGUAGE

	Number of Publications	Circulation
Weekly	1	5,000
Semi-monthly	1	6,000
Monthly	1	15.000
Other	1	3,970
(Subtotal)	(4)	(29,970)

BI-LINGUAL

Weekly	2	13,200
Monthly	1	12,025
Quarterly	2	5,600
(Subtotal)	(5)	(30,825)

ENGLISH

Quarterly	1	300
(Subtotal)	(1)	(300)
TOTAL	10	61,095

ROMANIAN

NATIVE LANGUAGE

	Number of Publications	Circulation
Bi-monthly	1	2,000
(Subtotal)	(1)	(2,000)

BI-LINGUAL

Semi-monthly	1	2,520
Monthly	3 +1	8,029
(Subtotal	(5)	(10,549)

ENGLISH

Monthly	+1	
(Subtotal)	(+1)	
TOTAL	7	12,549

Circulation not given for these publications:
LUMINATORUL
ROMANIAN BULLETIN

RUSSIAN

NATIVE LANGUAGE

	Number of Publications	Circulation
Daily	2	28,818
Semi-weekly	1	1,650
Weekly	1	2,584
Semi-monthly	1	1,600

RUSSIAN (cont'd)

NATIVE LANGUAGE (cont'd)

	Number of Publications	Circulation
Monthly	6	5,466
Bi-monthly	1	200
Quarterly	3	4,300
Other	4	4,050
(Subtotal)	(19)	(48,668)

BI-LINGUAL

Semi-annual	1	8,000
Other	1	500
(Subtotal)	(2)	(8,500)

ENGLISH

Monthly	1	5,020
Bi-monthly	2	3,750
Quarterly	1	1,850
Other	1	1,300
(Subtotal)	(5)	(11,920)
TOTAL	26	69,088

SCANDINAVIAN

ENGLISH

	Number of Publications	Circulation
Monthly	1 +1	6,300
Quarterly	2	7,015
(Subtotal)	(4)	(13,315)
TOTAL	4	13,315

Circulation not given for one publication:
SCANDINAVIAN-AMERICAN BULLETIN

SCOTTISH

ENGLISH

	Number of Publications	Circulation
Monthly	1 +1	550
Quarterly	1	4,700
Semi-annual	1	750
(Subtotal)	(4)	(6,000)
TOTAL	4	6,000

Circulation not given for one publication:
THE SCOTIA NEWS

SERBIAN

NATIVE LANGUAGE

	Number of Publications	Circulation
Weekly	1	3,500
Semi-monthly	+1	
Bi-monthly	1	3,500
(Subtotal)	(3)	(7,000)

BI-LINGUAL

Monthly	1	1,700
Other	2	25,760
(Subtotal)	(3)	(27,460)

ENGLISH

Other	1	5,000
(Subtotal)	(1)	(5,000)
TOTAL	7	39,460

Circulation not given for one publication:
RADNICKA BORBA

SLOVAK

NATIVE LANGUAGE

	Number of Publications	Circulation
Weekly	3	14,180
Monthly	3 +1	13,261
Bi-monthly	1	981
Quarterly	1	1,000
Other	1	500
(Subtotal)	(10)	(29,922)

BI-LINGUAL

Weekly	2	57,066
Semi-monthly	1	10,000
Monthly	6	38,508
Quarterly	+1	
(Subtotal)	(10)	(105,574)

ENGLISH

Semi-monthly	1	11,000
Monthly	2	9,000
Other	1	2,600
(Subtotal)	(4)	(22,600)
TOTAL	24	158,096

Circulation not given for these publications:
AVE MARIA
FLORIDSKY SLOVAK

SLOVENE

NATIVE LANGUAGE

	Number of Publications	Circulation
Semi-monthly	1	8,578
Monthly	1	2,760
(Subtotal)	(2)	(11,338)

BI-LINGUAL

Daily	2	17,832
Weekly	1	15,500
Semi-monthly	1	7,800
Monthly	2	12,087
Quarterly	1	1,700
(Subtotal)	(7)	(54,919)

ENGLISH

Monthly	2	15,330
(Subtotal)	(2)	(15,330)
TOTAL	11	81,587

SPANISH

NATIVE LANGUAGE

	Number of Publications	Circulation
Daily	5	238,940
Weekly	4 +1	27,296
Semi-monthly	4	80,000
Monthly	11 +1	878,100
Bi-monthly	1 +1	200
(Subtotal)	(28)	(1,224,536)

BI-LINGUAL

Daily	2	31,302
Weekly	6 +1	84,736
Semi-monthly	2	46,406
Monthly	6	128,000
Bi-monthly	1	2,500
Quarterly	3	2,300
Other	1	2,000
(Subtotal)	(22)	(297,244)

ENGLISH

Semi-weekly	1	1,843
Weekly	4	8,030
Monthly	+1	
Bi-monthly	1	400
Other	1	1,100
(Subtotal)	(8)	(11,373)
TOTAL	58	1,533,153

SPANISH (cont'd)

Circulation not given for these publications:
THE JOURNAL OF MEXICAN AMERICAN HISTORY
CORPUS CHRISTI AMERICANO
COSTILLA COUNTY FREE PRESS
EL MUNDO DE NUEVA YORK
GRAFICA

SWEDISH

	NATIVE LANGUAGE	
	Number of Publications	Circulation
Weekly	3	21,294
(Subtotal)	(3)	(21,294)
	BI-LINGUAL	
Weekly	2	8,885
Semi-monthly	1	1,050
Monthly	2	4,700
(Subtotal)	(5)	(14,635)
	ENGLISH	
Weekly	1	2,200
Semi-monthly	2	50,000
Monthly	7	72,807
Quarterly	1	1,521
Other	1	500
(Subtotal)	(12)	(127,028)
TOTAL	20	162,957

SWISS

	BI-LINGUAL	
	Number of Publications	Circulation
Weekly	2	5,500
(Subtotal)	(2)	(5,500)
	ENGLISH	
Monthly	1	3,600
Other	1	205
(Subtotal)	(2)	(3,805)
TOTAL	4	9,305

TURKISH

NATIVE LANGUAGE

	Number of Publications	Circulation
Quarterly	+1	
Semi-annual	+1	
(Subtotal)	(2)	

BI-LINGUAL

Monthly	3	6,397
(Subtotal)	(3)	(6,397)

ENGLISH

Monthly	1	3,000
(Subtotal)	(1)	(3,000)
TOTAL	6	9,397

Circulation not given for these publications:
NEWS FROM TURKEY
TURKISH REVIEW

UKRAINIAN

NATIVE LANGUAGE

	Number of Publications	Circulation
Daily	1	20,500
Weekly	1	1,670
Semi-monthly	3	5,000
Monthly	12 +2	30,400
Bi-monthly	8	10,365
Quarterly	14 .	13,425
Other	12 +2	11,185
(Subtotal)	(55)	(92,545)

BI-LINGUAL

Daily	1	6,500
Weekly	3	23,956
Semi-monthly	1	5,000
Monthly	2	8,330
Quarterly	2	2,000
Other	3	4,000
(Subtotal)	(12)	(49,786)

ENGLISH

Weekly	2	27,000
Monthly	1	2,000
Bi-monthly	1	800
Quarterly	2	5,557
Semi-annual	1	700
Other	2 +1	1,250
(Subtotal)	(10)	(37,307)
TOTAL	77	179,638

UKRAINIAN (cont'd)

Circulation not given for these publications:
UKRAINIAN TIMES
ANNALS OF THE WORLD LEMKOS' FEDERATION
NAZARETH
NOTATNYK
SUMIVETZ

WELSH

ENGLISH

	Number of Publications	Circulation
Monthly	1	2,000
(Subtotal)	(1)	(2,000)
TOTAL	1	2,000

INDEX

Numbers refer to entry numbers and not to page numbers. The ethnic group of a periodical is given in parentheses following each title.